1989

FUNDAMENTALS OF ELEMENTARY AND MIDDLE SCHOOL CLASSROOM INSTRUCTION

FUNDAMENTALS OF ELEMENTARY AND MIDDLE SCHOOL CLASSROOM INSTRUCTION

Earl J. Montague

James V. Hoffman

John P. Huntsberger

The University of Texas at Austin

MERRILL PUBLISHING COMPANY
A Bell & Howell Information Company
Columbus Toronto London Melbourne

Published by Merrill Publishing Company
A Bell & Howell Information Company
Columbus, Ohio 43216

This book was set in Eras.
Administrative Editor: Jeff Johnston
Production Coordinator: Anne Daly
Art Coordinator: Vincent Smith
Cover Designer: Cathy Watterson

Photo credits: All photos copyrighted by the author, Earl J. Montague.

Library of Congress Catalog Card Number: 88–062353
International Standard Book Number: 0–675–20851–3
Printed in the United States of America
1 2 3 4 5 6 7 8 9—93 92 91 90 89

Preface

This book is designed to be used in a one-semester course for beginning preservice teachers. It introduces fundamental skills of instruction involved in elementary and middle schools—skills most appropriately learned just before or concurrent with student teaching. The content and activities in this book would also be a valuable tool for the preparation of inservice teachers who were educated before much of the recent research on effective teaching strategies was published and in programs for the alternative certification of teachers.

Although teaching styles should and do vary, not all teaching behaviors are equally effective in promoting learning. The skills introduced in this book are those that studies have shown promote student on-task behavior and improve attitudes and achievement.

This book guides the preservice teacher from simple to more complex skills. Skills introduced in earlier chapters are reinforced throughout subsequent chapters. Text material, along with exercises and optional practicum teaching exercises, is used to introduce skills and provide for their practice. The emphasis is consistently on the ability to apply and use the skills introduced. References to research findings and additional sources of information are included in each chapter for students wishing to pursue a topic more fully.

Teachers must think about teaching in the context of a broad understanding of how schools are organized and the role teachers play in that organization. A brief introduction to elementary and middle school students, including special students and those who are culturally different, is also included. These understandings, introduced in chapter 1, circumscribe much of what teachers do and how they feel about what they do.

When planning instruction, teachers think about what they want students to learn. Although chapter 2 introduces students to the planning process, in reality, the whole book lays the groundwork for effective planning. Each chapter adds more specific things that teachers must think about when planning. By the end of the book, preservice teachers will have a fairly clear understanding of those things that must be considered when thinking about instruction. They will then be in a position to do long- and short-term planning. They will also be ready to learn possible formats for unit planning and daily lesson planning. The first two chapters, therefore, are merely introductions to the planning process, and additional implications for planning will be added in each chapter in a section called *Implications for Planning.*

In the earlier parts of the book, the preservice teacher is guided through simple instructional procedures used in more didactic or expository approaches to teaching, which is consistent with the preservice teacher's early conceptions of the teaching process.

Following these early chapters, more complex teaching processes involved in interactions and discussions with groups of students are introduced. For most preservice teachers, using questioning will be a somewhat novel concept of teaching, so detailed information is provided.

The text then introduces the strategies used to teach skills, concepts, and generalizations. Students should develop some understanding of the strategies involved through the information and activities provided. Mastery of these strategies is not expected, however.

This book also introduces the areas of classroom management, behavioral management, test construction, and grading. The exercises included in these chapters provide experiences in applying the skills introduced.

Far more exercises are included in the text than can be used during a one-semester course. This will allow your instructor to make choices, depending on the situation. If you are working in a classroom at the same time you are studying this material, some or all of the Exercises, Observation Exercises, and Practicum Teaching Exercises may be used. If your course is campus based, then you may do some or all of the Exercises and Practicum Teaching Exercises. If your campus situation does not allow you to practice the teaching skills found in the Practicum Teaching Exercises, then you may do some or all of the Exercises.

Not all of the chapters in this text will necessarily be used in a one-semester course. The instructor will undoubtedly need to make some choices about those chapters that will be included and the sequence in which they will be taught. The text is designed to allow for this flexibility.

Students using this text will master few of the skills introduced during a one-semester course. They will need further practice in subsequent courses or supervised classroom experience to develop and reinforce these skills. The ultimate transfer to the classroom will be enhanced by supervised classroom experience, during which these skills are reinforced and practiced. Expecting preservice teachers to transfer these skills to the classroom without this follow-up activity is unrealistic.

This book is not an introduction to educational foundations, nor is it a comprehensive treatment of various methodologies and curriculum alternatives. Rather, the skills introduced are fundamental; they represent a foundation on which to build subsequent skills. More complex sets of skills needed to adapt the curriculum to individual learning styles, to use new instructional technologies, to team teach, to organize cooperative learning groups, or to individualize instruction are not included. These more complex skills are not unimportant; in fact, they are essential for effective teaching. However, the basic skills that are prerequisite to higher-order instructional tasks provide a firm foundation on which to build subsequent skills.

We would like to express our appreciation to Dr. Elizabeth Stimson (Bowling Green State University), Dr. Duane Giannangelo (Memphis State University), Dr. Vivian Taylor (Jackson State University), Dr. Rita Jensen (Iowa State University), Dr. Ruth Shearer (Alderson Broaddus College), Carolyn M. Benitez (Buda Elementary School) and Mario A. Benitez (The University of Texas) who deserve our thanks for their helpful comments and suggestions. We also want to thank the students involved in trying out these materials. Their patience and suggestions were particularly helpful in developing and revising this text.

Earl J. Montague
James V. Hoffman
John P. Huntsberger

Contents

PART ONE

THINKING ABOUT TEACHING

The first two chapters of this book focus on how "students of teaching" and "teachers of students" think about their work. At one level, teachers need to think about teaching in the context of a broad understanding of how schools are organized, the nature of children, and the role teachers play. These understandings, introduced in Chapter 1, circumscribe much of what teachers do and how they feel about what they do. At another level, that of planning instruction, teachers need to think about their pupils and what they expect them to learn. What they expect children to learn is related to the goals that teachers recognize as having value. Goals are then translated into more specific learning outcomes when teachers think about day-to-day instruction. Teachers, when they think about instruction, try to anticipate what they must do to facilitate the intended learning. Chapter two will introduce you to these aspects of the planning process. While chapter two introduces you to some of the formal aspects of planning, in reality, the whole book develops the groundwork for effective planning. Each chapter of this text adds more specific things that teachers need to think about when planning. By the end of the book you will have a fairly clear understanding of those things that need to be considered when thinking about instruction. You will then be in a position to do long and short term planning. At that time, learning the possible formats for unit planning and daily lesson planning can occur. Until that time, plans that you write can be expected to be incomplete and lack some of the parts that you will ultimately come to recognize as vital.

An Introduction to Teaching in Elementary and Middle Schools 1

Thousands of books, professional reports, and articles have been written on the topic of teaching in elementary schools. Behind each of these texts is an author or team of authors with a particular purpose, a set of values, a vision of the future, and an audience in mind. This book is no exception. If this book is to become an important part of your learning experience, we think it is important to share with you from the very start some of our ideas about teaching. This first chapter has been set aside for just this purpose.

COMMONPLACES OF TEACHING

Joseph Schwab (1960) has used the term **commonplaces** to describe the essential pieces of the puzzle called teaching. He describes four commonplaces: the teacher, the learner, the content, and the milieu—the social and organizational context of the school. In any lesson, each of the four commonplaces is represented. That is, in teaching we always have someone (the teacher) attempting to get across something (the content) to someone (the learner) in some setting (the milieu). Let us explore briefly each of these commonplaces as you might experience them in an elementary school.

The Teacher

Just over one million elementary school teachers are currently employed in the United States. The number of teachers reached a peak around 1980 and has declined steadily since then. According to Emily Feistritzer (1983), the typical school teacher is

> a woman approaching her 40th birthday. She has taught for 12 years, mostly in her present district. Over those dozen years, she returned to her local college or university often enough to acquire enough credits for a master's degree. She is married and the mother of two children. She is white and not politically active. (p. 1)

Feistritzer (1986) found essentially the same profile of the typical teacher in a later survey. This survey also found that 69 percent of public school teachers were women, the majority of whom completed five or more years of college.

Considering both in-school and out-of-school responsibilities, the typical teacher puts in a work week slightly longer than the typical laborer and brings home a pay check that is slightly lower. The average teacher salary in the 1986 survey was around $24,600, which represented an increase of approximately 20 percent over the average salary in 1983.

Teachers are more satisfied with every aspect of their lives, including their jobs, than college graduates in general. Ninety percent of public school teachers are satisfied with their personal lives; 84 percent of college graduates indicate they are satisfied. Teachers do complain, however, of being paid too little (Feistritzer, 1986).

Teaching is apparently not as prestigious a profession as it once was. Considering that fewer college students are seeking teaching certificates, that the dropout rate from active teaching is increasing, and that the children of the baby boom generation are approaching school age, forecasters are predicting a teacher shortage in the next decade that will be unparalleled in our nation's history (Darling-Hammond, 1984).

The changes in teachers' attitudes toward the profession have been accompanied (some would suggest, caused) by changes in the public's perception of the quality of teaching in schools. Surveys suggest that parent ratings of the quality of teachers in schools have declined over the past two decades. Whether or not this perception is accurate, few would deny that the teaching profession is composed of individuals with varying levels of expertise (not to be confused with experience).

Teacher Expertise

What do expert teachers look like? How do they think and behave in their professional role? What can novices do to become experts? There are no simple answers to these questions, and yet any book about learning to teach must ground itself on a concept of expert teaching (Hoffman and Edwards 1986). What follows is a brief sketch of some of those characteristics essential to expert teaching.

☐ The expert teacher is organized and efficient in managing the complex social system called a classroom. The expert teacher's classroom is businesslike and academically focused and at the same time is a relaxed and friendly place to work.

☐ The expert teacher is a leader. In this capacity the expert teacher sets standards and holds high academic and social expectations for pupils.

☐ The expert teacher inspires students by example and support.

☐ The expert teacher is sensitive to the individual needs of class members in all realms, including the emotional, the intellectual, and the physical. She is compassionate with the children and responsive to the concerns, aspirations, and commitment of their parents.

☐ The expert teacher is knowledgeable in the content and processes to be taught. She is aware of and skilled in a variety of techniques for guiding students to learn.

☐ The expert teacher is diagnostic. She is constantly evaluating students in the class in order to decide what and how to teach so that they can learn.

☐ The expert teacher recognizes the importance of the school as a community of educators and learners. She actively works with other teachers to construct a school climate favorable to learning.

☐ The expert teacher understands that children have a life outside of the immediate environment of the classroom that also contributes to their development. The expert teacher seeks out and builds relationships with the parents and those working with children outside the school so that all can support students in their efforts to learn.

☐ Finally, the expert teacher is an enthusiastic learner. She recognizes that there is always room for professional growth. The expert teacher reads, attends workshops, enrolls in programs of advanced study, and conducts studies of teaching and learning in her own classroom.

Your goal is to become an expert teacher possessing the characteristics just described. Although we expect you are just embarking on the study of teaching in a formal sense, we recognize that you have likely developed strong impressions about teaching based upon your own years of experience as a student. You are a novice to teaching but you are not without preconceptions. Taking the time to reflect on the many teachers you have had will be helpful in working through this text. Are there teachers who stand out in your memory as being particularly good? What is it about these teachers that evokes a positive image in your mind? Are there teachers you recall with negative feelings? For what reasons? What is it about your experiences with these teachers that you would change if you could rewrite your personal history? Use these images, both positive and negative, as tangible points of reference for interpreting the information in this book.

Expert teachers did not start out that way. They achieved expertise gradually over the years, through effort and reflection. Some teachers never reach expert status. Some teachers with fifteen years or more of experience have, in reality, only one year of experience relived fifteen or more times with little or no development of expertise. The importance of continuous growth as a characteristic of expert teachers has been demonstrated in research in teacher development. For example, in a recent study of teacher attitudes and beliefs regarding the development of expertise, researchers found great differences among teacher perceptions as a function of school quality: the teachers in schools rated as lowest in quality tended to agree that it took around two years to learn to be a teacher; the teachers in schools rated as moderate in quality tended to agree that it took from four to six years to learn to be a teacher; the teachers in schools rated as most effective tended to agree that you **never stop** learning to be a teacher. For most of us, no short or easy paths to expertise exist, but, be assured, the outcomes are well worth the effort.

If you have the opportunity as part of this course to interact with expert teachers working in classrooms with their students, you are fortunate indeed. Expert teachers are a rich source of inspiration and ideas. As you watch and talk with these experts, keep two important points in mind: first, teaching that may appear effortless and easy is the product of years of learning; that is, for expert teachers, many aspects of their work have reached an automatic level. Their attention is free to focus on larger issues that you as a novice take little notice of, not because you don't believe these larger issues are important, but because you are so busy dealing mechanically with day-to-day events. Interestingly, this same phenomenon has been found in studies of experts and novices in many areas. For example, expert chess players have been found to remember and plan in terms of patterns and long-range strategies. Novice chess players focus their attention on specific parts of the playing board and are concerned primarily with their next few moves in a game. Experts deal with patterns, novices with details. This is a developmental difference, not necessarily a mistake on the part of the novices. As they master detail, novices pay more and more attention to the larger picture. They master detail through repeated and careful observation, participation, analysis, and reflection. The same point can be made about teacher development. Expert teachers are attentive to the larger patterns of classroom life; novices focus on events directly at hand. As you come to master the details, your ability to focus on the broader issues will emerge. Observation, interaction, practice, and reflection are the keys to moving forward. The details that require great effort at early stages will gradually give way to routine patterns and enhanced flexibility.

The second important point to remember is that when working with expert teachers, realize that most are far removed from the time they themselves were novices. Like all of us, they have forgotten the difficulties they experienced as novices and so may not start their explanations at your level of understanding. You must become an astute observer and inquisitor if you are to learn from expert teachers and be prepared to accept answers that are not as concrete as you may like. It may be helpful for you to think of something at which you are relatively expert that you have tried to teach, such as riding a bike, writing an essay, or windsurfing. Reaching back into your own ignorance (putting yourself in the learner's shoes) is difficult.

It is nearly impossible to prevent students' mistakes by trying to teach everything about a skill before allowing them to perform it. Any significant learning of complex skills involves in part a trial-and-error process. Expert teachers are often forced to rely on a combination of simple heuristics, the energy of the novice, and constructive feedback to promote learning. The expert teachers working to help you learn to teach face these same problems. Patience with others and with your own errors is a virtue that will serve you well in learning to teach.

The Learner

In 1982 approximately 24 million children were enrolled in elementary schools in the United States. The number of students has been steadily declining since peaking in 1968. Current predictions are for sharp enrollment increases over the next two decades (Feistritzer, 1983).

Not only is the number of students increasing, but the general nature of the student population is also changing. Nationally, minorities currently constitute about one quarter of the school-aged population, and by 1990 will reach 30 percent. The regional patterns in minority enrollment are even more dramatic. In Texas, for example, the majority of primary grade students in public schools are from minority ethnic groups. School is not an easy or familiar place for many of these pupils, who may enter school with a language background different from the English used by teachers. In addition, many come from economically disadvantaged homes where preschool experiences are not as rich and varied as in economically advantaged homes.

Achievement patterns for elementary students are also changing. Concerns have been expressed in recent years over the general decline in SAT scores of high school graduates. Recently, some mixed findings in patterns of student achievement have been reported from the National Assessment of Educational Progress (NAEP). The good

Learning to work with others

news comes in the form of reported gains in reading and mathematics for minority students from 9 to 13 years of age. The bad news comes in the form of declines in achievement levels among 17-year-old students in reading, science, and mathematics. This pattern of academic decline is also reflected in the NAEP data related to student attitudes toward school, which, at the elementary level, drop steadily with each grade.

Children as Learners

Not only have the general demographic characteristics of the school population changed in recent decades, but so too has the dominant view of psychologists about the nature of children as learners. Shulman and Carey (1984) have described three views of the learner and related these views to different conceptions of effective teaching. Different views of children as learners suggested by Shulman and Carey are the rationale view, the bounded rationale view, and the collective rationale view.

Rationale View.   One way of thinking about children as learners is to view learning as the development of stimulus-response bonds through exposure to material. Shulman and Carey call this the **rationale** view, which is represented best in the work of behaviorists like Hull and Skinner. In this view, associations on the part of the learner are strengthened primarily through repeated experience or practice. The learner is regarded as an organism that can be taught to respond in more desirable ways through training, practice, and reinforcement. The learner is portrayed as an "objective, passive recipient of sensory experience who can learn anything when enough practice is provided" (Shulman and Carey, 1984, p. 509). This view of the learner results in teaching being thought of as a form of **transmission:** the teacher's role is to transmit new information or skills to the learner; learners are the receivers and organizers of the new information and skills.

The rationale view of the learner grew to dominate the field of psychology from the time of Thorndike in the early twentieth century to its zenith in the 1960s. The influence of this view of the learner can be seen most directly in such curriculum approaches as programmed learning (e.g., the Sullivan Readers), DISTAR (Reading, Language, and Mathematics components), and early forms of computer-assisted instruction (CAI). This view is also evident in techniques for behavioral management, such as operant conditioning, that emphasize reinforcement, shaping, and extinction.

Bounded Rationale View. A second view of the pupil as learner, the **bounded rationale** view, is based on the recognition that humans have inherent limitations in making sense out of the complex world they perceive. In this view, the world is far too complex for any individual, particularly a child, to comprehend all at once. For this reason, the mind creates simple models of reality to reduce uncertainty and to achieve a state of equilibrium with the world as it is experienced. These simple models are used to anticipate, perceive, act on, and interpret experiences, and the learner carries them with him when entering into a new learning situation, and interpretation of new experiences is "bounded" by these models. Learning occurs when these simple models are modified in ways consistent with a more mature view of the world. Consideration of the models a person takes into a learning situation is therefore crucial to learning.

Shulman and Carey (1984, p. 509) describe the learner in the bounded rationale view as "active, inventive, knowledge bearing, and self-conscious." This view of the learner can be seen in the work of instructional psychologists who stress the importance of examining a learner's prior knowledge of a concept before attempting to teach it directly. This view can also be seen in the application of "schema theory" to reading comprehension instruction, where a great deal of emphasis is placed on ensuring that learners have the necessary prior knowledge before reading a text. Teaching under this view can be thought of as a **transaction,** that is, a process of replacing simple models with more sophisticated models. A learner's understanding comes as a result of connecting what is already known to what is experienced, and thereby constructing new models.

Collective Rationale View. A third view of the learner, the **collective rationale** view, emphasizes the understanding of meaning as socially constructed by groups of individuals. As in the bounded rationale view, the learner is actively constructing meaning by making use of prior knowledge as he interprets present experiences. However, he is also constantly examining the "bounds" of his own reasoning system in relation to others. The learner's interaction with other learners and knowledgeable others is the key to development. Grouping for instruction is seen more as an opportunity, or even a necessity, rather than as a compromise made necessary by the reality of schools. In this view, social interaction around the content is at the heart of all important learning.

In this view, teaching is thought of as helping learners transform simpler models into more sophisticated models of the world through interactions with others about experiences. The teacher supports the process of learning not only through direct instruction in skills and concepts, but also by engaging in instructional dialogues that help students connect the "known with the new" (Pearson and Johnson 1978). This view of the learner can be seen in the writing of Vygotsky (1978) and the applications of his work using such techniques as "dialogic teaching" (Palincsar and Brown 1986) and cooperative learning (Slavin 1980; Johnson and Johnson 1987).

Individual Differences

Students are not all alike. Some attempts are made to reduce the heterogeneity of classes by placing students in grades by chronological age and/or by abilities, but the students in any given classroom are very diverse. They have different cultural backgrounds, socio-economic levels, abilities, sets of experiences, attitudes toward school, preferences in learning experiences, and are concerned about different sets of problems. To assume that all children of a given age are alike is to deny these differences.

Special Students

It is important to recognize that all students are special in that they are unique human beings. Some, however, are different from the general population in ways that cause them particular problems in an educational setting. These "special" students may have impairments in sight, hearing, or mobility; they may have speech or language impairments; some may have learning disabilities or be mentally impaired; still others may be emotionally disturbed.

The rights of these students are protected under federal law. As a teacher, you must be aware of these particular pieces of legislation. The Rehabilitation Act of 1973, Public Law 93-112, Section 504, states that no otherwise qualified handicapped child or adult shall solely because of a handicap "be excluded from participation in ... any program or activity receiving federal financial assistance." Almost all public schools are receiving federal funds, so they fall under this law. Further, the All Handicapped Children Act of 1975, Public Law 94–142, requires schools to integrate special students into the regular classroom whenever possible. The act goes on to say that all handicapped children will have available to them

> a free appropriate public education which emphasizes special education and
> related services designed to meet their unique needs ... and [schools are]
> to assess and assure the effectiveness of efforts to educate handicapped children.

This means that school actions are bound by a set of procedures and guidelines. These include:

1. Parents of the child have the right to be present when the child is being evaluated, a placement is being determined, and an Individualized Education Program (IEP) is being developed.
2. The child, through his parents, has a right to question his placement.
3. Tests are to be a fair evaluation of the student's strengths and weaknesses, and assessment procedures should ensure that they contain no cultural biases.

4. The contents of IEPs should contain assessments of the student's present level of performance, ways that he will participate in the regular program, the kind of special services needed, the date when this service will begin, and the duration of the service. Long- and short-range standards are to be established along with the methods to be used to measure achievement. A description of the ways that educational progress will be assessed is provided and must include conferences between school officials and the parents.

5. The special student is to have a "least restrictive placement"; that is, he will be placed with nonhandicapped students to the maximum extent possible. Only when the severity of the handicap requires special programs may the student be removed from the regular classroom.

6. All students are educable. No child of school age can be denied an education. The child is to be educated at his present level of development, and the nature of this education is prescribed by an Individualized Education Program (IEP).

Even though special students may have a few characteristics different from those of the general population, the teacher must recognize that the child has many more characteristics in common with other students. Stereotyping these children does a disservice to them. Except in situations in which the impairment prevents the child from doing regular activities, few, if any, accommodations to the individual should be made. In all respects other than the impairment, the child is to be accepted as a fully functioning human being.

Cultural Differences

Many people view our society as monocultural. This perspective is insensitive to the many cultures that have built and are continuing to shape our nation. Teachers who have this kind of insensitivity may think of children who are different as inferior and may also set lower expectations for such students. Our society is composed of some individuals whose cultural heritage is native American; others are from Spanish-speaking countries such as South America, Central America, the Caribbean, and Spain; some are from Asian countries such as Japan, China, Korea, Vietnam, Samoa, the Philippines, and Indonesia; others are from Africa, the Middle East, and Eastern and Western Europe.

Knowing that a child is from a particular cultural group may be a starting point in getting to know that individual, but it may tell us very little about that particular child. Certainly we are all shaped by our cultural heritage to some extent, but this shaping may influence each person in very different ways. For example, within each cultural group there are individuals who practice different religions, use different languages, have different dietary preferences, and live at different socio-economic levels. Some are from rural areas; others are from urban areas. Some have been in the United States for many generations; others are recent immigrants. Some have had extensive travel experiences; others have traveled little.

The variation within any one of these groups is large. For a teacher to think in terms of a "typical" black person, for example, is to think in stereotypes. Avoid such thinking. One black child may have parents who hold advanced degrees. The child may have traveled extensively, read widely, been around well-educated people, have many friends of different cultures, enjoy fine food, prefer classical music, and be proud of his blackness. Another black child may come from a rural home and have hard-working parents who failed to complete elementary school. The child may never have traveled outside of the county, may have read few books, may have had little exposure to people other than poor blacks, may prefer gospel music, and may be ashamed of his blackness. Although the two children have race and some other cultural traditions and experiences in common (both for example, may have experienced some discrimination), in most respects they are quite different individuals. On the other hand, if you are teaching a group of Hispanic children whose parents are first-generation United States citizens from Mexico, you may find many more cultural traditions and attitudes held in common by these children than the two examples of black children. Avoid thinking that because children are from a particular culture they have all of the stereotypical characteristics of that culture.

To avoid cultural stereotyping, we must recognize differences within every cultural group. Cultural background is only a starting point in getting to know our children in the classroom. Another starting point is to realize that "different" should not be equated with being inferior or superior. People are people first, and as people, children have many characteristics in common. All children need to be accepted as they are, all need to experience success in school tasks, all need recognition for work well done, and all want to know that the teacher respects them. Approach each student as a unique individual who has certain needs and abilities. You are there to educate pupils as you find them.

The Content

Content for the curriculum is determined by the teacher's goals and objectives. An important distinction exists between the **intended** curriculum and the **actual** curriculum. The intended curriculum is represented most directly in the teacher manuals and curriculum guides prepared by the local school district, the state education agency, or commercial textbook publishers. A careful examination of these documents is helpful in revealing the intended curriculum. To find out if a teacher has accepted these goals as her own in practice, examine the actual curriculum, which is represented by the knowledge and skills that students are actually expected to acquire.

One useful way to examine the actual curriculum is to focus attention on the student tasks that teachers evaluate. Students see classrooms as places where academic work is to be completed. The work they must do is associated with products such as work sheets, essays, research reports, projects, tests, and other performance tasks that are to be produced for the teacher's evaluation. In exchange for this work the teacher assigns grades that are intended to represent the quality of the work completed. In the lower levels of the elementary school, teachers may rely on other mechanisms such as praise or other rewards rather than grades to let students know whether they are learning what the teacher intends. Let's examine one factor involved in choosing content to see how inconsistencies between the intended and actual curriculum arise.

Pupil art work

Risk and **ambiguity** are two terms useful in characterizing the academic work in classrooms (Doyle, 1986). At one extreme is the teacher who relies heavily on worksheets from the basal reader program to carry the load in the teaching of reading skills. The teacher introduces the worksheets in the morning (e.g., gives directions, mentions the skill involved) and then spends the rest of the reading period monitoring student work. The risk involved for the students is likely very low in that most students will be able to succeed. The ambiguity is also very low in the sense that the students are quite clear from the assignments and the structure of the worksheets what is to be done.

At the other extreme is the teacher who relies heavily on inquiry as the basis for improving reading comprehension. She assigns pupils a text to read and then places them in discussion groups. These groups are expected to do a literary analysis of the text and then present an oral report on this analysis, paying particular attention to author intent. The risk factor in this task is likely very high in that not all students and perhaps not all of the groups will produce a high-quality report. Ambiguity is also great because the task is rather loosely defined as to how the groups are expected to work together and what a high-quality report looks like.

An important relationship exists between the risk and ambiguity of academic work in classrooms and the learning that is likely to occur. When the amount of cognitive learning expected of pupils is small, low risk and low ambiguity are possible. However, when the amount of cognitive learning expected of pupils is great, high risk and high ambiguity will be present. If the teacher is working on simple associative learning (e.g., a phonic skill) or simple routines (e.g., addition of two-digit numbers without regrouping), then the risk and ambiguity associated with the work should be low. If the teacher is working on concept building (e.g., evaporation) or values (e.g., equality of opportunity), then greater levels of risk and ambiguity result. In general, work in which students have a great opportunity to construct meaning is inherently ambiguous and risky.

Most teachers agree that meaningful learning should take place in school. In a recent survey (Feistritzer 1986), 84 percent of public school teachers felt that one purpose of education is to teach students reasoning and analytical skills. In practice, one would expect that an inspection of classrooms would reveal students engaged frequently in risky and ambiguous tasks. Unfortunately, such is not always the case. The intended curriculum is not reflected in the actual curriculum. To understand this contradiction, you must recognize the relationship between maintaining order and conducting instruction; that is, keeping order in classrooms is more difficult when the academic work is high in risk and ambiguity. Creating meaningful learning opportunities in the classroom, while at the same time keeping students on task, requires a teacher skillful in management. Teachers who are weak in management skills and therefore need to rely on autocratic systems, or who are evaluated by administrators based exclusively on an orderly classroom, may find it necessary to fill the students' day with tasks low in risk and ambiguity. As a result, the intended curriculum is neglected.

The content to be learned in the typical elementary curriculum is organized around subjects that include mathematics, reading and language arts, science, social studies, fine arts, and health and physical education. In each of the subject areas, controversy exists over what should be taught: In reading, questions about the amount of phonics to be taught remain unresolved; in science, the process approach is contested; in mathematics, the "new math" is debated.

If a consensus exists in practice in a particular curriculum area, it is most often tied to similarities in commercial materials. The curriculum in elementary reading is dominated by a handful of basal publishers. Similarly, in science and mathematics, a small number of publishers account for most of the elementary curricula used nationwide.

Two broad issues with respect to the elementary curriculum are currently debated. The first concerns the choice of an "essentialist" versus "experiential" approach to the curriculum. The second is the issue of "dumbing down."

Essentialist Versus Experiential

In an essentialist curriculum the content or process to be learned is broken into small pieces. The student is expected to learn each piece to the mastery level before moving on to the next piece. In reading, this might mean working through a rigid sequence of phonic skills; in mathematics it might mean mastering a progression of simple-to-complex addition algorithms. The experiential approach to curriculum tends to emphasize a holistic interaction between student and content. The emphasis is on active participation by students in activities that may lead to different kinds and levels of learning, depending on what the learner brings to the experience. In reading, an emphasis on "free" reading in literature or "inquiry" reading in content areas, with teacher conferences to support learning, may result. In science, groups of pupils may conduct experiments and then be responsible for sharing findings publicly.

We take no stand about the merits of one approach to curriculum over the other. The strategies presented in this text are applicable to both approaches. You may find that some subject areas are tied to an essentialist philsophy and that others are more experiential in nature. You will need to be as flexible and adaptable in your teaching as the type of curriculum you are expected to teach allows.

"Dumbing Down"

The second general curriculum issue around which there is concerned debate is that of "dumbing down." The term, though not pleasant, is certainly provocative. Jeanne Chall (Chall, Conrad, and Harris 1977) has argued that publishers have been making their texts, particularly in the subject areas of mathematics, science, and social studies, increasingly easier to read over the past two decades. Vocabulary difficulty and concept load have been reduced steadily so that these texts do not present a significant challenge to the higher-ability and even average-ability students. Textbook publishers argue that such changes have been made in response to marketing surveys that indicated textbooks were too difficult for students to read. Chall argues that the decline in textbook difficulty is responsible in large part for the general decline in achievement levels already described.

At the heart of this trend toward dumbing down is an issue that represents something of a dilemma in teaching. The text, insofar as it represents the curriculum for the student, sets an expectation for learning. As texts are made easier, expectations are reduced, and the potential for learning is diminished. On the other hand, when pupils' background knowledge and skills are limited, a text that is too difficult can overwhelm and frustrate the learner. As a result, the learner may withdraw and learn nothing. Is reducing the learning demands for a student who does not have the minimum prerequisite knowledge or skills better or worse than retaining high expectations despite the learner's entering characteristics? For example, a second grade teacher has a class of 22 students with very different reading levels. Should the teacher determine reading levels and place students with books appropriate for their levels, or should the teacher take the second grade reader as the curriculum and use her knowledge of individual students to determine what different instructional approaches might apply best to each student? No simple answers exist, and the best approach is probably not represented by either of the them, but lies in some combination of them along with other alternatives.

The Milieu

From an administrative viewpoint, the basic unit for the nation's schools is the local school district. Since the 1930s there has been a steady decline in the number of school districts (due primarily to consolidations) from over 127,000 to slightly under 16,000.

The "graded" structure for schools has been an essential feature of American public education since the late 19th century. Mandatory school attendance laws that were put into effect at that time in states such as Massachusetts set the age for starting school at six. For the most part, students were expected to progress from one grade level to the next as they grew in chronological age.

By the turn of the century, most schools were organized with eight years of elementary school followed by four years of high school. Early in this century several commissions recommended that junior high schools be established and the number of years students spent in elementary grades be reduced. Districts across the country began experimenting with various grade level combinations. By mid-century approximately 6,500 junior high schools existed in the United States.

More recently we have seen the emergence of the "middle school," a long-standing feature in European educational systems, which generally incorporates grades five through eight. The middle school movement has gained momentum in recent years in response to such diverse issues as integration, subject matter achievement, and child development. This new structure for school organization is more than simply determining what building houses what grade levels; it reflects some important shifts in the treatment of students and subject matter.

Wiles and Bondi (1981) have suggested some important differences. In middle schools, teachers are more likely to work in interdisciplinary teams. This contrasts with teachers in self-contained classrooms at the elementary level and departmental organizations at the secondary level. The curriculum emphasis in middle schools is on exploration; in the elementary grades the emphasis is more likely on skills, and in the secondary grades on greater depth of coverage. Schedules in the middle schools tend to include blocks of time devoted to integrated subjects; at the elementary and secondary levels subjects tend to be treated more separately. In middle schools, students are often grouped according to developmental level; in elementary grades they are grouped by chronological age and in secondary classrooms, by subject and ability. Middle schools, then, are designed to help students in the transition from pre-adolescence through the early stages of adolescence, with particular concern for the growth and development of the learner.

The typical elementary school today has about 500 students, as compared with approximately 600 in 1973 (Feistritzer 1983). The individual elementary school is a complex organization. One way to think about the elementary school is in terms of how educators and learners are organized to carry out the business of teaching and learning. In contrast to most bureaucracies, schools can be characterized as relatively "flat" organizations typically composed of a principal with one level of authority and responsibility, possibly an assistant principal or lead teacher at the next level, and then the teachers who share equal authority and responsibility regardless of grade level or years of teaching experience.

The graded, self-contained classroom is still the norm in most elementary schools in the United States. Each teacher assumes primary responsibility for guiding the learning of a group of students for one academic year. Usually, students enter kindergarten in the September following their fifth birthday, and for the most part continue through the grades with their age group. When multiple classes exist at a given grade level, the typical pattern is to assign students to individual teachers without regard to ability levels.

Within the primary grades (kindergarten through third) the individual teacher typically instructs the whole class in the subject areas of science, social studies, and art and forms ability groups for reading and sometimes mathematics. At the intermediate levels (grades four through six in the absence of a middle school, grades four and five with a middle school present) a trend toward departmentalized instruction by subject areas seems to be occurring. Under this system each teacher at each grade level assumes responsibility for teaching a particular subject, and students are shifted from teacher to teacher on a fixed schedule. Departmentalization may or may not involve ability grouping of students. When using ability grouping, the teacher adjusts the content or methodology or both to accommodate differences in ability.

Issues related to self-contained versus ability grouping and other alternative organizational patterns for classrooms are fraught with controversy. With self-contained classrooms, the teacher has the advantage of coming to know the children better and has flexibility in time scheduling. The teacher is therefore in a better position to respond to individual students' needs in all areas. Ability grouping for instruction affords better opportunities for the teacher to differentiate curriculum and instruction, but the cost is often isolation of the better learners from the less able. Without models for good learning, the less successful students may find breaking out of a failure pattern more difficult.

The milieu for teaching is more than just the organizational structure of the school. It also encompasses what we can term the **norms** or **expected patterns of behavior** on the part of teachers and students.

As you observe and work in schools as part of your program, keep the following kinds of questions about norms of behavior in mind:

□ How do teachers relate to and interact with one another around the tasks of schooling?

□ What evidence exists that teachers are talking to one another about teaching?

□ What evidence indicates that the principal is supportive of teachers' efforts to be effective?

□ In what ways is the environment made orderly both within classrooms and in other school settings such as the lunchroom and playground?

□ In what ways are students exercising responsibility for learning both in individual and cooperative group settings?

From such observations you will come to recognize the norms of behavior in a school. The character of the school is something you can sense only by "living" there and becoming intimately involved in the daily school lives of the teachers and students.

The milieu for teaching also reaches outside the immediate school and school district. States have become increasingly active in educational decision making in recent years, particularly in the areas of curriculum, funding, student and teacher competency testing, and teacher certification. This activity influences what goes on in individual classrooms.

Education policy mandates that emanate from state education agencies are, of course, a reflection of the general public's opinions about the quality of schooling. Surveys indicate that the public's confidence in the quality of schools has been steadily deteriorating for the past two decades. Whether these concerns are valid or not, the fact is that teaching has become very political. The public's attitudes about schools and the policy activity that results are real, influential, and, at times, frustrating.

MAJOR FUNCTIONS OF TEACHING

Teaching is work. Schools are workplaces. These are stark images offered not with the intention of reducing teaching from the noble to the menial, but with the goal of emphasizing the real world that awaits you.

To discover the real world of teaching, you need to spend considerable time watching teachers at work. Imagine yourself as an observer in a "typical" classroom in a "typical" elementary or middle school, on a "typical" school day. What kinds of things do you expect to see the teacher in such a classroom doing? Surely the teacher will spend some time talking with students informally and formally as well as individually and in groups. This talk may be focused on the content to be learned (academics), on some ways of working in the classroom (procedures), or on some personal matter. The teacher uses talk to inform, direct, persuade, praise, correct, acknowledge, challenge, extend, interpret, evaluate, and build relationships with students. The teacher probably devotes considerable time to observing students as well, checking for compliance with rules and procedures or for signs of frustration or withdrawal. The teacher may spend some classroom time writing, either with students or alone. There are reports to complete, papers to check, grades to record, and plans to write. The teacher may also attend to the physical aspects of the classroom, such as arranging displays, moving furniture, and other housekeeping tasks. A teacher must attend meetings, monitor lunchrooms and halls, confer with parents and administrators, and chaperon students through the school to special classes, recess, lunch, and dismissal.

A typical teacher's work does not end even when she leaves the school. At home, materials must be constructed, plans written, and parents called. The teacher also reads professional magazines and books in search of teaching ideas, answers to questions, and for professional growth. The typical teacher likely attends workshops, seminars, and conferences devoted to improving teaching skills and knowledge and may even enroll in advanced coursework at colleges and universities. In addition, the teacher is now being called on to take tests designed to demonstrate her competence to the public.

Not all of what the typical teacher does is so easily observed. A teacher spends an enormous amount of time thinking about instruction, which serves to create plans and images for instruction and includes reflection on past instructional events. The typical teacher worries a great deal about her effectiveness in the task of helping students learn and develop. The typical teacher is also concerned with how she is perceived by others, including colleagues, administrators, parents, and students.

This is by no means a complete listing of what typical teachers do, but it does represent something of the array of activities that engage teachers. The "doing" of teaching is not as simple or clear as some texts suggest. The roles and responsibilities are many. The knowledge and skill base required to be successful is tremendous.

Our purpose in sharing these perceptions on teaching is not to discourage you from becoming a teacher, but simply to help dispel any romantic notions about teaching that, if embraced too tightly, may set the stage for disappointment and disillusionment. Recognizing that excellent or expert teachers seem able to rise above the difficulties, shortcomings, and trivialities that surround their work may also give you some encouragement to improve. Expert teachers find rewards in teaching that are far more important to them than salary or prestige. The findings from Philip Jackson's (1968) classic study of **Life in Classrooms** ring as true today as they did when published two decades ago. He found that among the rewards of teaching commented on most often by **excellent** teachers were those related to autonomy, immediacy, and spontaneity. Autonomy refers to the rewards experienced by making professional decisions about what is best for the students in your class; immediacy refers to the rewards of seeing your students learn as a result of your efforts those things you feel are important; spontaneity refers to the rewards of working in an unpredictable, ever-changing and exciting classroom. The true rewards of teaching are subtle and powerful and more likely to be experienced when a teacher becomes an expert.

As you strive to become an expert, it may be helpful to think about the requirements of teaching in terms of major functions. The types of activities involved in teaching just described can be categorized in terms of four major functions: (1) institutional, (2) managerial, (3) academic, and (4) professional development. The remainder of this chapter will be organized around a discussion of these four functions of teaching.

The Institutional Function

The institutional function requires the teacher to attend to student and teacher nonacademic and personal needs such as collecting lunch money, turning in attendance reports, filling out time sheets, and listening to announcements. Common sense and research findings (Brophy and Good 1986) support the notion that time devoted to institutional activities is time taken away from instruction. In more effective schools, and with more effective teachers, the time spent dealing with institutional functions is minimal.

The Managerial Function

The managerial function of teaching refers to the need to establish efficient and effective systems for students to get along and get work done in the classroom. A classroom is a problem space in terms of order—four walls surrounding a crowd of people. Teachers must manage students' lives during the school day in this confined space; they must create systems for working together that will ensure productivity and help students grow in self-discipline and independent work habits.

Some teachers manage classrooms by assuming most or all of the responsibility for management. The teacher is responsible for setting the rules and procedures and for monitoring and rewarding student performance. The teacher is the primary decision maker. Other teachers create work relationships that require cooperation and are based on democratic, participatory norms for student behavior. In such systems the students bear considerable responsibility for self-monitoring of behavior. The majority of teachers likely operate between the two extremes of teacher domination and individual student responsibility. Any approach has advantages and disadvantages; how a teacher approaches classroom management results in a broad array of short- and long-term consequences, some detrimental and others beneficial.

Each teacher presents through her management system a situation to which students must adjust. Students must determine and adapt to the rules for getting along and getting work done efficiently. Teacher-dominated classrooms are fairly low in ambiguity for the students; that is, students can easily know what is expected and respond accordingly. Most students, if they are motivated to do so, can learn to get along in such systems.

Teachers who organize the classroom toward more democratic systems make it more difficult for students to determine what is expected. These classrooms are inherently more ambiguous and risky. Rules for working together may not be clear and must be determined through uncertain processes. Because the processes involved require a degree of individual student responsibility, many students find it difficult to perform in such systems.

More autocratic systems of management are fairly easy to implement and maintain, but they may not be effective in nurturing student independence. The more democratic systems of management, which nurture independence, are more difficult to implement and maintain. Later in this text you will be offered some practical suggestions and guidance about workable management strategies for the beginning teacher.

The Academic Function

The teacher's academic function is to help students acquire knowledge and skills. Humans learn in essentially three ways:

1. through observation (i.e., watching others perform)
2. through direct experience (i.e., trying out or doing)
3. through being taught (i.e., a knowledgeable other helping us learn)

This simple framework is useful in thinking about how learning in schools sometimes differs from or resembles the learning that goes on outside the school. Outside the school, personal learning tends to result primarily from observing things and others (modeling) and from direct experience. Within schools, a greater emphasis on the help and guidance of knowledgeable others is commonly used to promote learning. This should not be taken to mean that no place exists for learning by observing or by doing; all three modes of learning must work in combination. The adequacy of learning restricted to knowledgeable others, while ignoring observation and direct experience, is questionable. Active observations and direct experiences along with input of knowledgeable others should be part of learning, whether inside or outside the classroom or school.

A teacher can help pupils acquire knowledge and skills by direct or indirect teaching. Direct teaching uses learning experiences in which the teacher actively guides students in the learning process. Direct teaching has a focused purpose and carefully targeted learning outcomes and typically includes three phases: demonstration, practice, and feedback (Rosenshine and Stevens 1984). Direct teaching can occur with the whole class, small groups, or individuals. A teacher presenting a reading skill to a small group, directing students in a mathematics drill, or demonstrating a science concept is using direct teaching.

Indirect teaching uses learning experiences that involve little or no direct instruction by the teacher. The teacher structures the experience toward specific learning goals, but the students are given the responsibility for carrying out tasks independently or in groups. The emphasis in indirect instruction is on learning by pursuing tasks with little or no direct supervision by the teacher. Learning centers, research projects, library corners, and journal writing are all examples of indirect teaching.

Both direct and indirect teaching are important parts of classroom life. Students spend their days in both direct and indirect learning experiences; the teacher spends most of her day in direct teaching. The appropriateness of direct or indirect teaching depends on the nature of desired learning outcomes. The role of the teacher is quite different, depending on the nature of the knowledge to be taught and the knowledge the learner brings to the lesson. How you approach the teaching of a particular piece of content or process is a decision that takes careful consideration of the learner's existing knowledge base and what is to be learned.

Substantial research exists to suggest that effective teaching strategies are dependent on the type of learning outcomes desired. For example, direct instruction works quite well in teaching basic skills (e.g., multiplying fractions); indirect instruction may be more appropriate in developing values (e.g., literary appreciation).

The Professional Development Function

Professions are characterized by the following:

1. a complex body of knowledge is used as the basis for performing
2. the purpose for the professional activity has significance for those receiving the service and for the society at large
3. the practitioner is actively and frequently involved in making important decisions and judgments about appropriate courses of action

4. the practitioner bears responsibility for contributing to and keeping abreast of knowledge in the field

5. entry into the profession and advancement within the profession are rigorous processes subject to standards set and controlled by the profession.

Teaching is a profession. Entry into teaching, and advancement once admitted, are becoming increasingly difficult as standards are being raised across the country. The skills and knowledge required to be an expert are complex. Good teaching has a direct and immediate impact on the lives of individuals and ultimately on society. Teachers have tremendous decision-making responsibilities that require knowledge and freedom to act. If teachers are to meet these responsibilities, and if they wish to consider themselves professional, then they must be concerned about their professional development.

Expert teachers devote a considerable amount of time and energy to this professional development function throughout their careers. Teachers who grow are those who work at not only learning from their own experiences but also by reaching out through professional reading, participation at the local school level in curriculum and program planning and evaluation, and involvement in professional organizations at the local, state, and national levels.

Recognize that activities related to the professional development function are not the same as those related to the institutional function. Teacher meetings involve both functions: When such meetings provide an opportunity for teachers to learn important things about teaching, or to work together to solve instructional problems, these activities relate to the professional development function. When such meetings tend to be given over to issues related to nonacademic functions (i.e., attendance procedures, schedules, or parking places), then they are institutionally related. If you have the opportunity to work or visit in schools as part of this semester's experience, then you should try to sit in on a teachers' meeting. Your observations of such meetings will give you a sense of the concern for professional development in the school.

SUMMARY

Our goal through this text is to assist you in becoming an expert teacher. You are a student of teaching striving to become an expert. We carry no illusions, nor should you, that you will achieve expert status by the time you finish this book. Expertise in teaching develops slowly.

We will present you with a great deal of information in this book that we believe is important in helping you become an expert teacher. However, in the final analysis, this book will raise more questions about effective teaching than it will answer. We believe that ignorance in a topic like teaching has less to do with not knowing the answers than it does with not knowing what the important questions are. We recognize that we can engage you in the interaction that gives birth to questioning only in the textual space that exists between authors and reader. We will assume that our dialogue of the minds will be augmented by your interactions with classmates, a course instructor, and perhaps even some practicing teachers and their students.

REFERENCES

Brophy, J.F. and T.L. Good. 1986. Teacher behavior and student achievement. In *Handbook of research in teaching*, ed. M. Wittrock. New York: Macmillan.

Chall, J.S., S.S. Conrad, and S.H. Harris. 1977. *An analysis of textbooks in relation to declining SAT scores*. New York: College Entrance Examination Board.

Darling-Hammond, L. 1984. *Beyond the commission reports: The coming crisis in teaching*. Santa Monica, CA: Rand Corporation.

Doyle, W. 1986. Classroom organization and management. In *Handbook of research in teaching*, ed. M. Wittrock. New York: Macmillan.

Feistritzer, C.E. 1983. *The American teacher*. Washington, DC: Feistritzer Publications.

Feistritzer, C.E. 1986. *Profile of teachers in the U.S.* Washington, DC: National Center for Education Information.

Hoffman, J.V. and S.A. Edwards. 1986. *Reality and reform in clinical teacher education*. New York: Random House.

Jackson, P.W. 1968. *Life in classrooms*. New York: Holt, Rinehart and Winston.

Johnson, D.W. and R.T. Johnson. 1987. *Learning together and alone: Cooperative, competitive and individualistic learning*. Englewood Cliffs, NJ: Prentice-Hall.

Palincsar, A.T. and A.L. Brown. 1986. Interactive teaching to promote independent learning from text. *Reading Teacher* 39(8):771–778.

Pearson, P.D., and D.D. Johnson. 1978. *Teaching reading comprehension*. New York: Holt, Rinehart and Winston.

Rosenshine, B., and R. Stevens. 1984. Classroom instruction in reading. In *Handbook of reading research*, ed. P. Pearson. New York: Longman, p.745–798.

Schwab, J.J. 1960. The teaching of science as enquiry. In *The teaching of science*, eds. J.J. Schwab and P.R. Brandewine. Cambridge, MA: Harvard University Press.

Shulman, L.S. and N.B. Carey. 1984. Psychology and the limitations of individual rationality: Implications for the study of reasoning and civility. *Review of Educational Research* 54(9): 501–504.

Slavin, R. 1980. Cooperative learning. *Review of Educational Research* 50: 315–342.

Vygotsky, L.S. 1978. *Mind in society: The development of higher psychological powers*. Cambridge, MA: Harvard University Press.

Wiles, J. and J. Bondi. 1981. *The Essential Middle School*. Columbus, OH: Merrill.

CHAPTER REVIEW

Commonplaces of Teaching: Four Essential Parts of Teaching
1. The teacher
2. The learner
3. The content
4. The milieu

The Teacher
The expert teacher is:

☐ organized and efficient in managing the classroom

☐ a leader

☐ an inspiration to students

☐ sensitive to individual student needs

☐ knowledgeable in the content to be taught and the methods to be used in teaching it

☐ diagnostic

☐ able to construct cooperatively a school climate favorable to learning

☐ able to build relationships with parents and others in the community

☐ an enthusiastic learner

☐ able to deal easily with the bigger picture and larger issues.

The Learner
1. The number of elementary-aged students is increasing.
2. The proportion of minority students is increasing.
3. Achievement appears to be in a pattern of decline.
4. Views of the learner by psychologists have changed in recent years. The learner is no longer regarded as a passive recipient of information, but as an active and socialized participant.
5. Students differ widely from each other.
   a. Some have impairments that may cause particular problems in an educational setting.
   b. All students come from different cultural backgrounds.
6. Pupils have many characteristics in common. They need
   a. to be accepted as they are
   b. to experience success in school activities
   c. recognition for work well done
   d. the teacher's respect

The Content
1. The curriculum
   a. Intended curriculum is indicated in teacher manuals, curriculum guides, and other state education publications.

    b. Actual curriculum is represented by the knowledge and skills that students are actually expected to acquire in the classroom.

2. Degree of risk and ambiguity
   a. Low risk and low ambiguity are
      (1) associated with academic work requiring little cognitive change.
      (2) more easily managed than high-risk and high ambiguity learning
   b. High risk and high ambiguity are
      (1) present in academic work requiring significant cognitive change.
      (2) more difficult to manage than low risk and low ambiguity learning
3. Curriculum Issues
   a. Essentialist vs. experiential approaches.
      (1) Essentialists promote mastery learning.
      (2) Experientialists promote holistic interaction between students and the content.
   b. "Dumbing down"
      (1) Curriculum content should be adjusted to the ability levels of the students.
      (2) Instruction should be adjusted so that students can learn content assigned to a course or grade level regardless of students' ability levels.

The Milieu

1. Graded, self-contained classrooms are the norm in elementary schools.
2. Departmentalized instruction by subject area is the norm for intermediate elementary grades and middle schools.
3. Public confidence in schools is declining.
4. Political influence in education is on the rise.
5. The 'ethos' of a school (i.e., norms of student and teacher behavior that emphasize academics) is related to school effectiveness.

Functions of Teaching

1. Institutional: the teacher attends to personal and nonacademic needs of students
2. Managerial: the teacher implements an ordered system for students to get along and get work done in the classroom.
3. Academic: the teacher plans for, initiates, sustains, and evaluates student work and related learning.
4. Professional: teachers assume increasing responsibility for their own professional growth not only by learning from their classroom experiences, but also by reaching out through professional reading, participation in curriculum development, and by involvement in local, state, and national professional organizations.

OBSERVATION EXERCISE 1

A Study of Pupils

The elementary or middle school classroom looks different to students and teachers. This exercise will help you become familiar with the characteristics and behaviors of students in classrooms from the teacher's viewpoint.

Directions. Record the following observations:

1. Record the number of boys and the number of girls in the classroom.
2. Record the percentage ethnic makeup of the students in the classroom. Include American Indian, Black, Anglo, Asian, and Hispanic.
3. Record the nature of any physical handicaps that students have. In what ways might these handicaps limit the handicapped students' activities in the classroom?
4. What do students do with personal belongings, such as pencils, paper, texts, combs, purses, and clothes, when they first enter the classroom? During lessons?
5. What do the students do when they first enter the classroom? When class starts?
6. Observe one girl for ten minutes and record what she does during those ten minutes. In what ways do other students, the teacher, or other stimuli affect her behavior?
7. Observe one boy for ten minutes and record what he does during those ten minutes. In what ways do other students, the teacher, or other stimuli affect his behavior?
8. In what ways are the girl's and boy's behavior similar? Different? In what ways do other people or things affect their behavior differently? Similarly?
9. What do students do when they leave the room at the end of the class?
10. What, if anything, surprised you about those things you observed?

OBSERVATION EXERCISE 2

The Content

This exercise will cause you to examine the content of the curriculum. Content and skills are taught to students to achieve certain goals and objectives. Some of these goals and objectives may be more valid than others.

Directions. Observe a complete lesson and record the following observations and answer the related questions.

1. Briefly describe the content or skill being taught in the lesson.
2. What did the teacher do at the start of the lesson to help the students recognize the importance of the content or skill being taught?

3. What did the teacher do at the end of the lesson to help the students recognize the importance of the content or skill being taught?

4. What level of risk and ambiguity were involved in the lesson? What reasons support the judgment?

5. In what ways does the content or skill being taught have significance in the lives of students?

6. What evidence do you have that students either had success or difficulty in learning the content or skill being taught?

Planning Instruction **2**

Planning is thinking about instruction in order to make decisions about what will be taught and how one will teach it. The more carefully and thoroughly a teacher thinks about instruction, the better his decisions and the more effective his instruction will be. Planning for instruction is therefore essential.

Good decision making is a central part of effective teaching and professional life. All of the areas of planning discussed in this chapter are part of what has been termed **pre-active** teacher decision making. The decisions a teacher makes before instituting instruction are an important part of successful teaching.

This chapter will introduce six planning-related tasks that research suggests are critical to successful teaching. These are:

1. identifying content and goals
2. assessing pupil abilities
3. organizing for instruction
4. pacing instruction
5. developing units
6. preparing lessons

The first five areas will be described in fairly general terms; the sixth will be introduced in considerable detail in this chapter and then continued throughout most of the remaining chapters. Do not interpret the depth or order of treatment in this chapter to mean that any one area is more or less important than another. Extensive consideration is given to lesson preparation throughout this book because your initial direct involvement in teaching as a part of an introductory course will most likely be focused at the lesson level. As you move further into your teaching preparation program you will begin to assume greater responsibilities in the other five areas.

IDENTIFYING CONTENT AND GOALS

Although the individual classroom teacher retains some flexibility in determining the curriculum in the classroom, the time when individual teachers were expected to determine everything to be taught is gone. Today, most school districts have identified an intended curriculum for each of the major subject areas at the elementary level.

In some school districts, particularly the larger ones, the intended curriculum may be presented in curriculum guides for the subject areas. These guides have often been developed by teachers in the district working together with instructional coordinators and curriculum experts. A comprehensive curriculum guide identifies goals and objectives for the subject, prescribes a sequence for teaching, suggests activities to be followed, and identifies resources for the teacher to use. Of course, the quality and detail provided in curriculum guides can vary enormously among districts and even among subject areas within a district.

Rather than working to develop individual curriculum guides for each subject area, many districts choose to identify the curriculum through the commercial materials and programs they adopt. Publishers develop materials for teaching that reflect a particular representation of the content. In the major subject areas of the elementary curriculum, publishers typically develop a set of materials, usually referred to as a **series,** that purport to offer a comprehensive and coherent treatment of the subject across grade levels. When schools adopt a particular series for use in a subject area, they are, in effect, making a commitment to a particular curriculum.

The subject area of mathematics, science, and reading can be used to illustrate the need, importance, and role of an explicit curriculum in successful teaching. Each of these subject areas is composed of both content and processes that are important in the curriculum. Mathematics is composed of computational procedures (e.g., simple addition, subtraction with regrouping) and processes (e.g., problem solving, estimation). Science is composed of content topics (e.g., gravity, magnetism) and skills (e.g., observing, hypotheses formation). Reading includes the study of literary genre (e.g., poetry, fables, myths, mysteries) and strategies (e.g., word analysis, comprehension).

The content and processes for each of these subject areas is sequentially ordered in the curriculum. In some cases, sequencing decisions with respect to content are justified on developmental grounds. Thus, in mathematics, learning to add without regrouping is an important prerequisite to learning to add with regrouping. In science, content must be chosen that is consistent with the child's stage of cognitive development.

In other cases, sequencing decisions are based on convenience or personal preference. In reading, for example, a curriculum may include an introduction to folktales at one level and myths at another. The order in which these are taught may be arbitrary, because one is not a prerequisite to the other; however, administrators may desire consistency among teachers to ensure that both are included in the curriculum.

What would schools be like if each teacher were free to determine the curriculum in each subject area without regard to other teachers and classes? Obviously, the curriculum would be disjointed, with many repetitions and omissions. Curriculum guides and instructional materials help teachers avoid these problems. Through the use of guides and instructional materials all students are more likely to experience a coherent and continuous exposure to all important subject areas.

The effective teacher recognizes the importance of the school curriculum and devotes a considerable amount of time studying the materials that represent the content to be taught. This study includes looking not only at the curriculum at the grade level to be taught, but also the curricula immediately preceding and following the targeted grade level. The effective teacher, while doing this kind of review, often engages in curriculum revision. The teacher, working alone or in collaboration with other teachers, should enhance or improve the curriculum by building on the teacher's past experiences and growing professional knowledge in the various subject areas.

ASSESSING STUDENT ABILITIES

Instructional materials and curriculum guides for a subject area are developed and written without a full knowledge of the situation in which they are to be used. Curriculum guides and instructional materials are based on a whole set of assumptions about learner characteristics that may or may not be true for individual teachers or learners. The mathematics curriculum designed for use at the second grade level is based on the assumption that the students entering second grade have learned the skills identified in the first grade curriculum and have not learned those in the second grade curriculum. For some students (presumably the majority) such assumptions may hold true; they may not for many others. This situation is common in all schools. Treating students as if they are all alike because the curriculum guide is interpreted too rigidly or literally can cause serious problems. Effective teachers know that the curriculum guide is a reference point from which to make decisions. The teacher assumes responsibility for assessing student abilities in the various subject areas so that the appropriateness of the intended curriculum for individuals can be determined and modified when needed. Assessment will be considered in several places in this text, but for the present, a brief introduction to assessment as it relates to planning is provided here.

Assessments are conducted most intensely during the first few weeks of the school year or at the beginning of extended units of study. The results of these assessments then influence the decisions that will shape the instructional program. In conducting these assessments the teacher may test students individually or in groups. Often these tests are informally constructed by the teacher, although in some cases tests may be provided by the publishers of the programs being used.

In mathematics, for example, the teacher may construct some simple tests that check on computational skills identified in the preceding year's curriculum guide. Even for students who are skilled in these areas, these tests often provide the opportunity for review of important skills needed in the current academic year. The results of these tests may also identify students who need intensive instruction on prerequisite skills before launching into the intended curriculum.

In reading, the effective teacher may take the time during the first few weeks of school to listen informally to students read from a text they completed the previous year or perhaps even from a text to be read in the current year. The teacher notes student strengths and weaknesses in word analysis, fluency, and comprehension. These are important data for the teacher when making decisions about where individual children might best fit into the curriculum and what instructional strategies might best be used with the learner.

Of course, informal testing is only one of many possible sources of information on students. The effective teacher may also study cumulative records looking for long-term patterns in performance. The effective teacher takes note of learning or physical disabilities that might be important in constructing an instructional program that is suited to the individual children or the class.

Assessment is a common part of the effective teacher's classroom throughout the year. If teachers are to provide needed feedback and proper instructional decisions for the students, then teachers must actively and continuously monitor how students are responding to the instructional program (sometimes referred to as **formative evaluation**) and not wait until the end of the year (sometimes referred to as **summative evaluation**) for such assessment. The importance of the assessment that goes on in the first few weeks of school should not be underestimated, however. During this crucial period many important decisions are made, such as whether to provide remedial activities and how the early activities will be sequenced.

ORGANIZING FOR INSTRUCTION

Teachers have limits on the amount of time available each day to accomplish all of the assigned tasks in and out of the classroom. Effective teachers use this time efficiently through careful organization and planning. Establishing schedules, establishing management systems for indirect instruction, planning the pacing of instruction, developing units, and preparing daily lesson plans are all tasks that require organization and planning.

Establishing Schedules

A part of organizing for instruction is establishing a schedule for academics. Research indicates that teachers who are particularly effective in promoting the academic growth of students are those who maximize the amount of time allocated to academics during the school day (Brophy, 1986). Part of the available time in any school day is taken up with institutional and management functions. Effective teachers work to minimize the time taken away from instruction by setting up a schedule of academic work for the day or week that wastes little time on procedural tasks and makes a strong effort to adhere to the schedule.

The actual schedule is based on consideration of several factors. The amount of time scheduled for the teaching of certain subject areas may be (and often is) prescribed by state law. These time regulations are often expressed in terms of the minimum number of minutes per week in subject areas. In middle schools, subjects are usually scheduled in discreet periods, so the time students spend in certain subjects is set by the school consistent with state laws. At the elementary level, these "minimums" often leave some leeway for the teacher to be flexible in scheduling and expanding the time in subject areas as needed. Elementary teachers must consider the schedule for special classes such as music, art, and physical education that are scheduled by the school. Given the fact that the scheduling of these "special" classes for the entire school is such a complex problem, teachers are expected to be flexible when planning for their classrooms. In those elementary and middle schools where there is partial departmentalization or other forms of shared teaching responsibilities for a group of students, teachers work together to determine a schedule that allows an orderly transition between classes.

Planning Indirect Instruction

A second part of organizing for instruction is the establishment of work routines or a management system for indirect instruction. Direct instruction is characterized by active participation of the teacher working with the students; indirect instruction is characterized by students engaged in independent learning. Learning through indirect instruction is maximized when it is well organized and managed.

Indirect instruction is commonly managed at the elementary level through the use of "centers" and "contracts." In a center management system, physical areas of the room (e.g., corners, desks partitioned off) are identified by a theme (e.g., writing, library, science, mathematics). Each area has specific tasks set up for students to complete independently or cooperatively that are related to that theme (e.g., solve a puzzle, read a book and make a cover, write a story about a picture, make some estimations). Students move from center to center, completing tasks based on some planned schedule. This movement may be based on a specific amount of time in a center or on task completion. Many variations are possible.

In contract management systems, students are typically given a written form that identifies the tasks to be completed independently in a given period of time. Students may or may not be given choices about the order of task completion and optional (as opposed to required) tasks. The effective teacher is able to plan and implement a system that allows students to pursue the tasks on the contract independently while the teacher is engaged with other students in direct instruction.

Pacing Instruction

Decisions about the pacing of instruction are among the most complex and least understood aspects of planning. In its simplest terms, **pacing** refers to the rate at which content is taught in a classroom. For example, a teacher working in science has to decide on how much class time to spend on magnets. In reading, a teacher must decide whether to move through a basal at two stories or three stories per week. Pacing decisions involve all of the areas of planning discussed so far—the consideration of the curriculum, the abilities of the students, and the organization of the instructional program. Pacing is far more complex than simply taking the number of chapters in the social studies text and distributing these evenly across the time available in the year.

The effective teacher must be responsive to how well the students are learning and be willing to adjust the pace of lessons accordingly, either for individuals or the entire class. The effective teacher also plans so as to be able to adjust the pace of instruction as needed during lessons. For example, novice teachers may find it difficult to anticipate the number of examples students may need to master a particular skill. To accommodate for this in a lesson, teachers can plan more examples than they think they need, then use all or only some of the examples as the lesson progresses. The teacher can also plan short optional activities to allow the extension of lessons when needed to maintain schedules. These could include such things as addition/subtraction or carrying facts with which the students may need more incidental practice. The teacher may have the letters of the alphabet or common colors displayed in the room, and plan to ask students to name letters or colors for brief periods of time when time becomes available. An optional story related to the lesson could be planned so that if time becomes available the teacher can enrich the lesson by reading the story.

This kind of planned flexibility also allows the teacher to take advantage of unexpected "teachable moments" that arise. At times students suddenly indicate an intense interest in some part of a lesson. Pursuing that interest could result in some unplanned but significant learning. Thorough planning makes it easier to pursue those moments when they occur.

Providing for optional activities or planning where the lesson could be stopped and delayed until the next day also has its advantages. When students are not learning at the rate the teacher anticipated, allowing more time for additional explanation or practice is essential. Occasionally, administrators may suddenly shorten the school day (more common in middle school than in the elementary grades). When these kinds of things occur, some of the planned activities will need to be eliminated or delayed until later lessons.

The effective teacher recognizes the importance of holding high academic expectations for students while also recognizing that expectations that are too high may only produce frustration and, ultimately, failure. Teachers must maintain high but reasonable standards, and communicate these to students most directly through the pacing of instruction.

DEVELOPING UNITS

If you talk to elementary or middle school teachers about what they are teaching in subject areas such as social studies and science, they generally tend to respond in terms of a topic; for example, "I'm teaching the Constitution," or "We're studying the water cycle." Instruction that is organized around a particular topic or theme is often referred to as a **unit**. Planning units is an important part of an effective teacher's responsibility. The topics to be taught in any given academic year are typically identified in the school district's curriculum guides or in the adopted textbooks for subject areas. These curriculum materials or guides identify broad goals and objectives and suggest activities to be followed over an extended period of time.

Units are often designed around three phases. The first is an **initiating event** that introduces the topic and provides some overview of the study and piques student interest. The initiating event may be a guest speaker, a film, a field trip, a demonstration, an experiment, or a brainstorming session. The second phase of a unit involves a series of **focused lessons** around the topic that introduces and develops new information.

The final phase of a unit typically involves some **culminating activity** that serves to pull all of the information learned about the topic together for one final view. This is a time during which students might share with one another work they have completed over the course of the study. The unit may be augmented by **correlated activities** such as field trips, guest speakers, movies, or group projects such as model building or research reports.

Effective teachers recognize that units provide an opportunity to integrate skills being learned in the diverse subject areas of the curriculum. Thus, the study of ants in science provides an opportunity to use in an applied way the mathematics, writing, and reading skills developed elsewhere in the curriculum.

PREPARING LESSONS

The lesson can be thought of as the smallest unit in direct instruction. The lesson is a teacher-directed learning experience to accomplish specific objectives or learning outcomes. As a student teacher in the early stages of learning to teach, you will find yourself in a position of planning daily lessons, with someone else making most of the long-term planning decisions. Considerable emphasis will therefore be placed at this time and throughout the rest of this textbook on learning lesson planning. This chapter focuses attention primarily on the thinking needed to establish instructional intent. The issues related to planning activities are covered in later chapters that expand on the tasks of active teaching and lesson frameworks.

Focused Instruction

Research on learning has shown that student achievement can be enhanced if the instruction is directed toward particular outcomes (Lawson, 1974; Melton, 1978; Roberts, 1982). Analyzing what students should be able to do following instruction that they could not do prior to instruction is important. By starting with this analysis, the teacher will be better able to choose content or skills and design activities that will result in student learning. What students are expected to learn to do as a result of instruction should determine the nature of the learning experiences.

For example, if I want to teach students about graphs, I will be better able to focus my instruction if I first decide what I want students to be able to do with graphs. Do I want them to be able to plot bar graphs? Do I want them to be able, given one variable on one axis of a line graph, to determine the quantity of the variable on the other axis? Do I want them to be able to extrapolate from a line graph? An affirmative answer to any one of these questions would dictate a different set of learning activities as well as different kinds of assessments of student learning.

Instructional objectives should increase student achievement and improve student attitudes toward classroom instruction by helping teachers to design learning activities and assessment instruments that are more likely to be congruent with their instructional intent.

Teachers assess pupils before instruction.

INSTRUCTIONAL OBJECTIVES

An instructional objective is **a desired outcome of learning that is expressed in terms of observable behavior or performance of the learners**. The learners should be able to do something that they could not do prior to the learning experience provided by the teacher. The observed behaviors at the end of the lesson are going to be either new behaviors or extensions of existing behaviors. An instructional objective obviously will not measure all of the possible outcomes of a learning experience, but it should measure those outcomes specifically desired by the teacher.

An instructional objective is composed of three parts:

1. a verb or infinitive defining some observable action

2. a description of the task to be performed

3. an indication of the criterion to be used to judge whether students can perform the task satisfactorily

Imagine you are a teacher who wishes to teach students about writing sentences using correct verb tenses. You could choose several possible things for students to learn, each requiring a different kind of instruction. You could choose to teach students to be "able to write ten sentences, five using present tense and five using past tense, and be able to do this with 90 percent accuracy." Notice the observable action is described by the infinitive "to write," the task is "to write ten sentences, five using present tense and five using past tense." The criterion for success would be "to do this with 90 percent accuracy." On the other hand, you might want to teach the students to be able "to identify and list ten errors of verb tense found in a 100-word paragraph and write the correct verb tense with an accuracy of 80 percent." Notice the observable actions are described by the infinitives **to identify, to list** and **to write**. The task is one of identifying and listing ten errors in verb tense found in a paragraph, then writing the correct form. The criterion is to do this with 80 percent accuracy.

The two objectives are different even though they involve similar content. The nature of the learning activities is also different. To achieve the first objective, the appropriate learning activities might involve practice in writing sentences using present and past verb tenses. To achieve the second objective, the activities would involve practice in analyzing sentences for verb tense errors.

Here are a few illustrations of correctly stated instructional objectives:

1. Students will be able to identify the situation that involves magnetism from a list of four written descriptions, only one of which involves magnetism.

2. When given photographs of ten different kinds of hats, students will be able to list the occupation associated with each with an 80 percent accuracy.

3. When given a mixed-up sequence of eight different length sticks, students will be able to arrange the eight sticks in order from longest to shortest.

4. When given the photographs of ten animals, students will be able to group the animals into three groups based on different characteristics for each group and list the characteristics used to group the animals.

5. When given ten Spanish sentences, students will be able to translate at least seven sentences into English without error.

A few nonexamples may illustrate common errors in developing instructional objectives. Nonaction verbs (representing actions that cannot be observed) should not be used. For example, "Students will gain an understanding of the major premises of democracy" is an inappropriate instructional objective. An "understanding" is not observable. Also, "an understanding of the major premises of democracy" could mean anything from a one-sentence description to a large book on the subject. This kind of ambiguity gives no guidance in the choice of learning activities.

"Students will learn to appreciate music in our society" sounds like a very desirable goal. However, knowing what to teach, how to teach it, and how to assess successful instruction cannot be determined from such a vague statement. Though as statements for overall goals they may be adequate, if lessons are to have clarity and if learning outcomes are to be clearly communicated to students and others, they need to be translated into specific learning outcomes before planning instruction.

This initial emphasis on how to write instructional objectives should not mislead you into thinking that writing instructional objectives is an end in itself. The process of writing instructional objectives involves a clarification of a teacher's instructional intent. The thinking that is required to generate and use instructional objectives is the important factor (Roberts 1982). Being able to write them merely insures that the kind of thinking needed for clearer choices of learning activities and assessment measures has been done.

EXPRESSING DIFFERENT INSTRUCTIONAL OBJECTIVES

The first chapter introduced you to the idea that the kind of instruction is dependent on the kind of learning expected. As you engage in the process of lesson planning and, in particular, the formulation of instructional objectives, you will find two ways of classifying instructional objectives. The first method, using Bloom's (1956), Krathwhol, Bloom, and Masia's (1964), and Harrow's (1972) taxonomies, is perhaps more common. The second method, which will be referred to as the **lesson framework perspective,** is one suggested by classroom research on effective teaching, and the one that will be developed extensively throughout the remainder of this text.

Traditional Approach

Learning outcomes can be classified into three categories: (1) cognitive (dealing with knowledge), (2) affective (dealing with attitudes, values, and feelings), and (3) psychomotor (dealing with the coordination of muscular movement with sensory perception). All three have relevance when planning for elementary or middle school instruction.

Cognitive Learning

Cognitive learning deals with knowledge and understanding and may involve recall, comprehension, application, analysis, synthesis, or evaluation of knowledge. Teachers should be concerned that pupils learn knowledge in ways that are useful, which implies their ability to use knowledge in some fashion beyond merely being able to recall it. Benjamin Bloom (1956) suggested a classification system for different kinds of cognitive learning that others have found useful (Furst 1981; Moore 1982). The six categories of Bloom's system are knowledge, comprehension, application, analysis, synthesis, and evaluation. The following list contains simplified definitions and an example of each. More detailed descriptions will be studied in the chapters dealing with classroom questions (Chapter 4) and test construction (Chapter 9).

1. Knowledge: The ability to remember facts in a form similar to that in which they were presented.
   Objective: Students will be able to list the colors of the Mexican flag correctly.

2. Comprehension: The ability to translate some knowledge into your own words.

Textbooks are one source of content.

Objective: Students will be able to identify correctly eight of ten correctly spelled words found in a list of twenty verbs.

3. Application: The ability to apply learning to new situations.
   Objective: When given a list of possible ingredients, students will be able to choose from the list the ingredients that could be used to make a sandwich.

4. Analysis: The ability to break down a situation into its component parts and to detect relationships between the parts or of a part to the whole.
   Objective: When given a small plant in distress, students will determine if the plant needs water, light, fertilizer, or some combination of the three.

5. Synthesis: The ability to organize or assemble parts to form a new whole.
   Objective: When given a pencil and blank sheet of paper, students will create a picture of happiness.

6. Evaluation: The ability to make judgments based on identified criteria or standards.
   Objective: When given a set of three short essays, the students will be able to select one as the "best," and list two criteria used to make the selection.

When planning lessons, you should think about the kinds of learning that could be promoted when teaching a particular topic or unit. Writing objectives at different cognitive levels when free to choose any topics for the objectives, as in our previous example, is relatively easy. Writing objectives at different cognitive levels concerned with the same topic is more difficult. To understand this process, examine the objectives dealing with the story "Goldilocks and the Three Bears."

☐ Knowledge: Student will be able to list the names of the three bears.

☐ Comprehension: Students will be able to list the common name of the grain that is used in making porridge.

☐ Application: Students will be able to list two things the bears could have done to cool their porridge other than take a walk.

☐ Analysis: Students will be able to list one similarity and one difference that would likely exist between the bears' beds and those used by humans.

☐ Synthesis: Students will be able to write an alternate ending to the story that contains an element of surprise.

☐ Evaluation: Students will be able to list two values they used to write an alternate ending that contained a element of surprise.

Affective Learning

Affective learning refers to the values, attitudes, feelings, and appreciations that may result from a learning experience (Krathwohl et al. 1964). Writing appropriate instructional objectives of this kind is extremely difficult but possible (Anderson and Anderson 1982; Hughes and Frommer 1982). In any event, it is essential to realize that **all** instruction will affect students' attitudes and feelings positively, negatively, or in both ways. The extent to which you can define affective outcomes and teach for them will determine the success you will have in achieving them.

At the elementary and middle school levels, teachers are constantly involved with and concerned about enhancing and developing affective attributes in students. This implies that during the formative and adolescent years, students begin to show a willingness to receive information; respond to information; begin to value and show a conviction for particular affective concepts such as honesty, sharing, establishing habits productive to both themselves and their environment; and perhaps work toward conceptualizing a value system by the time they enter the secondary level.

David Krathwohl (1964) suggested a classification of affective objectives that are useful when thinking about teaching for affective learning. Krathwohl classified affective objectives into five categories, the first three being of particular interest to elementary grade teachers. Simple definitions and examples are:

1. Receiving—the ability to attend to a stimulus and show a willingness to focus on it.
   Objective: Students will be able to list two reasons they are or are not interested in physical exercise.

2. Responding—the ability to show a willingness to respond and having satisfaction in doing so.
   Objective: When asked to write a short essay, students will use neat handwriting.

3. Valuing—the ability to accept, show a preference for and a commitment to a value.

Objective: When asked the reasons for supporting classroom rules, the students will be able to list one value of the rules.

4. Organization—the ability to demonstrate that a particular value has been conceptualized and organized into a personal system.
   Objective: Students will be able to list two reasons honesty is important and be able to describe one consequence of honesty and one of dishonesty.

5. Characterization by a value or value complex—the ability to respond consistently to a value-laden situation with a personal view of the world.
   Objective: When in a testing situation, students will not copy from other students.

Psychomotor Learning

Psychomotor learning refers to the ability to coordinate muscular movement with sensory perception. Simple motor skills such as typing or more complex skills such as talking and writing may be involved. Anita Harrow developed a model for classifying physical movements (Harrow 1972), which was specifically designed to aid educators and curriculum developers in clarifying and categorizing behaviors involving physical movement. She categorized movements into six categories (the first two being of little interest to teachers):

1. Reflex movements—involuntary movements.
   Objective: No specific objectives would be written at this level because reflexes are physiological phenomena.

2. Basic-fundamental movements—movements that emerge without training and serve as starting points for further improvement of physical abilities.
   Objective: Students will be able to throw a ball to another person.

3. Perceptual abilities—the ability to discriminate kinesthetically, visually, auditorially, tactily, and to use eye-hand and eye-foot coordination.
   Objective: Students will be able to correctly state the names of three different musical instruments heard in a recording of a band.
   Objective: Students will be able to identify the penny, dime, and quarter when handed the three while blindfolded.

4. Physical abilities—the ability to demonstrate muscular endurance, strength, flexibility, reaction-response time, dexterity, and agility when starting, stopping, and changing direction.
   Objective: Students will be able to do ten pull-ups.
   Objective: Students will be able to hit a tennis ball over a net three consecutive times without hitting the ball into the net or out of bounds.

5. Skilled movements—the ability to achieve a level of difficulty and proficiency when performing a particular skill.
   Objective: Students will be able to balance on one foot for at least one minute.

6. Non-discursive communication—the ability to demonstrate a style of moving that communicates one's feelings.
Objective: Students will be able to demonstrate two body movements and two facial expressions that would depict an excited person.

Lesson Framework Perspective on Instructional Objectives

While the taxonomic view of learning outcomes is conceptually elegant, findings of classroom research suggests that most teachers don't use it when they plan (Yinger 1979). A simpler way of viewing objectives that may have greater utility and appeal is one of classifying learning outcomes into four categories: (1) skills and strategies, (2) concepts, (3) laws and law-like generalizations or principles, and (4) values.

Skill and Strategy Learning

Skill and strategy learning deals more with the "learning to" side of teaching and less with the "learning that" side. When choosing lesson outcomes, the effective teacher recognizes that many different skill types exist. A **simple** or **basic** skill can be thought of as an associative response. Show a child a card with "3 + 3 = _____" and the response from the child is "six." The child is said to know the number facts of addition when this response reaches a highly automatic level; that is, when she does not rely on fingers or objects to arrive at the answer. Similarly, show a child a card with the letter **P** on it, and the response is /p/. This is a phonics skill. Automatic response with all of the phonic elements is considered by many to be a basic skill of reading. Some examples of skill instructional objectives include:

When given a list of 100 simple addition fact problems, the students will complete all of the items with at least 98 percent accuracy in less than 5 minutes.

Students will immediately identify with 100 percent accuracy the six new sight words for the story "The Boy Upstairs" when the words are displayed on flashcards.

Students will correctly form the first eight letters of the alphabet (in capital and lower case) in less than one minute.

Complex skills require the coordination and synchronization of many basic skills. Solving for long division problems in mathematics involves, among other things, the use of multiplication and subtraction skills. Identifying an unknown word when reading may involve the coordinated use of phonics, structural analysis, and context skills. Some examples of complex skill learning outcomes include:

Students will apply their knowledge of phonics, structural analysis, and context skills to successfully decode 98 percent of the words in the story "The Blue-Tailed Horse."

Students will identify the main idea of a paragraph in which the main idea is represented in a single sentence by reading silently for comprehension, identifying the topic of the paragraph, determining the most important comment on the topic in the paragraph, and locating the sentence that states the main idea. They will do this with four paragraphs with 75 percent accuracy.

A third type of skill outcome, **higher-order skills,** relates to the mental processes we associate with analytical and critical thinking abilities. Higher-order skills include such things as observing, classifying and synthesizing.

Some essential differences exist between the kinds of teaching used for the three types of skill. The designs of lessons for the three types of skill learning (basic, complex, and higher order) will be introduced in more detail in chapter 5.

Strategy learning is associated with skill learning, but is different in important ways. Strategy learning refers to the knowledge of when it is appropriate to use a particular skill and the knowledge of whether the application is functioning properly as it is being used. Thus, a student approaching a thought problem in mathematics must have knowledge about which particular skill algorithm can be used to solve the problem. The student also has strategic knowledge as she works through the problem that tells her whether the algorithm chosen is leading to success or another needs to be chosen ("I need to go back and divide instead of multiplying."). The student also has knowledge that leads her to recognize a successfully completed problem.

Some authorities refer to this type of strategic knowledge that governs or directs skill use as **metacognitive**. In many areas of academic performance this type of strategic knowledge is what distinguishes the "good" from the "poor" student. In reading, for example, some students are skilled in phonics but lack the strategic knowledge to use the skill at appropriate times. Strategies must be taught along with the skill if students are expected to use the skill appropriately.

Concept Learning

A concept is a category or set of objects, conditions, events, or processes that can be grouped together based on some characteristics they have in common. This category of things can then be represented by a single symbol. Concept learning involves learning the similarities and differences between categories of things. The most basic distinction between concept learning and skill or strategy learning is the difference noted in chapter 1 between "learning that" and "learning to." In developing concepts, the student is expanding her declarative knowledge of the world.

Pearson and Johnson (1978) developed a framework that is useful in discussing the nature of concept learning. They argue that any concept is comprised of three kinds of relationships: class relations, example relations, and property relations. **Class relations** refer to the larger set of concepts to which a given concept is tied. Thus, the concept of "dog" is tied to the larger class of things we refer to as animals. **Example relations** refer to the set of concepts that are subsidiary to a given concept. Thus, collies, poodles, and mutts are all examples of dogs. **Property relations** refer to the characteristics or traits that we associate with a concept. Property relations are sometimes referred to as variable or critical attributes or characteristics that describe and define the concept. For example, dogs are mammals who do not have retractable claws, who walk on four legs, who have canine teeth, and who have tails.

Concept learning involves changes in our understanding of class, example, and property relations. This learning in turn causes changes in our mental representations of the world. In learning about dogs, for example, the students could expand their understanding of class relations, such as the fact that dogs are not the only mammals, but so are cats, monkeys, and human beings. They could expand their understanding of property relations by learning about the reproductive processes of dogs. They could expand their example relations by coming to know that wolves are also dogs. Whether the activity is focused on class, example, or property relations, concept learning takes place. The network of knowledge of the world in the child's brain is being refined, expanded, and more extensively interconnected when concept learning occurs. Some examples of instructional objectives related to concept learning include:

> Students will be able to list the five characteristics of mammals with 100 percent accuracy.

> When presented with a map of the United States, students will be able to label the names of the fifty states with 90 percent accuracy.

These two examples require that the students do something that can then be used to evaluate their success in learning. You might wonder then whether we are focused on "teaching that" when the objective stresses performing. Isn't this "teaching to"? The answer is no; the focus on performance is part of any instructional objective no matter what type of learning we are interested in achieving. In skills or strategy learning we can observe directly the performance we are trying to nurture. In concept learning, and the other types of learning yet to be discussed, we infer something about success from observations of performance. In labeling the states, for example, our goal is not to develop the skill of labeling at an automatic level, but to ensure that the learner has all of the examples of the states of our country in simple memory.

Laws, Principles, and Generalizations

Laws, law-like principles, and generalizations learning is the third type of learning to be considered when formulating instructional objectives using the lesson framework perspective. Learning laws and other forms of generalizations is common in the elementary and middle school curricula. The areas of science and social studies are filled with examples of this type of learning, which often involves the analysis of cause-and-effect relationships. Thus, in science we might focus on general descriptions of the laws of gravity (but certainly not on the mathematical forms of the laws). In social studies we might focus on the general relationships of climate to clothing and shelter characteristics of a particular culture. In learning such generalizations, the student is manipulating concepts into propositions or assertions about the world. The following instructional objectives are examples of such learning outcomes.

Students will be able to draw an illustration of the water cycle in a way that correctly represents each of the five major stages of transfer.

When given a description of the geography and climate of an area unfamiliar to the students, they will be able to identify two types of clothing, shelter and food that would be characteristic of the communities residing in the area.

Learning of laws, law-like principles, and generalizations is similar to the learning of concepts in that both deal with "learning that." The difference comes in the fact that the learning of laws, principles, and generalizations is focused on relating two or more concepts that have an existence independent of one another. With this kind of learning students begin to expand their knowledge of the relationships between concepts not related by class, example, or property.

Values

Although some claim that the development of values is outside the scope of what schools should attend to, the fact is that teachers are constantly concerned with and working to promote values that are consistent with our society. The attention to values may come at the personal level, involving honesty, sharing, and respect for authority, or the teacher may be concerned with more formal and systematic instruction of societal values. The basic rights established through the Constitution are values to which we as a society are committed. Few would deny that such values should be taught. Examples of instructional objectives dealing with values include:

When asked the reasons for supporting classroom rules, the students will be able to list one value derived from the use of rules.

After reading "Our First Congresswoman," students will be able to offer a judgment on Hanson's behavior and support that judgment with one reference to the rights guaranteed by the Constitution.

Implications

In planning a lesson, you should identify at the start the kind of learning that you want to occur; that is, you specify your instructional intent by formulating an instructional objective. Recognizing the type of learning you want to occur will help you plan activities that will result in that learning.

As with any classification system, the distinctions among the various categories of learning may not always be clear. One thing is clear, however: effective teaching practices are different, depending on the kind of learning expected. The kinds of activities and lesson organization appropriate to skills teaching are not the same as those that contribute to successful concept teaching. The instructional strategies that are appropriate to each of these areas will be examined in subsequent chapters.

Having simplified matters, let us complicate planning a bit by returning to the real world. Seldom will you find yourself engaged in teaching a lesson that falls neatly into just one area of learning. Thus, in a single lesson with an instructional intent of teaching children how to find the main idea of a passage of text, a teacher may become involved in concept learning (a main idea is...), and strategy learning (to find the main idea you...) at the application level (find the main idea...). In a lesson of this type, you should have at least three instructional objectives: one focused on the concept of **main idea,** one focused on knowing the strategy of finding the main idea, and another of the actual demonstration of finding a main idea. Together, these instructional objectives will also ensure that the instructional intent is accomplished. The actual lesson unfolds in a series of activities designed to achieve the instructional objectives. Many lessons cross over these categories, but the principle of formulating instructional objectives in this fashion will serve you well in planning instruction.

SOME CAUTIONS ABOUT INSTRUCTIONAL OBJECTIVES

The instructional objectives chosen and taught do not determine all of the outcomes of learning. Students will learn many things during instruction—some intended and some not. Instructional objectives should define what you intend students to learn and what you will try to ensure they do learn. You may also introduce students to additional content without the expectation that they will learn predetermined outcomes. Also, although you may have some intended outcome, the actual outcome may be quite different. For example, you may intend that the students learn a given concept, but the students may learn the concept incorrectly or not at all. They may also have such a disagreeable experience that they learn to hate the content being taught. Being aware of the possible incidental outcomes of instruction is important if such detrimental outcomes of instruction are to be avoided.

Don't assume in using instructional objectives that all students must pursue the same or similar objectives. When you begin to work with students in the elementary or middle school classroom, you will find tremendous variations in students' interests and abilities. You will need to learn how to individualize instruction by having different objectives and learning activities for different students, by having the same objectives but allowing students to pursue the objectives at different paces, or by having the same objectives but different learning experiences for different students. Individualizing the curriculum will be necessary when working with highly heterogeneous classes of students. How to individualize instruction cannot be considered a fundamental instructional skill and thus will not be dealt with at this time. Later, when working in the classroom, you will have opportunities to learn the processes involved in individualizing instruction.

Using instructional objectives will not necessarily result in higher achievement (Melton, 1978). Research findings suggest that the use of instructional objectives may not result in higher achievement when students are unaware of the objectives, and when the objectives are too easily accomplished or are too difficult to accomplish given the ability levels of the students or the adequacy of the learning experiences provided.

Instructional objectives may enhance learning if you tell the students the objective prior to instruction. However, such a practice may inhibit incidental learning; that is, learning of things not intended. Most of the time, incidental learning is advantageous and should be encouraged. Evidence suggests that giving objectives, or making the objectives clear, immediately after instruction may enhance incidental learning without depressing intended learning (Melton 1978). Therefore, do not assume that students must be told the instructional objectives at the beginning of the lesson unless you want to emphasize the intended outcomes. Rather, ensure that the objectives become clear to the students by the end of the lesson.

Using instructional objectives to guide instruction has some limitations. Most teachers, when first trying to use instructional objectives, will have a tendency to teach and evaluate trivial outcomes because these can more easily be specified by instructional objectives. Specifying an outcome such as "Students will be able to list at least three of the authors from a list of the titles of four books" is easy. Teaching for and measuring this outcome is also relatively easy. On the other hand, specifying the outcome that "Students, when given two novel opposing persuasive arguments for and against using playground equipment, will be able to identify at least two distortions in each argument resulting from the use of persuasive tactics" is not only difficult, but the instruction required for students to be able to do this would be quite complex. And any test designed to measure this outcome would be a challenge. Yet, which of the two objectives is more significant? Because significant learnings are more difficult to teach and to measure, teachers may tend to focus on the trivial. Avoid focusing on the trivial.

Another risk in using instructional objectives is that the teacher will start to believe that things that cannot or should not be specified should therefore not be taught. A teacher may decide that visiting an art gallery would be a nice experience for students, but may not have any specific outcomes in mind, only an intuitive sense that such a visit could be a valuable experience. In this case, what the individual derives from the experience should be left to the individual to seek out. Should the teacher deny students this experience because specific outcomes for the group cannot be specified? Not at all. These experiences should be provided.

Sometimes something unexpected happens that becomes a teachable moment. Taking advantage of such moments, even though the learning outcomes have not been previously specified and may be uncertain, is recommended. Teachers can and should use such occasions to provide students valuable learning experiences without being concerned about specific outcomes. As long as this does not become the primary mode of instruction, taking advantage of these moments is an appropriate occasional alternative.

SUMMARY

The quality of planning largely determines the quality of instruction. Quality of planning relates to how well a teacher thinks about what to teach and how to teach it. Thorough planning does not mean just writing a unit or lesson plan to be followed. The thinking that must occur before instruction includes an identification of the goals of instruction. These goals then need to be translated into specific instructional objectives consistent with the entering abilities of the students. Activities are then chosen to accomplish these objectives. Another part of the thinking about teaching involves a mental rehearsal of a lesson. This rehearsal should include all of the actions the teacher will take as well as all of the things the students will be doing. During and following lessons, careful assessment of student learning occurs and instruction is modified based on those assessments. Good planning, therefore, occurs long before, immediately before, during, and even after lessons are written. Writing plans takes a small fraction of the time needed for adequate planning. Thorough thinking about teaching prior to instruction should result in greater teacher flexibility when teaching a lesson, more clarity in the instruction, more student on-task behavior, less disruptive behavior, and ultimately, greater student achievement. These are all worthy goals.

REFERENCES

Anderson, L., and J. Anderson. 1982. Affective assessment is necessary and possible. *Educational Leadership*, 39:524–525.

Bloom, B.S., ed. 1956. *Taxonomy of educational objectives, handbook I: Cognitive domain*. New York: David McKay.

Brophy, J.F., and T.L. Good. 1986. Teacher behavior and student achievement. In *Handbook of research in teaching*, ed. M. Wittrock, New York: Macmillan.

Furst, E.J. 1981. Bloom's taxonomy of educational objectives for the cognitive domain: Philosophical and educational issues. *Review of Educational Research* 51 (4):441–453.

Harrow, A.J. 1972. *A taxonomy of the psychomotor domain: A guide for developing behavioral objectives*. New York: David McKay.

Hughes, A.L., and K. Frommer. 1982. A system for monitoring affective objectives. *Educational Leadership* 39:521–523.

Krathwohl, D.R., B.S. Bloom, and B.B. Masia. 1964. *Taxonomy of educational objectives, handbook II: Affective domain*. New York: David McKay.

Lawson, T.E. 1974. Effects of instructional objectives on learning and retention. *Instructional Science* 3:1–22.

Melton, R. 1978. Resolution of conflicting claims concerning the effect of behavioral objectives on student learning. *Review of Educational Research* 48 (2):291–302.

Moore, D.S. 1982. Reconsidering Bloom's taxonomy of educational objectives, cognitive domain. *Educational Theory* 32 (1):29–34.

Pearson, P.D., and D.D. Johnson. 1978. *Teaching reading comprehension*. New York: Holt, Rinehart & Winston.

Roberts, W.K. 1982. Preparing instructional objectives: Usefulness revisited. *Educational Technology* 22 (7):15–19.

Rosenshine, B., and N. Furst. 1971. Research in teacher performance criteria. In *Research in teacher education: A symposium,* ed. B.O. Smith. Englewood Cliffs, New Jersey: Prentice-Hall.

Slavin, R.E. 1984. Component building: A strategy for research-based instructional improvement. *Elementary School Journal,* 84(3):255–269.

Yinger, R.J. 1979. Routines in teacher planning. *Theory Into Practice* 18:163–169.

CHAPTER REVIEW

Six Tasks Critical to Successful Teaching
1. Identifying content and goals
2. Assessing student abilities
3. Organizing for instruction
4. Pacing instruction
5. Developing units
6. Preparing lessons

Identifying Content and Goals
Early in the academic year, even prior to the arrival of students, teachers engage in a systematic analysis of the intended curriculum for each objective area.

Assessing Student Abilities
Early in the year, teachers conduct informal assessments to determine individual student abilities in each subject area.

Organizing for Instruction
1. Establishing schedules based on the analysis of the intended curriculum, the assessment of student abilities, and the adoption of an organizational pattern, teachers allot specific time periods to academic subject areas.
2. Planning Indirect Instruction
   a. centers—physical areas of the room are identified by a theme with each area having a specific task for students to complete either independently or cooperatively.
   b. contracts—students are given a written form that identifies the tasks to be completed and a period of time for completion. Some options in sequence and choice of activities may be provided the students.

Pacing Instruction
1. Pacing refers to the rate at which content is taught in the classroom.
2. Pacing decisions are based on a consideration of the curriculum, the abilities of the students, and the organization of the instructional program.

Developing Units

1. Unit—a sequence of instruction organized around a particular topic or theme.
2. Units are designed around three phases
    a. an initiating event in which the topic is introduced to the students
    b. a series of lessons and correlated activities in which new information is introduced
    c. a culminating activity that pulls together all of the information learned about the topic.

Role of Instructional Objectives

Instructional objectives help teachers

1. design learning activities that are more likely to be congruent with their instructional intent
2. design assessment instruments more congruent with their instructional intent.

Definition of an Instructional Objective

An instructional objective is a desired outcome of learning that is expressed in terms of observable behavior of the learner.

Parts of Instructional Objectives

1. a verb or infinitive describing some observable action
2. a description of the task to be performed
3. a description of the criterion to be used to judge the adequacy of the performance

Expressing Different Instructional Objectives

1. Traditional Approach
    a. Cognitive learning: learning dealing with knowledge
    b. Affective learning: learning dealing with feelings and beliefs
    c. Psychomotor learning: learning associated with coordinating muscular movement with sensory perception
2. Classification of Cognitive Objectives
    a. Knowledge: the ability to remember facts in a form similar to that in which they were presented
    b. Comprehension: the ability to translate some knowledge into your own words
    c. Application: the ability to apply learning to new situations
    d. Analysis: the ability to break down a situation into its component parts and to detect relationships between the parts or a part to the whole
    e. Synthesis: the ability to organize or assemble parts to form a new whol
    f. Evaluation: the ability to make judgments based on identified criteria or standards
3. Lesson Framework Perspective
    a. skill and strategy learning
        (1) skill—a simple associative response
        (2) strategy—the coordination and synchronization of multiple skills
    b. concept learning—learning the similarities and differences between categories of things, or changes in the student's understanding of class, example, and property relations

    c. laws, principles and generalization learning—learning to manipulate concepts into propositions or assertions about the world

    d. value learning
      (1) personal values—honesty, sharing, respect for authority
      (2) societal values—basic constitutional rights

Cautions about Instructional Objectives

1. Teachers tend to teach and evaluate outcomes that are trivial because these outcomes can be easily defined and measured.

2. Teachers may tend to deny students experiences if the outcomes cannot be identified and defined.

3. Teachers may tend not to deviate from a plan, and thus ignore teachable moments.

Advantages of Planning for Instruction

1. more teacher flexibility when teaching a lesson

2. more clarity in the instruction

3. more student on-task behavior

4. higher student achievement

EXERCISE 3

Practice in Identifying Instructional Objectives

Directions. Identify which of the following are inadequate statements of instructional objectives. Recognize that ambiguity in statements allows many possible instructional objectives to be derived and should therefore be avoided. Write one correctly stated instructional objective for each inadequate statement.

1. To learn the main distinctions between the plants and animals.
2. To gain knowledge concerning how eating habits affect the individual.
3. Students will be able to identify and record all of the acronyms presented during a thirty-minute national newscast.
4. Students should be able to write the correct form of the present tense of *to be* with an accuracy of 80 percent when it is encountered in a paragraph.
5. Students will improve their critical thinking ability.
6. To teach students the methods needed to use the library properly.
7. To learn why littering is a problem in the school.
8. To be able to list some of the characteristics of social insects.
9. To identify some of the relationships between magic and reality.
10. To show the effects of smoking on the student.

EXERCISE 4

Justifying Objectives

The purpose of this exercise is to provide an experience that will allow you to think about the value and appropriateness of certain instructional objectives. This exercise also allows you to share your ideas with a small group of peers and them to share their ideas with you.

Directions
1. Write instructional objectives for a content lesson (as opposed to a lesson involving some skill such as reading, writing, or arithmetic) that could be taught appropriately to elementary or middle school students. If your class is using the "Practicum Teaching Exercises" with peers, then the objectives could be those you would try to accomplish in the "Teaching for Instructional Objectives" exercise.
2. List the reasons you feel these objectives would be interesting, useful, or in some way beneficial to those students whom you will be teaching. If you are using these objectives for a "Practicum Teaching Exercise" with peers, you may be asked to list reasons for teaching this content to your peers.

3. Come prepared to share this information with the group of peers. The discussion could be facilitated if you provide copies for each group member.

Discussion
1. Pass out a copy of your objectives and the reasons for teaching them.
2. Each person should then share his/her candid opinion about the merits of the content and the objectives, as well as the validity of the reasons given. In addition, the appropriateness of the objectives in terms of level of difficulty should be discussed.
3. If all are in agreement that the objectives and content are consistent with the reasons, the reasons are valid, and the level of difficulty is appropriate, then no reason exists to change them.
4. If your peers do not perceive that the objectives and content are useful and appropriate, then you will need to convince them of the merits of the content and objectives, or ask them to offer suggestions about the ways the objectives could be reworded to be appropriate and have value. You will probably choose the second option.
5. Using the input from your group, revise your objectives and turn them in along with the reasons supporting their use the next class period.

EXERCISE 5

Writing Instructional Objectives at Different Cognitive Levels

This exercise will help you think about the different kinds of instructional objectives that could be taught when teaching a particular topic. This exercise will help you view the possible outcomes of learning in ways not restricted to the memorization of knowledge.

Directions
1. Choose some topic that could appropriately be taught at the elementary or middle school level. Write the name of the topic at the top of the paper to be submitted.
2. Write a one- or two-sentence description of the topic.
3. Write one instructional objective that could be a possible outcome of instruction on this topic for each of the six cognitive levels: knowledge, comprehension, application, analysis, synthesis, and evaluation. Label each objective with the cognitive level of the outcome the objective is designed to describe.

EXERCISE 6

Curriculum Analysis

This activity provides experiences in analyzing curriculum materials available in reading. Basal reader systems form the core of developmental reading instruction in the elementary and middle school classrooms. Basal systems are typically referred to by the name of the publisher (e.g. Scott Foresman, Ginn). Most basal reader systems contain similar components such as basal readers, teacher's manuals, tests, and workbooks. Typically, one or more "levels" of the series are designed to be covered at particular grade levels. The system in place in a school or district serves to define the developmental reading curriculum. The manual provides directions to the teacher in how to guide the students through the content.

Directions.   In completing this task you will need to identify a reading system for analysis. Locate a teacher's manual for the level that corresponds most closely to the level you hope to teach. Examine the manual for the answers to the following questions:

1. What is the basic philosophy of reading espoused by the publisher?
2. What are the major word-recognition skills taught at this level?
3. What are the major comprehension skills taught at this level?
4. What kind of detail is offered in the manual to help you plan lessons to teach these skills?
5. What kind of detail is offered in the manual to help you guide the reading of stories?
6. List three reasons to support your judgment of the quality of the literature included in the student books.
7. What suggestions does the manual offer for placing students in the program?
8. What suggestions does the series offer for organizing and scheduling reading groups?
9. What suggestions does the manual offer for managing and pacing students through the levels in the series?
10. In what ways do you feel the program would be useful to you in planning for effective teaching? In what ways might the program have negative effects on planning and instruction?

OBSERVATION EXERCISE 7

Analyzing the Classroom Arrangement

This exercise provides an experience in thinking about optimum arrangements for elementary or middle school classrooms. This practice offers you a valuable opportunity to analyze situations, identify potential problems, and then find solutions to those problems before you have the responsibility for arranging your own classroom.

Directions. Observe the arrangement of an elementary or middle school classroom and then draw a sketch of the room, noting the following:

heating and cooling units	storage cabinets
fire extinguisher	overhead projector
safety equipment	pencil sharpener
location of doors	attendance pick-up clip
light switches	bulletin boards
teacher's desk	chalkboards
students' desks	learning centers
tables	reading area
chairs	other instructional areas

Answer the following questions.

1. What problems, if any, related to each of the following may be caused by this arrangement?
    a. movement of children with impaired movement, sight, or hearing
    b. movement of children during an emergency
    c. dealing with in-room fires or other emergencies
    d. movement of children when changing activities
    e. student on-task/off-task behavior
    f. starting class
    g. sight and hearing of students in general
    h. taking attendance
2. For each of the problem listed, indicate the ways the arrangement of the room might be altered to alleviate these difficulties.

OBSERVATION EXERCISE 8

Managing the Environment

This exercise provides you with the experience of analyzing what teachers do to ensure that tasks are accomplished in an orderly fashion. Without observing and analyzing what teachers actually do, many of these small but essential tasks could go unnoticed.

Directions. Observe an elementary or middle school classroom and record the following observations and answer the related questions.

1. What do the students do when class first begins?
2. What procedures does the teacher follow when taking attendance?
3. What are the students doing while the teacher is taking attendance?
4. What do students bring with them to the classroom?
5. What does the teacher do when students do not have needed materials? How much time is lost in supplying them?
6. What responsibilities do the students have in helping manage the classroom (such as collecting or handing out materials)?
7. What procedures does the teacher follow in handing out and collecting materials?
8. What steps does the teacher follow, and what does he say at each of these steps, when students are shifting from one activity to another?
9. What other kinds of things did you observe the teacher say or do that reduced confusion in the classroom?
10. List those things you observed that you felt were done ineffectively. For each item listed, indicate what you would do or say differently in order to accomplish the task more effectively.

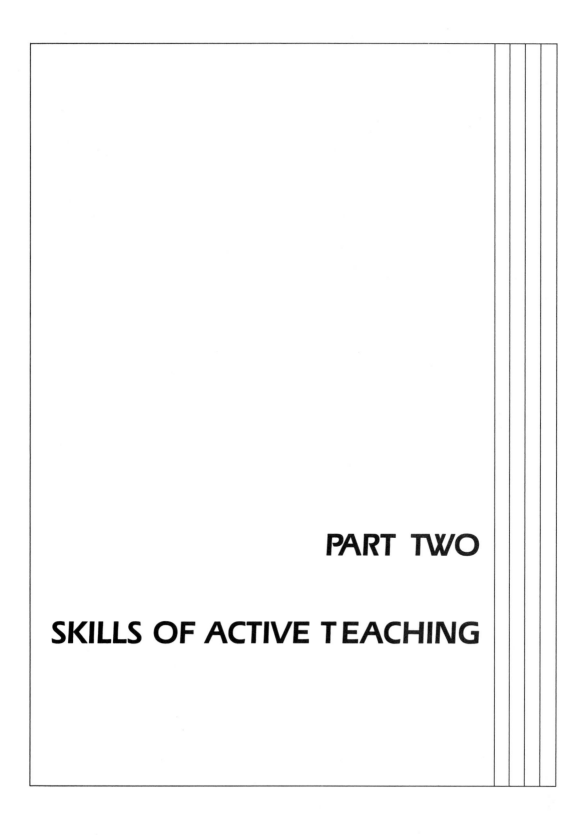

PART TWO

SKILLS OF ACTIVE TEACHING

The sequence and kinds of skills that are used with different teaching strategies or lesson frameworks may vary, but some skills are consistently used when teachers are involved in direct instruction, regardless of the strategy being used. The skills introduced in the next two chapters are such skills. The skills introduced are those used when performing the tasks of preparing for and teaching individual lessons. Some of these skills are important in improving the motivation of students, others are useful in helping children stay engaged in the lesson, others help bring clarity to lessons, and still others provide children with opportunities to think about the topics of the lesson.

Keeping children motivated and engaged involves a complex set of tasks. Doing any one teaching task poorly can significantly affect student motivation. This part of the text, while introducing some additional important teaching tasks affecting pupils' motivation and engagement, does not introduce all such tasks. Subsequent parts of this text will continue to add to your repertory of skills and strategies known to enhance students' motivation and learning.

Chapter 4, "Questioning," will introduce you to the teaching strategy of teacher-directed discussions. Teacher-directed discussions are one of the ways that teachers use questioning to provide students opportunities to think more in depth about things. This will be the first of several teaching strategies with which you will become acquainted.

Some Basic Teaching Tasks 3

Before and during the teaching of lessons, certain basic tasks must be performed if lessons are to be effective. Properly performed, these tasks can do much to help children stay on task with high degrees of motivation to learn. The skills introduced in this chapter are basic tasks that are not unique to certain teaching strategies, but rather will be used with most, if not all, strategies.

CREATING A CLASSROOM ENVIRONMENT

Teaching can do much to help improve student motivation by creating a classroom environment conducive to learning. Bulletin boards, maps, equipment, and models are much more effective than barren walls in rousing students' curiosity toward the subjects being taught as they enter your classroom. An elementary classroom should look as though interesting topics are being taught there. Students walking into classrooms displaying interesting visuals representing the content areas to be taught will be stimulated to begin to think about those areas. If science is the focus, many items related to science should be displayed. If writing creative stories is currently a major class project, then a bulletin board with students' or other exemplar stories should be in view. Many primary teachers have one bulletin board with a calendar that becomes a focal point for discussion each morning. In this way a teacher can reinforce basic concepts concerning calendars.

One empty surface not used in many classrooms is the ceiling! Large maps, star charts, art work, written work, models, and awards over the seat of the students who won them are all things that can be suspended from or attached to the ceiling.

On the other hand, a teacher should avoid placing things in locations likely to distract students from learning. Placing a gerbil or other animal in the students' line of vision is usually counterproductive. Children should not be seated facing windows, nor should the teacher stand in front of a window when talking to the class. Things happening on the outside, as well as glare from the windows, tend to distract students.

Students at times start to wander off task because they start to get comfortable with those sitting around them. For example, when the same students have been seated next to each other for an extended period of time, they will be less inhibited about talking with each other. While changing seating is not an effective long-term strategy to maintaining good behavior, it can be used to help students become temporarily less distracted by others.

Students' attention can sometimes be improved merely by introducing a freshness to the classroom by rearranging seating areas, learning centers, reading areas, and other work spaces as well as by changing bulletin boards and other displays.

The main criterion for arranging materials in a classroom, deciding on seating arrangements, decorating a classroom, or arranging field trips, is the degree to which the setting will make learning easier and provide a safe environment. If you are studying trees or seeds, students will more likely stay on task if they are in front of a tree or planting seeds in a garden. When planning room arrangements, decide what will stimulate the interest of pupils without distracting them.

Creating a climate for reading

ASSESSING READINESS

Before planning and conducting lessons, assessing what students know or don't know about a topic is vital (Ausubel *et al.*,1978). Teaching something students already know makes little sense except in certain situations where overlearning may be desirable. Attempting to teach something if the students do not possess the prerequisite knowledge and/or skills to learn the material being presented also makes little sense. Preassessment is something you are going to do at the beginning of the school year and continue doing throughout the year when introducing any unit or lesson (Hartley and Davies 1976). Preassessment will help you avoid teaching something students already know, or teaching something for which they lack the necessary prerequisites.

    Many prepared assessment instruments are available, particularly in the areas of reading and mathematics, that provide specific information about the students' current achievement levels so that the teacher can organize students and lessons to accommodate for differences among students. The common practice of asking students to write about their summers at the beginning of the school year can provide much useful information about the students' writing and spelling skills. It also provides insights into the student's life outside the school. This information is valuable not only for planning instruction but also in relating better with individual students. Prepared assessment instruments are not commonly available in social studies and science. As a result, you will need to give some attention to preparing your own written or oral assessments. These assessments need not be elaborate, however; a few questions at the beginning of units and lessons may provide the needed insight into students' levels of knowledge in these areas.

Another aspect of preassessment often overlooked by teachers is determining the readiness of students to want to learn the material to be introduced—not their knowledge of the material, but rather their feelings about the material. Part of the preassessment process involves considering the present level of interest students have about the topics of a new lesson. If students have little or no interest in the topics, you need to provide some initial experiences to create an interest. On the other hand, stimulating an interest in students already possessing a high degree of interest may be unnecessary.

This assessment of interest is accomplished through the use of questions dealing with how students are feeling. Questions that ask students how they feel are called **affective** questions, as opposed to questions that assess student knowledge, called **cognitive** questions. Both cognitive and affective questions should be a part of preassessment.

ORGANIZING CONTENT

When the focus of lessons is on the learning of content, the logical arrangement of content is crucial. If the arrangement is confusing, then students will not understand the relationships among the elements taught (Bush, Kennedy, and Cruickshank 1977). Two ways of organizing content are commonly used: First, content can be organized from the general to the specific, or **deductively**. When using this type of organization, the teacher must assume that students have a clear understanding of the initial generalization based on direct experience with illustrative examples. This understanding is then used as a basis for identifying additional applications or other elaborations of the generalizations. Second, content can be organized from the specific to the general, or **inductively**. If you are using an inductive strategy, your students must have had, or be provided with, some direct experience with the specific examples being used.

For an example of the general to specific strategy, a middle school social studies teacher may choose to introduce the concept of scale as it is used in making maps. An outline as part of a lesson plan of a deductively arranged lesson, beginning with the generalization and developing specific applications, might look like this:

A. Generalization: A scale is a description of the fraction a real object or area is reduced when placed on a map. This number represents the number of times larger the real object or area is than the object or area on a map.
B. Explain the terms
   1. reduced size
   2. real object of area
   3. fraction
   4. map
C. Give examples
   1. Use an example from the room, such as a table top.
   2. Give the students the scale and a drawing of the table top and have them calculate the actual size.

3. Give the students the scale and the actual size of another table top and have them calculate the size on a map of the room.
4. Now do similar examples using a scale on a road map and calculating the distances between cities.

On the other hand, the same lesson could be taught inductively. The following would be an example of an outline in such a lesson plan.

A. Preassess the students' understanding of
   1. Map
   2. Division skills
   3. The term **fraction**
B. Provide the following experience
   1. Use an example from the room, such as a desk or table top.
   2. Measure the length and width of table top.
   3. Determine what length and width would fit on an $8\frac{1}{2} \times$ -11 inch piece of paper, allowing for some margins.
   4. Now divide the actual length of a table by the length you want to use on the paper. This number represents the number that would be divided into the actual length to arrive at the size of the object that would be drawn on a map. The word **scale**, which represents this number, is now introduced.
   5. Now take the actual width, divide by the scale, and then draw a diagram of the table on the paper.
   6. Provide an additional example of another object in the room.
   7. Have the students go outside and pick some area near the school and draw a map of the area after determining a scale that would allow them to draw the map on an $8\frac{1}{2} \times$ -11 inch piece of paper.
   8. Provide additional examples using the scale on a road map and calculating distances between cities.

A primary teacher, on the other hand, may choose to introduce rules concerned with household poisons. An outline of a deductive lesson beginning with the generalization to be taught might look like this:

A. Generalization
   1. Rule: Do not put anything in your mouth that wasn't given to you by an adult you know and trust.
   2. Many household medicines and kitchen products can cause serious sickness and even death.
   3. Sometimes a very poisonous product is marked with a skull and crossbones.
B. Introduce
   1. Household medicines
   2. Kitchen products
   3. Poisonous products marked with a skull and crossbones
C. Show examples and tell students the effects each product can have on their health.
   1. Household medicines
   2. Kitchen products
   3. Poisonous products marked with a skull and crossbones
D. Show some "nonexamples" of safe products such as table salt, coffee, bread, and vinegar.
E. Ask students to identify additional examples and nonexamples

The teacher may reverse the order and teach an inductive lesson by outlining the lesson in a lesson plan as follows.

A. Examine examples of empty containers that once held kitchen products, medicines, and poisons marked with a skull and crossbones.
B. Explain the health risks associated with each and where each might be found.
C. Classify the examples as
   1. Household medicines
   2. Kitchen products
   3. Poisonous products marked with a skull and crossbones
D. Introduce some nonexamples of safe substances such as table salt, coffee, bread, and vinegar.
E. Introduce rule: Do not put anything in your mouth that wasn't given to you by an adult you know and trust.

Recognizing the assumptions underlying the organization of content is important regardless of the pattern of organization chosen. If any of the assumptions are violated, students may have difficulty in understanding and learning the content and thus lose the motivation to learn. For example, if in a deductively sequenced lesson students cannot relate the generalization being used to examples they have experienced, then they may misunderstand the applications of the generalization being taught (Tennyson and Park 1980). If in an inductively sequenced lesson students are not provided sufficient experience with the examples being used to develop the generalization, then their understanding of the generalization will be limited.

CHOOSING ACTIVITIES AND ASSOCIATED TECHNOLOGY

Think of classes you enjoyed in school versus those you dreaded. What kind of things affected your attitudes toward your classes? Very likely your attitudes were influenced by the nature of classroom activities. For example, when the teacher used the same activity with most lessons, or the same sequence of activities day after day, you were more likely to be bored and less interested in what occurred. Nothing is deadlier to student interest and motivation than a teacher who follows the same passive sequence of activities every day. Some middle school teachers have students quietly read a section in a book and fill out a worksheet on the written material; afterwards they conduct a class review of the answers on the worksheet and, finally, they administer a test over the material. The same pattern is used repeatedly. It is not surprising that their students lose interest.

Selecting Activities

Your choice of activities can do much to help maintain student motivation. A teacher who consistently uses hands-on activities and is clear, well-organized, and businesslike will have students who are more motivated and who achieve more than the teacher who does not behave this way (Rosenshine and Furst 1971).

You have an amazing choice of activities available to you as a teacher. Some of your options include

1. field trips
   a. to see something new
   b. to collect data
   c. to explore a particular place
   d. to collect specimens
   e. to have a unique or new experience
2. laboratory activities
   a. to show and tell or verify
   b. to collect data
   c. to explore
   d. to practice skills
3. demonstrations
   a. to show and tell or verify
   b. to collect data
   c. to create interest
   d. to make observations and inferences
   e. to explore
   f. to participate in silent demonstrations
   g. to present discrepant events
   h. to generate discussions
   i. to introduce a concept
   j. to introduce a learning center or bulletin board
4. small and large group discussions
   a. to identify differences in views
   b. to reach consensus on views
   c. to examine data and draw inferences
   d. to develop plans of action
   e. to brainstorm
   f. to examine current events
   g. to examine controversial issues
   h. to review
5. tests
   a. to diagnose
   b. to measure achievement
   c. to preassess
   d. to measure practical/laboratory skills
   e. to measure performance
6. games
   a. simulations
   b. computer
   c. small group
   d. individual
7. projects—group or individual
   a. model building
      1. creating a model
      2. replicating a model

    b. making video tapes
    c. making films
    d. doing research investigations
       1. laboratory
       2. library
    e. constructing dioramas
    f. drawing art work or making crafts
    g. making posters and bulletin boards

8. peer instruction
    a. remedial
    b. enrichment
9. drill and practice
    a. whole class
    b. games
    c. worksheets
10. debates
11. dramatizations and skits
12. story-telling
13. reading current publications and book reports
14. oral reports
15. panel discussions
16. creative writing
17. individual study
18. guest speakers
19. individualized learning centers
20. cooperative learning groups
21. contests

Selecting Instructional Technology

Many activities can be enhanced by the use of supporting instructional technologies. We all know how easily some television programs can hold the attention of children; similar results can be obtained by many other kinds of technology, as well. We also know that some children learn better when they use the senses of seeing, smelling, and feeling in addition to that of hearing. Technology provides many opportunities for students to use their senses and thus learn more easily. A wide variety of such supporting technology is available in most schools. They include

1. films
    a. documentary
    b. fiction
    c. investigative
    d. review
    e. topic introduction
    f. motivational
    g. simulated experiences

Children learning with the aid of computers

2. slides/overhead projector transparencies
   a. show and tell
   b. data collection
   c. data analysis
   d. simulated experiences
   e. topic introduction
   f. review
3. records or tape recorders
   a. nature sounds
   b. role playing
   c. simulations
   d. outside speakers and events
   e. interviews
   f. creating music
   g. story-telling
4. television
   a. current events
   b. enrichment
   c. rewards
5. film loops
   a. enrichment
   b. review concepts
   c. simulations

6. computers
   a. laboratory simulations
   b. drill and practice tutorials
   c. interactive video
   d. problem solving
   e. story writing
   f. programming
   g. robotics

Individual Differences

Providing different kinds of activities and lessons introduces stimulus variation for your students. Different students prefer to learn in different modes (Arlin, 1975; Dunn and Dunn, 1978; Witkin et al., 1977). Some prefer visual learning; others prefer tactile, auditory, or a combination of styles. Some like to work alone; others like to work in groups. Some students need quiet surroundings; others need the stimulus of music. By providing a variety of learning activities you will not be catering to a particular set of students. Over a period of several lessons you will at least be meeting the needs of most of the students some of the time. When you fail to provide a variety of learning activities, some students will be unmotivated and uninterested in lessons, off-task, and disruptive. Successful teachers vary their instructional styles and strategies (Brophy and Evertson, 1976). Varying your style is critical (Turner, 1979), and yet we do not know conclusively how teaching styles should be matched to individuals' learning styles (Levy, 1983). Given present knowledge, teachers should at least accommodate all students some of the time by using a variety of teaching activities and strategies.

STARTING LESSONS

The introduction of a lesson is crucial to student motivation and learning (Hartley and Davies 1976). It should focus the students' attention on what is going to be taught and help them see how the lesson is going to fit into a larger framework. Providing a framework for a lesson can be done by relating the lesson to students' past experiences, knowledge, and interests; stating the purpose of the lesson in language appropriate for the student; and relating the lesson to past and future goals of the unit or larger topic.

The introduction of a lesson should make the students ready and eager to learn and provides a framework for the lesson. It should be part of the introduction of all activities and lessons. **This process of inducing a readiness to learn is called set induction**; it is also known as inducing set, anticipatory set and lesson focus. The ultimate purpose of the set induction is to increase student motivation to learn. Research has indicated that the quality with which set induction is accomplished will affect the motivation of students and, ultimately, their achievement (Schuck 1981). Providing effective set inductions is something you will want to learn. Four tasks to be completed during a set induction, but not necessarily in this order are

1. relating the lesson to students' past experiences
2. stating the purpose of the lesson in the students' language without necessarily telling them the specific objectives or contents of the lesson (Melton 1978)
3. relating the lesson to future goals the lesson will help to accomplish
4. doing something to get the students' attention and interest

A set induction at the primary level may take the form of a statement such as, "We have just studied frogs and we took a field trip to a pond to see frogs where they live; now we are ready to see how important frogs are to us." This statement could then be followed by a question such as, "What could happen in ponds if frogs suddenly disappeared from the earth?" Or, in the upper grades, "We have studied the role leaders have played in establishing new countries, including our own. Today we are going to take a look at other roles leaders may play in the survival of countries by examining some of the actions taken by former presidents when faced with threats to the welfare of our country, and comparing them to some of the actions of our current president. We will also examine alternative ways these threats could have been handled in the absence of a strong leader."

Photographs, models, paintings, puzzles, demonstrations, or objects could also be used to add interest or understanding to the introduction. Providing some direct experience as a lead into some topic could serve this function, and you will want to become familiar with this process. For example, if the teacher is going to introduce adjectives she could relate a brief story to the children in which no adjectives are used. The teacher could then tell the students a short story in which adjectives are used, and then explain that today's lesson will teach them the difference between the two situations as well as the advantages and disadvantages of each.

Set inductions should usually be brief. Occasionally the instructional objectives will be stated as part of the set induction, but the usual pattern will be to refer to them only in a general way so as to allow for incidental learning. Later, in the closing, the instructional objectives will be stated and made clear.

PRESENTING INFORMATION

Teaching, in the minds of many teachers, means **presenting** or **lecturing**; that is, taking information and telling the students what you want them to know. In practice, presenting is only one of many tasks that teachers perform in the process of teaching. Presenting may be used when giving directions, using a set induction, providing an explanation, introducing a topic or giving summaries. Although teaching is more than presenting, presenting is something you will want to do well.

To present information, you must take ideas and put them into words that communicate the essence of those ideas. Clear communication is difficult because it requires you to have some knowledge of what words mean to the students. Remember, you will probably have more knowledge about a subject than your students will. Your knowledge and experiences allow you to know the denotations and connotations of words that your students may not understand. Students hearing your words will need to associate these words with what they know from their experiences. Since their knowledge and experiences will differ from yours, the meanings they derive from words they hear may be quite different from the meanings you intend. For young children, the meaning of words you communicate may be the first meaning they attach to the word. Using words correctly is imperative. Failure to recognize this will result in a lack of communication.

The basic purpose of a presentation is to introduce information that you believe the students can grasp without hands-on experience, to give directions or explain procedures for an activity, or to summarize some activity in order to draw generalizations. For example, if students have had considerable experience with some concept or generalization, then drawing on that experience to provide new insights may constitute an effective presentation. Or, if students have just completed a set of activities, generalizations to be drawn from those activities may be presented by the teacher. If students have had no prior experiences with examples of the content to be taught, then using a presentation to teach it would be inappropriate. Usually, pure presentations are short and part of a larger lesson. Conducting lessons using only this strategy is undesirable and ineffective.

Presentations need to be organized well and delivered smoothly. This requires careful planning and rehearsal, particularly for beginning teachers. The extent to which you must stop and refer to notes, or hesitate in order to think of the next idea, will diminish effectiveness. You will find it helpful to outline the content to be included in a presentation for reference during the lesson. Do not make the outline too extensive, or you will have difficulty in finding the appropriate point during the lesson. On the other hand, do not make the outline too brief, or you may neglect needed ideas. Experience will indicate the appropriate amount of direction you will need to provide yourself in your lesson plan.

Clarity may be aided during a presentation by the use of examples and nonexamples with which students are familiar (Armento 1977; Tennyson and Parks 1980). A teacher could explain perspective in paintings or photographs by showing students a photograph of the street outside the school and pointing out the horizon and vanishing point. For a nonexample, the teacher could show drawings done by young children that have no vanishing point or horizon, which distorts perspective. Examples chosen from the daily life experiences of students will not only add clarity, but will also help make the content more interesting and useful and thus help motivate them to learn.

To avoid misunderstandings, ask questions to ascertain whether students understand the essential elements of the presentation. Uninterrupted teacher talk should rarely exceed 2 to 5 minutes. If the content is complex or abstract, then more frequent questions may be necessary. If in doubt whether students understand something, ask questions. Failure to follow this practice may cause you to lose contact with students during a presentation.

Asking discussion questions during a presentation will merely interrupt the flow of ideas you are presenting; avoid asking questions likely to lead to distractions from the main thrust of the presentation.

Since students remain passive during presentations, presentations should be stimulating. Using audio-visual aids, including the overhead projector, the chalkboard, models, charts, or objects, and using voice control, have marked effects on students' attention.

Outlining and note-taking are usually introduced as part of presentations in the upper elementary or middle school grades. When students are taking notes, allow them time to think about what they are placing in their notes. When they first learn to take notes, place an example on the overhead projector or chalkboard immediately after the information is presented to the students to ensure that they will place needed information in their notes. Let students know what material should be remembered from the material presented. Some information will merely be explanatory; some must be learned. Not all material presented will be equally important, so tell students those things that should become part of their notes. Teaching upper elementary and middle school students how to take notes, therefore, is something you will need to do. Without instruction, students are unlikely to be successful note takers.

Some teachers have the mistaken notion that providing note-taking aids such as outlines or copies of the teacher's notes prior to a presentation will help students. Research on older students has shown the opposite to be true (Petrich and Montague 1981). Outlines or other organizational aids given students before presentations will actually lower achievement. The more students are expected to organize their own notes, the more mental involvement they will have in the activity, and the higher their resultant achievement will be.

When writing on the chalkboard or overhead projector during a presentation, your writing should be neat and organized. Avoid using abbreviations of words you wish students to learn to use and spell. Students will have the tendency to copy only those things you have written on the chalkboard or overhead projector: if you abbreviate, they will abbreviate; if your writing is poorly formed and illegible, their writing will be poorly formed and illegible. Try to set a good example. If you are one of those individuals who write poorly when writing on the chalkboard, then practice the appropriate manuscript and cursive handwriting skills on a chalkboard until you improve.

MAINTAINING ATTENTION DURING LESSONS

During lessons it often happens that students lose motivation and drift off task. Teachers can avoid this by varying the methodology and instructional technology used for lessons as well as by using specific responses when students begin to lose interest in a lesson. The latter responses are sometimes called **refocusing, which is the process**

of interjecting stimuli into a lesson to gain, maintain or increase student attention.

During lessons a teacher has a variety of ways to gain, maintain, or regain the attention of pupils. Choosing a specific refocusing skill to use will depend on the particular situation. Teachers must be aware of student reactions to class activities and be able to use refocusing when it is most likely to be effective. For example, when you have talked too long, students will lose eye contact with you, move around in their seats, play with some object, or in other ways communicate that they are no longer listening. When these signs **first become apparent**, you must regain your students' interest. As you learn to recognize these early signs of noninterest, and as you learn how to refocus attention, you will more likely be successful in keeping students on task and in reducing misbehavior. Let's examine some of these skills that can be used to maintain high interest and motivation.

Questions

During many activities in the classroom, either the students or the teacher is talking. Whenever the teacher has been talking for a while, students will begin to lose interest. Teachers are rarely able to provide enough stimulus variation in their voices to maintain student interest over long periods.

Students in the primary grades are less able to listen quietly than are students in the upper-elementary and middle-school grades. Even students in middle school, however, have difficulty listening to uninterrupted teacher talk for more than a few minutes. When you see students losing interest in what you are saying, one way of regaining this interest is to ask the class a question. Providing opportunities for students to talk will regain the attention of the student responding as well as those in his immediate vicinity.

Gestures

Gestures using the hand, arm, face, or body can direct the attention of the student and can do much to help students recognize important ideas and facts. Since students cannot remember every word spoken and every idea introduced during a class period, they need clues about the ones that are very important or somewhat important, and the ones introduced just to elaborate, clarify, or explain. A teacher can differentiate importance by gesturing at appropriate times; for instance, walking up to the blackboard and pointing to something written while telling the students it is important will more likely convey the word's importance than merely telling them it is important.

Overuse of gestures, on the other hand, should be avoided. The continuous use of the same gesture will cause it to lose all effectiveness. Overuse may also result in a gesture's becoming a distracting mannerism. Become purposeful in the use of gestures; use gestures when you have a specific purpose in mind, but avoid using them otherwise.

Giving Directions

When students' interest and attention stray, you can reclaim their attention by telling them to look at you, to look at what you are showing them, or to pay attention. Use words to direct their attention. Again, this is a simple tactic, but an effective one. Do not confuse this kind of direction-giving with the directions given before students are to perform some task. Directions for tasks will be explained in a later chapter.

Movement

When you have remained in one location of the classroom for some time, changing your location can gain students' attention. Students far from you feel the distance. Merely changing the amount of physical distance between you and these students will increase their awareness and attention. The more the teacher stays at the front of the classroom, the higher the incidence of student off-task behavior will be. Conversely, the more the teacher moves around the classroom, the more students are likely to remain on task. When teachers move to different parts of the room, they tend to make eye contact and interact with different students, which makes these students more attentive. When students are working independently or in small groups at their seats, moving near them will help them stay on task and will help you recognize more readily when students are losing interest in or are having difficulty with a task so you can respond more quickly to their concerns.

Sensory Change

Students should be provided with a variety of stimuli in a lesson. A change in the senses the student must use can provide such variety. For example, after a student has been listening for a while, introducing something that will require the student to use a different or an additional sensory mode helps promote attention. Recognize that some students learn better by seeing, and others may learn better through hearing. Sensory preference can be partially accommodated by using multiple sensory channels and changing the senses students are called upon to use as activities progress. Avoid overloading sensory channels, but plan for students to use a variety of senses during any given lesson.

Use of Voice

A teacher's voice should not be used solely to convey information to the students. Your voice should indicate the relative importance of information, convey the feelings you may be experiencing or would want the students to experience, and serve as a source of stimulation. When students start to lose interest, you can help them regain interest by merely increasing the volume of your voice. Importance of information can be indicated by slowing your speech and raising your voice. Varying the rate, volume, and inflection of your voice will help you maintain your students' interest.

Silence

The use of silence in unorthodox situations can be a source of stimulation for students. One use of silence is the pause that indicates to the students that what has just been said is important and takes some time to think about. You can also use silence at the beginning of an activity or when students are being inattentive; remain silent until the students become silent and direct their attention toward you. Attempting to talk when students are inattentive ensures that some students will not hear what is being said.

Silence is used at other times when you are asking students to respond to questions. This use of silence will be introduced in more detail in the next chapter, "Questioning."

Distractors

Any tactic used to gain students' attention can become a distracting affectation or mannerism when overused and actually interfere with their learning. Other sources of distraction include verbal mannerisms, such as "you know" and "OK," and indeed, almost any verbal behavior, gestures, or movement can become distracting when overused. Use refocusing tactics when appropriate, but be careful not to overuse them.

CLOSING THE LESSON

At least two tasks must be accomplished during the closing of a lesson. First, at least partially assess the attainment of the instructional objectives either by asking the students to respond verbally to questions congruent with the instructional objectives or by using some other means of obtaining feedback, such as a brief quiz or an individual writing exercise. This assessment should not be conducted merely by asking questions such as "Are there any questions?" or "Do you understand?" If you want to find out if students have actually learned what you want them to learn, and you wish to reinforce that learning, then ask questions directly assessing your instructional objectives. Asking such questions will also allow you to correct any misconceptions students may have gained from the lesson. You do not want students to use misconceptions in any practice exercises. Such practice may "set" misconceptions and make eradicating them later very difficult.

Second, restate and reinforce the important generalizations to be learned from the lesson, and the purpose and value of the lesson stated in the set induction. At this time, if the instructional objectives have not been introduced, state the objectives of the lesson and give reasons for their importance (Wright and Nuthall 1970; Armento 1977). Studies on learning have clearly demonstrated that students tend to remember better those things presented at the beginning and ending of a lesson (Armento 1977; Wright and Nuthall 1970). They remember less well those things in between. Therefore, the closing should include all information you want the students to remember from the lesson. Referring to your set induction and showing students how the learning from the lesson fits into the context brought up in the set induction is also a way of helping students to assimilate the learning into their memory.

If you find that most of the students have not learned what you intended, then you may need to plan additional lessons dealing with those instructional objectives. This is particularly important when teaching content or skills that are sequential in nature. If particular students do not achieve the expected outcomes, then additional instruction or practice may be necessary for them. This additional instruction should use activities different from those used for the initial instruction. Merely repeating the initial instruction that did not result in success will likely end up with the same lack of success and in students who are even more frustrated. Try to make remedial instruction fresh and interesting rather than dull drill-and-practice activities.

IMPLICATIONS FOR PLANNING

Including students in the planning of the classroom arrangement at the beginning of the year, semester, or major unit can be rewarding for the students and the teacher. Students often have good judgment about arrangements that might minimize distractions. When you respond to students' suggestions, they may be more likely to stay on task because they have a stake in the arrangement.

Include diagrams in your plans of the placements of materials, learning centers, bulletin boards, seats, and discussion areas. These diagrams may help you arrive at more effective arrangements, and will simplify your planning the next time you are faced with a similar situation. Consider your movement as well as the students' when planning.

Check each activity in your plans to see that the duration is not too long, and that students frequently change the senses they use. When activities are too long or do not call for sensory change, try to modify the activities so that more variety does occur. Avoid having a series of very similar activities over long periods.

When planning lessons, consider the nature of the preassessment required. Whether formal or informal, the preassessment must be conducted prior to the planning of lessons. This enables you to modify your plans, depending on what insight about student background understandings you gain. If students are found to have little interest in the topic, for example, then planning some initiating event to generate interest is crucial.

In order to preassess the students' current knowledge or skill level, a task analysis of what is to be learned as well as what they need to know is necessary. Students must be assessed on their ability to accomplish the tasks defined by the prerequisite objectives. For example, if students are to learn to multiply, then assessing their ability to add is imperative. If you find that some of your students are unable to add, then instruction on addition is indicated before you introduce the process of multiplying.

Since set inductions may have an impact on motivation and achievement, carefully plan the introductions of activities and lessons. When planning set inductions, try to put the lesson into contexts related to the lives of students. If doing a lesson on poetry, for example, you may find that using some familiar source of poems such as pop songs or greeting cards in your introduction will increase motivation.

If a content outline is to be a part of your plans, think about the prerequisite knowledge students must have to understand the content being introduced. Use this thinking both as a source of possible preassessment items and as a help in sequencing the content. You would not want to introduce, for example, the notion of drug dependency if students had no understanding of the concept "drug."

To avoid misspellings and awkward arrangements of things written on the chalkboard, include notes to yourself in your plans that guide you on what and where to write on the chalkboard. With experience you will learn how much detail to include in plans to accomplish your purposes effectively.

Placing reminders to yourself within your plans to use certain refocusing tactics may help you to use them when needed. For example, if you know that you will need to give a lengthy description of some procedure, place a note midway through your plan outline to remind yourself to ask an appropriate question.

When writing your plans, include a verbatim list of the questions you will ask in the closing to check the accomplishment of your objectives. Do the questions actually ask the students to do the task described in the objective? Writing the questions in your plans will help ensure that you ask the questions as intended.

Remember, a lesson plan is merely something you carry into the classroom to help you do the job of teaching. Include those reminders, outlines, questions, and suggestions that will help you work effectively. If you find that you are not doing something that you had intended to do, then your lesson plans need to be changed in ways to make it more likely that you will do that thing. If you find you are putting something in your plans that you never use, then that something is probably unnecessary. With experience, the plans you develop will be effective instructional aids.

REFERENCES

Arlin, M. 1975, The interaction of locus of control, classroom structure, and pupil satisfaction. *Psychology in the Schools,* 12: 279–286.

Armento, B.J. 1977. Teacher behaviors related to student achievement on a social science concept test. *Journal of Teacher Education,* 28(2): 46–52.

Ausubel, D.P., J.D. Novak, and H. Hanesian. 1978. *Educational Psychology: A Cognitive View.* (2nd ed.). New York: Holt, Rinehart and Winston.

Brophy, J.E. and C.M. Evertson. 1976. *Learning from Teaching: A Developmental Perspective.* Boston: Allyn and Bacon.

Bush, A.J., J.J. Kennedy, and D.R. Cruickshank. 1977. An empirical investigation of teacher clarity. *Journal of Teacher Education,* 28(2): 53–58.

Dunn, R. and K. Dunn. 1978. *Teaching Students Through Their Individual Learning Styles: A Practical Approach.* Reston, VA: Reston Publishing.

Hartley, J. and I.K. Davies. 1976. Preinstructional strategies: The role of pretests, behavioral objectives, overviews, and advance organizers. *Review of Educational Research* 46(2): 239–265.

Levy, J. 1983. Research synthesis on right and left hemispheres: We think with both sides of the brain. *Educational Leadership,* 40(4): 66–71.

Melton, R.F. 1978. Resolution of conflicting claims concerning the effect of behavioral objectives on student learning. *Review of Educational Research,* 48(2): 291–302.

Petrich, J.A. and E.J. Montague. 1981. The effect of instructor-prepared handout materials on learning from lecture instruction. *Journal of Research in Science Teaching,* 18(2): 177–187.

Rosenshine, B. and N. Furst. 1971. Research in teacher performance criteria. In *Research in teacher education: A symposium,* ed. B.O. Smith. Englewood Cliffs, New Jersey: Prentice-Hall.

Schuck, R.F. 1981. The impact of set induction on student achievement and retention. *Journal of Educational Research,* 74(4): 227–232.

Tennyson, R.D. and O. Park. 1980. The teaching of concepts: A review of instructional design research literature. *Review of Educational Research,* 50(1): 55–70.

Turner, R.L. 1979. The value of variety in teaching styles. *Educational Leadership,* 36(4): 257–258.

Witkin, H.A., C.A. Moore, D.R. Goodenough, and R.W. Cox. 1977. Field dependent and field independent cognitive styles and their educational implications. *Review of Educational Research,* 47(1): 17-27.

Wright, C.J. and G. Nuthall. 1970. Relationships between teacher behaviors and pupil achievement in three experimental science lessons. *American Educational Research Journal,* 7(4): 477–491.

CHAPTER REVIEW

---

1. Creating a Classroom Environment
   a. Arrange seating to reduce distractions and facilitate on-task behavior.
   b. Classroom furnishings should reflect the nature of the activities being conducted.
   c. Classroom furnishings should be placed so as not to distract ongoing activities.

Purposes of Assessing Readiness

   1. to find out if students possess prerequisite knowledge or skills

   2. to determine if students already possess the knowledge and skills to be taught

   3. to determine if students have an interest in learning what is to be taught

Organizing Content

   1. Organize content from the general to the specific when it is clear that students understand the generalization and you want merely to provide additional examples of applications of the generalizations.

2. Organize content from specific examples to generalizations when it is clear that students have had experience with the examples, or you are going to provide the experience.

Selecting Activities and Associated Technology

Using a variety of activities and supporting technology will enhance the achievement and engagement of pupils.

Starting Lessons

1. Set Induction is the process of inducing readiness to learn.
2. Steps in Set Induction
    a. relate the lesson to be taught to students' past experiences
    b. state the purpose of the lesson in the students' language
    c. relate the lesson to past and future goals of the topic
    d. do something to get their attention and interest

Presenting

1. Purposes of Presentations
    a. to introduce information or knowledge
    b. to give directions or explain procedures
    c. to summarize some activity in order to draw generalizations from the activity
2. Conducting a Presentation
    a. Ask questions during the presentation to ensure that students have understood important ideas as they are presented.
    b. Do not ask discussion questions during a presentation.
    c. Use examples and nonexamples with which students are familiar to bring clarity to ideas being discussed.
    d. Introduce or change the kind of stimuli being used during a presentation.
    e. Allow time for students to take notes during a presentation.
    f. Let students know the relative degree of importance of the material being presented.
    g. Do not provide note-taking aids such as outlines to students prior to a presentation.
    h. Write notes on the chalkboard or overhead projector as you want them to appear in students' notes.

Maintaining Attention During Lessons: Refocusing Skills

Refocusing is the process of interjecting stimuli into a lesson in order to gain, maintain, or increase student attention.

1. Questions: Whenever a teacher has been talking for an extended period and students show signs of losing attention, then the teacher should direct questions to some students.
2. Gestures: Gestures should be used to call attention to things you want students to remember.
3. Giving directions: Telling students to direct their attention to you or to some other point of interest can help them regain attention.

4. Movement: Teacher movement about the room during lessons and seatwork can help students remain attentive and on task.

5. Sensory Change: Whenever students have been required to use one sensory mode for an extended period, changing the sensory mode can help students regain or maintain attention.

6. Voice: Variety in the volume, speed, and inflection of the teacher's voice can help students stay attentive and distinguish between more and less important points.

7. Silence: Unexpected use of silence can gain the students' attention.

8. Distractors: Overuse of any refocusing tactic can become distracting and cause students to lose attention.

Closing Lessons

1. Ask questions congruent with your objectives in order to assess attainment of the instructional objectives for the lesson.

2. State the instructional objectives of the lesson.

3. Give reasons for the importance of the learning outcomes and refer to the set induction in doing so.

EXERCISE 9

Classroom Environment

Arranging a functional classroom that is conducive to learning is valuable to you and your students. This exercise will provide experience with this process by requiring you to draw a classroom arrangement that provides stimulation to students, maintains their interest, and provides for movement by you and the students.

Directions

1. Select a grade level and subject that you will be teaching either on a continuous basis or for a special unit. Record this information at the top of your report and title it "Subject and Level." If you are planning for an elementary self-contained classroom, then title your report "Self-Contained Classroom."

2. List and describe briefly the kinds and sequence of activities that will be used with this arrangement. If you are planning for a unit, list a possible sequence of activities to be used with one lasting about seven class days. If you are planning for the usual activities of an elementary self-contained classroom, list the activities to be used in a typical day. Include such things as learning centers, individualized instruction, small group instruction, whole class instruction, hands-on activities, projects, and audio-visuals to be used. Title this section "Sequence of Activities."

3. Draw a layout of the classroom arranged as you intend to use it for the activities just described, including seats, table, chalkboard(s), bulletin board(s), learning center(s), activity area(s), teacher's desk, and project area(s).

4. List the advantages and disadvantages of this arrangement in conducting the activities listed in the second step above. Include the advantages and disadvantages for each activity as well as the transitions that must be made from one activity to the next. Title this section "Advantages and Disadvantages."

OBSERVATION EXERCISE 10

Room Arrangement

This exercise is designed to provide you with the experience of analyzing the effectiveness of a room arrangement in promoting instruction.

Directions

1. Observe a teacher's classroom arrangement. Draw the room and all of the major furnishings of the room to scale. Include the teacher's desk, students' desks, worktables, chalkboards, overhead projector, learning centers, and other furnishings used as part of instruction.

2. Observe the teacher teaching a lesson, and briefly describe the nature and sequence of the activities used during the lesson.

3. Briefly describe any problems you observed that arose because of the arrangement of the furnishings in the room.

4. For each of the problems, briefly describe what changes in the room arrangement could be made to alleviate the problems.

5. List the ways the room arrangement facilitated instruction.

EXERCISE 11

Preassessment of Interest

One of the purposes of preassessment is to determine the interest students have in the material to be taught. The purpose of this exercise is to provide experience in determining the appropriateness (in terms of amount, level of difficulty, and relevancy) of the content and instructional objectives for a group of elementary or middle school students.

Directions

1. Write instructional objectives for a lesson you might use in teaching some of your content to a class of elementary or middle school students.

2. List the reasons you feel this content and these objectives would be interesting, useful, or in some way beneficial to students you will be teaching.

3. Come prepared the next class period to share this information with the group of peers. Provide copies for each group member.

The Discussion

1. Pass out a copy of your objectives, the reasons for teaching them, and the length of time you feel would be devoted to teaching them.

2. Each person should then share his/her honest opinion about the merits of the content and the objectives. Discuss both the level of difficulty and the amount of content to be taught in the time period indicated.

3. If all are in agreement that the objectives and content are consistent with the reasons, the reasons are valid, and the level of difficulty and amount of content are appropriate, then there is no reason to make changes.

4. If the objectives and content are not perceived as being useful and appropriate for elementary or middle school students, then you will need to convince your peers of the merits of the content and objectives or ask them to offer suggestions about the ways the objectives could be changed so as to be appropriate and have value for students. The latter is probably the option you will need to choose.

EXERCISE 12

Preassessment of Content

One of the concerns a teacher should have prior to any lesson is the current level of experience and understanding of the students. If students have not had the prerequisite experience or understanding necessary for a lesson, then these will need to be provided prior to the intended lesson. Asking questions that assess the adequacy of students' prerequisite knowledge and skills is essential. This exercise provides you with an opportunity to write questions to assess prerequisite knowledge and skills. These questions could be designed to be used to assess students orally or in writing.

Directions

1. List instructional objectives you would teach to a class of elementary or middle school students.

2. After each objective, list the questions you will ask to assess the students' prerequisite knowledge and/or experiences.

3. During the next class period your instructor will assign you to a group of two to four peers. Your task will be to review each of your objectives and the questions assessing prerequisite experiences and understandings. Arrive at a consensus on one objective and associated questions that you feel represent an effective assessment.

4. Choose one person in your group to present your objective and questions to the entire class. Your instructor may have you place this information on the chalkboard, or she may ask you to prepare a transparency for a presentation during the next class period. The purpose of this presentation to the whole class is to analyze the objective and related questions for adequacy. Reviewing your objectives along with related preassessment questions will ensure that no misunderstandings about the process of identifying prerequisite knowledge and skills will be perpetuated. This exercise will also provide members of the class practice in judging the adequacy of preassessment questions.

EXERCISE 13

Set Induction

Using a set induction to start lessons will facilitate student learning. This exercise is designed to provide an experience in developing set induction strategies. A set induction should include the following elements, not necessarily in the order listed:

1. relating the lesson to be taught to students' past experiences

2. stating the purpose but not necessarily the objectives of the lesson in the students' language

3. relating the lesson to future goals

4. doing something to get their attention and interest

1. Write a brief description of the content or skills that could be taught to a class of elementary or middle school children. Title this section "Content (or Skills) to be Taught."

2. Write the instructional objective(s) for the lesson. Title this section "Instructional Objectives."

3. Describe the set induction you could use to start the lesson. Be sure that each of the elements is included in your set induction. Where your set induction involves something you are going to say, or questions you are going to ask, list each **verbatim** and in proper sequence.

4. Your instructor may ask some of you to present your actual set induction to the whole class as you would if teaching a lesson using this set induction.

EXERCISE 14

Outlining Content

Producing an outline of content to be introduced in a lesson as part of a lesson plan is sometimes difficult; therefore, this exercise provides some practice and feedback before you are asked to use an outline in teaching.

Any outline to be used in a lesson plan should list the content in the order it is to be discussed. Include in your outline

1. important generalizations to be made either prior to or following the specific examples to be used

2. brief descriptions of specific examples or points to precede or follow the generalizations

3. verbatim lists of questions to check understanding to be included at the point they will be asked.

Directions

1. Write the instructional objectives to be used in teaching a class of elementary or middle school students.

2. Write a content outline following the description above just as you intend to use it in your teaching lesson.

3. Turn your outline in to your instructor for her comments.

Questioning 4

The use of questions is an important part of teaching. Effective questioning is essential for conducting a variety of activities and tasks in the classroom. The purposes of questioning students include:

1. to preassess students' knowledge prior to instruction
2. to determine students' current understanding during a lesson
3. to assess the attainment of objectives at the conclusion of a lesson
4. to determine students' understanding of procedural directions
5. to increase student involvement in the lesson
6. to provide students with opportunities to think about a topic in more depth

Checking for student understanding throughout a lesson ensures better communication and clarity of instruction. Checking for understanding of directions reduces confusion and resultant off-task behavior. The effect of increased involvement in the lesson will be to increase student time on task and student achievement. Providing opportunities to think about the content of a lesson will increase student understanding of the content. Increased depth of understanding may make the application of what is learned more probable.

KINDS OF QUESTIONS

A teacher can ask many different types of questions during classroom instruction that may serve different functions. Being able to use certain types of questions at appropriate times is a valuable skill.

One way of analyzing questions is to consider their effect in promoting student responses. If a teacher asks a question that has only one correct answer, called a **closed** question, then he can assess something specific a student knows. This kind of question will result in a restricted and usually relatively short response on the part of the student. Examples of this kind of question would be:

What is the capital of the United States?

What is the verb in this sentence?

What is the English word for **si**?

What is the definition of **mineral**?

What is the name of a four-sided figure?

What is the sum of 3 plus 2?

Closed questions are important for finding out whether students have understood something specific. Closed questions are usually asked at the beginning of a lesson for purposes of preassessment, during a lesson to check understanding of something that has been said or taught, and at the end of a lesson to assess students' learning. They may also be asked during a lesson to check student understanding of some directions just given.

Questions that call for one of a limited number of possible correct answers are commonly called **convergent** questions; that is, they converge on a particular set of answers. While convergent questions will likely result in slightly more student talk than closed questions, responses will still be rather limited. Some examples of convergent questions would be

What are some of the colors of the blocks?

Who was one of the last five presidents of the United States?

Who is one of the best known of contemporary American authors?

What are some other words for **food**?

What are some combinations of two numbers that when added result in the sum of 12?

What is one of the most common flowers found in our state?

Convergent and closed questions, which call for specific correct answers, pose some threat to students because they can be embarrassed by incorrect answers. This threat may prevent some students from volunteering to answer and getting involved in the lesson. Convergent and closed questions reduce students' opportunities and willingness to present their beliefs and opinions. If getting students to talk and think is a major concern in a given lesson, then teachers should ask less threatening questions that call for longer answers.

Because getting students to state their beliefs and opinions is an essential part of effective discussions, questions that allow several possible correct answers, called **divergent** questions, may be helpful in fostering more willingness and ability to respond. Some examples of divergent questions are:

What are some similarities between plants and animals?

What are some of the differences between folk and classical music?

What are some rules that different ball sports have in common?

What are some different words that could be used in place of the word **good** without changing the meaning?

What are some things that are done to increase the number of people voting in elections?

The least threatening kind of question of all, and the kind of question that would allow any student to respond, is the question that has no correct or incorrect responses—the **open** question. Open questions are valuable in encouraging student responses. Since there are no correct or incorrect answers, students can respond without embarrassment. An answer need only relate directly to the question to be appropriate. Some examples are:

What are some things that could result if we had no rules at school?

What might happen if no clocks were in our classroom?

What are some of the reasons you like some foods more than others?

What are some of the possible effects on you if you do not like certain people because they go to different churches or have different color skin?

If a teacher wants to find out if students know certain facts, then closed and convergent questions are appropriate; however, if a teacher wants to encourage students to talk, then divergent and open questions are appropriate. The appropriate use of a question is determined by its function.

COGNITIVE LEVELS OF QUESTIONS

Another way of analyzing questions is to consider their use in the kinds of cognitive thinking students are able to demonstrate. During the instructional process, determining what students know, and the extent of this knowledge, is crucial to effective instruction. Studies have shown that many teachers restrict the cognitive level of their questions to the memory level; they merely ask students to repeat memorized facts (Centra and Potter, 1980; Clegg, 1971; Gall, 1970). The ability to repeat memorized facts is not a good indicator of a student's understanding of a topic. In fact, it is fair to say that if rote memorization is the extent to which students understand a topic, then they will not be able to apply the knowledge of that topic. That knowledge is therefore meaningless or useless (Ausubel, 1963). The constant use of memory questions conveys the message to the students that memorization is the kind of learning important to the teacher. If a teacher wants students to be able to use knowledge in any meaningful way, then he must provide opportunities to use knowledge in the ways intended, in addition to mere memory, through teacher questions.

Classifying questions according to their cognitive level may be useful in helping you generate more effective questions in your classroom. The sequence in this classification also implies different complexities of understanding. Demonstrating comprehension of something would be more complex than merely knowing something (at the knowledge level), applying something would be more complex than merely comprehending it, and analyzing something would be more complex than applying it. The cognitive levels suggested by Benjamin Bloom (Bloom, 1956), from less complex to more complex, are

- knowledge
- comprehension
- application
- analysis
- synthesis
- evaluation

Knowledge

Questions at the knowledge level ask students to remember facts about or ways of dealing with specifics. Some examples of questions about specifics are

> What is the distance from the earth to the moon?
>
> Who is the president of the United States?
>
> What are the colors used in the American flag?
>
> What is 3 times 4?

Questions about facts can include questions about rules, past trends, sequences, criteria, classifications, or generalizations.

□ Examples dealing with rules:
  What is the rule for proper use of _____ ?
  What does the symbol _____ mean?
  What kind of question should a teacher use to start a classroom discussion?

□ Examples dealing with past trends:
  What has happened to size of humans in the last 500 years?
  What changes in our country occurred as a result of the introduction of the automobile?
  What changes in the size of the population of the United States have occurred since 1940?

□ Examples dealing with sequences:
  What steps must you take in making a telephone call?
  What are the steps involved in calculating an average value of a series of numbers?
  What are the stages a space shuttle goes through on launching?

□ Examples dealing with criteria:
  What are three characteristics of a good student?
  What are the criteria used to judge the quality of a library project?
  What conditions cause sleet to fall?
  What do we use to decide if we are going to add or subtract two numbers?

□ Examples dealing with classifications:
  What are the names of the five senses?
  What are the names of the different sections of books in the library?
  What are some names of different kinds of insects?

□ Examples dealing with generalizations:
  In what ways must two magnets be arranged to attract each other?
  When the subject of a sentence is plural, which form of the present tense of the verb "to be" is used?
  When reducing a proper fraction to a decimal fraction, which number is divided by the other?

Comprehension

Comprehension questions help a teacher assess students' understanding of a literal message. This assessment can be done by asking students to translate, interpret, or extrapolate.

- ☐ Examples dealing with translation:
  What is the meaning of "being cool" in your own words?
  Define the word **temperature** in your own words.
  What does the phrase **improper fraction** mean?

- ☐ Examples dealing with interpretation:
  What does it mean when you say "That's dumb"?
  What is the main idea you get when you hear the word **lonely**?
  What does the rising line on this graph represent?

- ☐ Examples dealing with extrapolation:
  From our study of what happens to us when we don't eat properly, what would happen to your pet if you don't feed it properly?
  From the growth rate of the plant shown in the graph, what will the height of the plant be at the end of next week?
  If we mix paint of the primary colors yellow and blue we get green, and if we mix red and blue we get purple. What color might we get if we mix the primary colors yellow and red?

Application

Questions at the application level assess the ability of students to apply the knowledge they possess without having been told the particular application they are to identify. Application questions ask students to identify solutions to problems, or in some other fashion demonstrate their ability to use knowledge in a novel or new circumstance.

- ☐ Examples of application questions:
  What is one way you might be able to put out a fire?
  What are three examples of sentences using the correct present tense of the verb "to be"?
  What is the product of 33 times 24?
  What are some ways of keeping warm on a very cold day?

Analysis

Analysis questions assess students' ability

1. to examine a novel or new situation and break it into its component parts
2. to identify the elements making the whole
3. to identify the possible relationships that could exist between the parts
4. to recognize principles that might govern the operation of the whole

□ Examples dealing with identification of elements:

What are some things that students do in a classroom to make it a happy place to learn?

What parts of your clothes help keep you warm?

What are some fast ways to travel across our city?

□ Examples dealing with relationships between elements:

What would happen to a bird if we clipped its wings?

What could you do to get out of this classroom if the doors wouldn't open?

In what ways would the addition of four-digit numbers be similar to the addition of three-digit numbers?

□ Examples dealing with principles:

In what ways has the artist of this painting used color to emphasize happiness?

What would cause a person to give money to help someone in need?

What would be likely to happen when riding a bicycle if suddenly there was no friction?

Synthesis

Synthesis questions require students to organize knowledge in order to arrive at unique (for them) solutions or products of thought. Synthesis questions allow students to demonstrate their creativity.

□ Examples include:

What could you do to make your room at home a nicer place to spend time?

What kinds of things could be done to attempt to reduce the incidence of drug use on the part of students?

What are some contributions art makes to better the lives of people who are not artists?

What would be one example of a plot that could be used for a short story?

Evaluation

Evaluation questions require students to make judgments about relative values and to identify the bases for their judgments. Students are asked to analyze a novel or new (for them) situation, compare the situation with certain criteria or standards, then use the results of this analysis to make decisions about the degree of fit between elements in the situation and the criteria or standards. This process is fundamental to decision making in life, and this level of understanding is essential for making wise decisions. When students' understanding reaches this level, they are able to use the knowledge in ways likely to have significance in their lives. A few examples illustrate evaluative questions:

What are some considerations for best arranging our classroom so that we can read quietly without being bothered by other classmates?

What criteria can be used to determine the value of poetry in the lives of people?

What are some things you would want to consider before deciding on a place to take a family vacation?

What criteria would you use to decide what knowledge is of most value to students you teach?

What things would help you decide which television programs would be best for you to watch?

What kinds of things determine whether you are being successful in school?

USES OF COGNITIVE QUESTIONS

Do not become overly concerned with the classification of cognitive questions into the categories just described. Bloom's taxonomy helps teachers determine the nature of the questions they tend to ask. Most educators think that effective teachers use a variety of cognitive questions. Early research studies indicated that using higher-level questions in the classroom had little effect on achievement (Andre, 1979; Winne, 1979; Medley, 1979; Centra and Potter, 1980). Andre suggested that if teachers communicate the fact that they expect their students to achieve higher-level objectives, then students perceiving their task as one of acquiring as much as possible from instruction will be influenced little by higher-level questions. On the other hand, learners who want only to get through the instruction with the least amount of effort will be more affected by higher-level questions. Later, more careful analyses of prior research (Redfield and Rousseau, 1981) found that when teachers predominantly use higher cognitive-level questions, gains in achievement are positive. At present it appears that if the objectives and the tests used to measure achievement are essentially knowledge level, then the use of higher cognitive-level questions will do little to aid achievement and, in fact, could be detrimental. On the other hand, if the objectives and the tests used to measure achievement deal with higher cognitive levels, the **predominant** use of higher cognitive-level classroom questions may result in achievement gains.

As is the case with any classification, questions do not always fall easily into the designated categories. Use this classification to guide the formulation of questions when planning lessons. Planning questions that are clear, that will serve the purpose intended, and that will assess not only knowledge levels of understanding, but also higher levels, is important.

FORMULATING QUESTIONS

Clarity in phrasing questions is critical for effective questioning (Land, 1980; Gall and Gillett, 1980). The two predominant problems teachers have in phrasing questions are asking questions that call for only two alternative answers (e.g., yes or no) and questions that are ambiguous.

Ambiguity can lead to frustration for you and your students; therefore, stating questions with clarity is essential for effective interactions. When the intent of the question is unclear to students, fewer students will be willing to respond, students will attempt to guess at answers, students will ask the teacher for clarification, and lessons will tend to lose clarity. For example, what responses would the teacher expect from the following questions?

What about the Middle East?

How is sound made?

What do you know about life?

How did the War of Independence begin?

What exercises are good for you?

What can you do to become better?

Obviously, the teachers asking these questions have not made the intent of the answers clear. The nature of the responses expected is so open-ended that students would find answering these questions difficult.

Questions that call for one of two alternative answers also rarely reflect the teacher's intent. For example, the question "Should there be a rule about raising your hand before talking?" calls for a yes-or-no answer, which is probably not the response the teacher really wants. In all likelihood an ambiguous follow-up question, "Why do you think that?" will be asked. A better question (and one that probably reflects the teacher's true intent) would be "What are some of the reasons for or against raising your hand before talking?" Questions calling for one of two alternative answers will cause the student to guess or will require an immediate follow-up question by the teacher because the intent of the questions would be unclear.

Here are some additional examples of undesirable phrasing taken from actual transcripts of classrooms:

Which is more important in a workout, the warmup or the warmdown?

What is more important in writing a short story, having precise descriptive detail of actions and mannerisms or having abstract generalizations?

Could we think of ourselves being the same without being able to see color?

Commonly, questions calling for yes-or-no answers start with auxiliary verbs such as **do, could, is, are, have, can, should, was,** and **does**. Ambiguous questions quite often start with the words **how** and **why**. Avoid starting any questions with these words. When asking cognitive questions, try to start with the verbs **what, which, when, who,** and **where**. Starting with these words will not ensure lack of ambiguous or two-alternative questions, but it will help. Clearly phrased cognitive questions will be precise, have a proper grammatical arrangement, and use easily understood terminology.

Do not think that all questions need to take the form of interrogative statements. Declarative statements indicating that you wish students to say something can be as effective, if not more effective, than interrogative statements (Dillon, 1979; Dillon, 1981). For example, rather than ask, "What is the evidence to support _____," the teacher might say, "Describe the evidence that supports _____." Each calls for a similar response, but Dillon has found that declarative statements can often elicit longer and more complex student responses.

Do not expect that the cognitive level of the student responses will always correspond to the intended cognitive level of the questions. Dillon found that about 13 percent of the responses will occur at a lower level and about 27 percent at a higher level (Dillon, 1982). On the other hand, Willson (1973) found that the level of elementary student responses to teacher questions was significantly affected by the level of teacher questions.

ELICITING

A question used to evoke a pupil response is called an **eliciting question**. The process of indicating which student you wish to respond to your question is called **eliciting**. One of three patterns can be used to indicate who is to respond:

1. Ask a question and allow any student or group of students to respond spontaneously without indicating who is to respond.

2. Call on a student by name and ask the question that particular student is to answer.

3. Ask a question, pause, call on a student by name to respond, and then have that particular student respond.

The first option usually creates behavioral problems. Such a pattern allows and encourages uncontrolled talking, resulting in disruptive student behavior. Also, interacting with students in this fashion is impersonal, and students quickly feel that they are not being recognized as individuals. As a result, social constraints are removed, thus making disruptive behavior more likely. Allowing students to call out answers indiscriminately will not only create behavioral management problems, but will also make it impossible to conduct questioning in ways likely to encourage student thinking. Effective teacher responses to student answers become difficult, if not impossible, when students are allowed to answer without being called on to respond. The quality of thought in the classroom is thereby diminished.

Allowing unison responses, and even encouraging unison responses, does have some advantages in helping students at the primary level stay on task during drills. At those times, the students should be directed to respond in unison when given the signal to do so. A teacher would likely use this pattern when showing flash cards with names of colors, addition and subtraction problems, or some similar simple task.

Although using this pattern may have advantages at these times, avoid using it at other times.

The second pattern, calling on a student and then asking a question, is also undesirable. First, as soon as one student is identified to answer the question, other students cease to feel a need to think about the question. Second, the student being asked the question is put in a position of potential embarrassment, making it less likely that the student will respond successfully. The second pattern is often used by teachers as a means of behavior control after using the first pattern with the resultant calling out of answers by students. The second pattern is a poor substitute for good behavioral management and should be avoided.

The third pattern, asking a question, pausing, indicating a student to respond, and then getting a response from that student alone, is preferred for several reasons (Brophy 1979; Anderson, Everston, and Brophy 1979). First, using this pattern avoids the difficulties presented by the other two patterns. Second, calling on individual students allows you to interact with individuals to the extent you desire.

You may feel that asking students to raise their hands and wait to be called on before responding to questions may stifle their participation. Keep in mind that deliberative bodies all have rules for recognition. While each individual has the right to speak in such a body, each also has an equal right to be heard. The only way to ensure that each person's rights to speak and be heard are protected is to ensure that not all individuals speak at once. Without rules, a deliberative body could not function. The value in allowing others to speak and be listened to is an important lesson for students to learn.

Until you are able to develop other options, the best means of ensuring that you will protect the rights of individual students in your class is to expect students to raise their hands to be called on. The only students talking during a discussion will be those recognized by you and asked to respond by name. At least for the present, you should develop the pattern of asking a question and then calling on a student by name to respond. Do not allow any other students to answer, and if some call out unsolicited answers, do not accept those answers. This may seem rigid, but until your skills in behavioral management are well developed, you would be wise to follow such a pattern.

When eliciting responses from students, use silence to allow them to think about their answers. The use of silence requires effort on the part of most novice teachers. Their natural tendency is to fill in any silent periods that arise during questioning with teacher talk. The usual amount of silence can be measured in fractions of seconds (Rowe, 1974). However, using such short periods of silence will reduce the quality and frequency of student responses. The use of longer periods of silence, or wait time, during questioning can have several well-established beneficial effects (Rowe, 1974; Rowe, 1978; Honea, 1982; Tobin, 1984). Silence can be used when eliciting in one of two ways:

1. The use of a brief silent period immediately following your stated question, but before you indicate the student who should respond, will result in students' being more likely to respond and respond correctly or appropriately.

2. When calling on a student to respond and not getting an immediate reply, allow some silence so that the student can think about the question. The student will be more likely to respond with time.

The use of wait time is not a natural behavior for most teachers. Developing this skill will take some practice. Initially, the use of silence will seem strange and artificial. One method of learning to use silence when needed is to start counting to yourself when you know silence could be used. Do not say anything until you have counted to seven. With practice, you will begin to develop a habit of waiting, and you will not dread the use of silence (Rowe, 1974).

TEACHER RESPONSES

Questions are used in the classroom as an instructional aid to find out what students know so that you can help them with their learning. Effective learning is not errorless. Students will make mistakes, and that is to be expected. One of the reasons for asking questions is to discover the difficulties in learning that students may be experiencing. All answers, correct or incorrect, provide valuable information about what students are understanding and not understanding and should be viewed as opportunities for you to promote learning. Viewing student responses objectively is essential. Avoid getting your ego involved in the adequacy of student responses: you should not feel elated when students respond correctly, nor should you be upset when they respond incorrectly. Asking good questions is not enough; responding appropriately to student answers, even incorrect ones, is also essential (Good and Brophy, 1978; McKeown, 1977).

Responses to Correct Answers

If students are going to respond freely to your questions, then they must be encouraged to do so. One form of encouragement is to praise correct replies. This form of reinforcement, however, can be insidious if not used properly. If you constantly tell students that their answers are excellent or good, then students will depend on your response as a measure of the quality of their answers. Constant praise also implies a criticism of students' answers when such praise is not forthcoming, because praise tends to be evaluative and judgmental. Praise implies approval, while encouragement conveys acceptance. Forms of encouragement other than praise are sometimes preferred (Grey, 1974).

Encouragement may take the form of pointing out that a student's response was certainly justified on the basis of the evidence the student presented. A student given this kind of feedback may be encourage to continue to do that kind of thinking. This form of encouragement, commonly referred to as **labeled** praise, attempts to point out to the student how her response or the thinking leading to the response will benefit her.

When using praise, avoid overuse of unthinking praise like "Good!" "Very good!" "I like that answer!" and similar kinds of global praise. Try to encourage student responses and thinking by specifically pointing out examples of effective thinking and why the thinking was effective.

The most effective form of reinforcement is using something a student has said earlier in the lesson. Do this by mentioning the name of the student and what he or she said, and then expanding on that idea or incorporating that idea into the lesson in some fashion. In essence you are telling the student, "I not only heard what you said, but what you said has value to us in this lesson." That idea is powerful reinforcement indeed! Unfortunately, this form of reinforcement is seldom used by teachers; you should learn to incorporate it into your lessons often.

If you find yourself constantly saying things like "That's correct!" or "That's right!" then you may be asking too many convergent or factual recall questions. These questions do not encourage student responses or thought and should be avoided except for purposes of drill and practice, for assessing student learning at the conclusion of lessons, or as a preassessment of student learning at the beginning of lessons.

When responding to students' answers with encouragement, try to develop a variety of responses rather than merely repeating the students' answers or adopting some repetitious expression of praise. Repetitious forms of praise and acceptance soon lose their effectiveness. Using students' ideas and recognizing those ideas by name is a powerful form of reinforcement. If you use other forms of encouragement, try to indicate the reason the student's contribution would likely help the student; that is, use labeled encouragement or praise. Also guard against giving more encouragement and praise to high achievers than low achievers. Studies have shown that this is a tendency on the part of many teachers (Braun, 1976). Since high achievers are more likely to give correct answers to questions, try to avoid such disparity in your responses.

When students respond correctly to higher-level types of questions such as application, analysis, synthesis, and evaluation, they may have responded with little thought. The intention of using such questions is to provide opportunities for thinking. To encourage pupils to think about their responses, ask them to describe the reasoning that led to their answers when they answer such questions. If you do this on a consistent basis, students will become less likely to respond unthinkingly to higher-level questions.

Responses to Incorrect Answers

Some teachers have the mistaken notion that students who provide incorrect answers should not be corrected or in any way criticized. No evidence has been found to support the notion that teachers should avoid letting students know when they have replied incorrectly and providing help in correcting the misunderstanding (Soar and Soar, 1979). In fact, available research suggests that correcting students when they are wrong may be more important than praising them when they are correct (Anderson and Faust, 1973). When correcting high-ability students, an instructor who gives occasional, justified, mild criticism indicating that they could or should have done better tends to contribute more to their motivation and achievement than does one who only praises (Good and Brophy, 1977; Soar and Soar, 1979).

Many teachers react to incorrect answers by repeating the original question and asking students to try again (Dunkin and Biddle, 1974). Repeating the question does nothing to correct the student's misconceptions or lack of knowledge. Failure to correct students when they respond incorrectly may indicate to them a teacher's lack of interest in the student's progress. Look on your response not as a criticism but as a response to correct misunderstandings—as corrective feedback that provides information to the student without any evaluation of the person.

When students are unable to respond correctly to knowledge-level questions, they should be given the correct answer. Do not encourage them to guess at the answer or call on others for the answer (Good and Brophy, 1977; Anderson and Faust, 1973). When the problem is a lack of specific information, simply furnish the student with the information. Inaccurate factual responses should be corrected; to do otherwise is to show a lack of respect for the truth.

When a student has responded incorrectly to a higher cognitive-level question, you have two viable ways of responding. The first kind of response is to deal with the error in a fairly direct manner. This direct corrective feedback will

1. indicate that the student answered incorrectly, with phrases such as

   "Your answer was partially correct, but _____"

   "That's not quite right."

   "No, that would not usually be considered correct."

2. provide background information that appeared to be lacking in the student's understanding, including definitions or examples

3. provide another opportunity for the student to answer

The other method of responding is one that some would call a Socratic method, which may take one of two approaches. The first approach may be to ask the student to describe the thinking she did to arrive at an answer. Then specific questions about faulty steps in her thinking process may help her recognize the error made. The second approach involves breaking the original question down into a logical succession of smaller questions. The student is then asked to respond to each of these questions in sequence until she is led to a position of being able to answer the original question. She is then asked the original question, followed by a question similar to the first question. The latter question will then determine if the student can do the kind of thinking required to answer that kind of question (Brophy, 1979).

Responses to Correct but Inadequate Answers

Some student answers to questions will obviously be memorized, textbook responses, others will be unclear or incomplete, and still others may be unsubstantiated assertions. All such answers are opportunities to help the students improve on their understanding

Pupil listening to teacher's response

(Brophy, 1979) by asking additional questions. These questions are referred to as **probes**. A probe is a question **about a student's response** that requires a student to say more about her answer, clarify something that she said, or justify her response. The teacher, when probing, can also ask another student to do one of these three tasks based on something another student has just said. Kinds of probes are:

Extending

Asking a student to say more is called **extending**. After a student has responded, the teacher can ask the student to continue to respond. Asking students to extend their replies can be done in many ways, such as:

"Say more."

"Tell us a little more about that."

"Please add to that."

"And then what?"

"What is the next step, if what you said is true?"

A student should be asked to extend a response if the response is incomplete or if you have some reason to think the student might like to say more about the response. Sometimes, students will respond impulsively. If encouraged to continue, they may give their original comments more thought and proceed to expand on an initially limited answer. Asking students to extend their replies will allow them to respond with more deliberation and completeness.

Clarifying

Asking a student to explain more clearly is called **clarifying**. Any word or phrase used by the student that represents memorized answers can be a source for clarification. A teacher could ask:

> "Would you please say that in your own words?"
>
> "Please give me an example of what you mean."
>
> "Please rephrase your answer."

If, on the other hand, the student uses ambiguous words or phrases, then a teacher might ask:

> "What did you mean by _____?"
>
> "Please give me an example of _____."
>
> "Would you clarify what you meant by _____?"

If a student responds to a question in a way that clearly indicates the answer is merely a memorized one, then you should ask for clarification. Asking the student to clarify a response will enable you to find out if a student has any understanding beyond memorized answers. Ask students who use ambiguous terms to define the terms or give examples. This process will ensure clear communication between the student and you as well as between the student and other students. Clarity in communication is a valuable skill all students need to develop. This kind of probe encourages growth in clarity of communication.

Justifying

Asking a student to give the reasons or evidence for an assertion is called a **justifying probe**. When a student responds to a question in a manner indicating lack of thought, or you are uncertain as to the basis for the response, you can ask questions such as the following to encourage thought:

> "What reasons do you have for believing that?"
>
> "What evidence suggests that?"
>
> "Is there any evidence to the contrary?"

One important goal of education is to help students think more critically. Students must learn to recognize the evidence or reasoning that leads them to adopt certain positions, beliefs, or understandings. One of the mechanisms teachers have to encourage this kind of thinking is to ask students to justify responses.

Redirecting

There may be times when you will want to get as many students as possible to respond during a discussion. One of the ways this can be accomplished, and at the same time encourage the whole class to think about responses, is to redirect some of the students' responses by asking another student to extend, clarify, or justify a student's response. This tactic is called **redirecting**. For example, a teacher may call on a second student following a student response and ask the second student:

"What reasons do you have for agreeing or disagreeing with _____?"

"Would you please expand on _____'s answer?"

"What reasons do you think would lead someone to _____'s position?"

"What evidence would support _____'s position?"

"What do you think _____meant by _____?"

Silent Probe

When a student's answer to a higher-level question is incomplete, unclear, or unsubstantiated, you can accomplish much the same result as with verbal probing by just remaining silent. During the silence you continue eye contact with the student, nod, or in other nonverbal ways communicate a desire for the student to continue talking. This silence should extend for a period of at least 3 to 5 seconds. If the student does not extend, clarify, or justify her answer, then use verbal probes. Avoid using verbal probes if a 3-to-5-second silence will accomplish the same result. This most important use of silence **following a student's response** is rarely used by teachers (Rowe, 1978). If you can remain silent at the conclusion of a student's response, the student will almost always continue talking. This additional talk will take the form of extending, clarifying, or justifying the initial response; in essence, probing without the necessity of a question. This use of silence will increase length of student responses, increase number of speculative responses, increase number of student questions, decrease failure to respond, increase student involvement, increase student reasoning, increase number of slower students responding, and increase evidence-inference statements (Rowe, 1978). These are powerful reasons for developing this skill. Again, using silence at this time is unnatural and requires effort on your part.

Some caution in the use of silence, or wait time, is in order. When you are teaching, you must be aware of a possible tendency to vary the amount of silence you allow different students, depending on your expectations for those students. This is true of all the wait times that have been introduced. For example, if you have low expectations for students, you may have the tendency to allow less silence to occur when interacting with them. If you associate ethnicity with certain expectations, then you may allow varying durations of silence, depending on the ethnicity of the student. Be aware of such differences in your behavior if you expect not to discriminate against students based on expectations you have for them. The appropriate use of silence is something that you will want to examine carefully in your teaching, and then practice its use in order to use it naturally.

TEACHER-DIRECTED DISCUSSIONS

A teaching strategy can be thought of as a sequence of teaching tasks designed to accomplish some particular kind of learning. The skills introduced to this point are those used when planning and conducting lessons, regardless of the teaching strategy that is being used. The rest of this chapter and the next part of the textbook will introduce you to some of the teaching strategies commonly used in elementary and middle schools.

One common teaching strategy in the upper elementary and middle school grades that uses questions is class discussions. Many kinds of discussion strategies exist, but the most fundamental is that of the teacher-directed discussion. The purpose of a teacher-directed discussion is to allow students, under the direction of the teacher, to examine some topic with which they already have some familiarity in order to develop a deeper understanding of the topic. The teacher's role is to help students remember what they already know and to help them to analyze that knowledge in ways that will allow them to come to a new (for them) understanding. **Students must have some knowledge and prior experience with the topic to be discussed if the discussion is to be successful**. Some characteristics of effective group discussions are:

1. most, if not all, of the students have an opportunity to express their thoughts
2. most, if not all, of the students have opportunities to talk approximately equal lengths of time
3. most, if not all, of the students listen to what other students have to say
4. students are permitted to examine their own and others' views in a nonthreatening environment.

Several kinds of topics are appropriate for discussion. These include:

1. possible positions on issues
2. making predictions or hypothesizing
3. identification of problems that need further study
4. interpretation of experiences
5. exploring beliefs or attitudes.

Starting a Discussion

The initial question used to start a discussion defines the topic. This first question should be an open or divergent question in order to encourage as many responses as possible. Students who respond early in a discussion are more willing to continue to respond. If students have not responded early in a discussion, they will be less likely to want to respond later. Thus, calling on as many students as possible early in a discussion is crucial.

Although the initial question should be open or divergent, many teachers tend to begin with an ambiguous question, thinking such a practice is desirable. **Open** is not synonymous with **ambiguous**. While open questions will have many acceptable answers, they should not be ambiguous. For example, if you wish to have a discussion about the effects of discharged sewage on the wildlife in and along a stream, a question like "What do you think are some of the possible effects of pollution on our environment?" opens the subject up to any number of answers that would be totally unrelated to the subject to be discussed. You need, therefore, to phrase the question so that any answer focused on the topic would be acceptable. A properly worded question for the example just stated would be "What kinds of things do you think might happen to the wildlife in and along a stream when untreated sewage is discharged into the stream?" Notice that this question is open in the sense that any answer directly related to the question would be acceptable, but it lets the students know the context of the discussion.

Similarly, divergent questions also must have clarity even though these questions allow several answers to be correct. For example, if discussing the health effects of littering on society, you could ask, "What are some effects of littering?" Notice that student replies to such a question could range far afield of the intended topic. The question, "What effects on the health of people would littering have?" would provide for a variety of answers, but would restrict the context to the topic being discussed.

Further, the initial question should not be one beginning with threatening phrases, such as

Can you tell me _____?

Do you know _____?

Who can tell me _____?

Such phrases are somewhat threatening and may make students less willing to respond. Another undesirable result of using these phrases is that they encourage students to respond by calling out an answer. Such "call outs" can disrupt the discussion and lead to other kinds of misbehavior.

The initial question should also not call for a yes-or-no answer. One word answers do little to stimulate further discussion. Questions asking students to state their positions on issues also stifle student thought. Students have a tendency, once they have stated a position, to feel a need to defend that position. They will also then have the tendency to remember selectively data that supports their position and forget data that contradicts their position. When examining issues, teachers must try to ask questions that will allow a free examination of a multitude of positions without forcing a student to take a position prematurely. These questions can take the form of asking students to identify the advantages and disadvantages of certain positions, or you could ask them to identify unanswered, interesting questions about a particular issue. For example, you might ask students to discuss the advantages and disadvantages of eating fast foods. They may also then identify questions that must be answered before anyone could take a reasonable position on the question.

Questions used to initiate a discussion should be stimulating, focus on the topic to be discussed, be in the students' vernacular, and be open or divergent. Kinds of phrases likely to stimulate discussion would include:

What kinds of things might happen if _____?

In what ways do you think your lives would change if _____?

What kinds of things might you do if you were placed in the situation of ?

In what ways could a change in _____affect your lives? What would be some of the problems created and some of the benefits derived from _____?

What possible changes could occur if _____?

When using open or divergent questions to increase the number of students responding during a discussion, attempt to get maximum mileage from such questions. When asking an open or divergent question, keep in mind that many answers will be acceptable in response to the question. After the first student responds to the question, you are encouraged to probe, use silence, and use reinforcement to the extent that these make sense for use with that student. You could use a rather extended period of time with that one student if you fully used all of these skills. However, focusing on one student would clearly not be desirable because you will want to include as many students as possible. Therefore, after you think you have interacted with the first student sufficiently, then, **using the same question** or a redirecting probe, move on to another student. Usually you should be able to repeat the initial open question several times before moving on to another question. You will need to sense when dropping a given question is advisable, but do not do so too quickly in an effort to hurry through a lesson. Discussions should not be hurried. Hurrying promotes superficiality and sloppy thinking. Discussions should promote deliberate thought, so do not try to cover too much in a limited time.

During a Discussion

As you move through the discussion, a sequence of open or divergent questions should allow an exploration of ideas. Eventually, you will want to begin to narrow the discussion through the use of convergent questions. Do not be too quick in closing down the exploratory phase. You will want as many students as possible to contribute to the exploratory phase. You will also be trying to ensure that all participate equally. Eliciting with names and requiring students to wait to be called on to respond will be crucial for accomplishing equal participation.

Probing student answers and using wait time will be very profitable in a discussion situation. Remember, the purpose of discussions is to help students explore ideas they already possess. Students should examine their positions on topics and identify ambiguities and inconsistencies, as well as recognize when positions held are based on incomplete, incorrect, or unsubstantiated information. Probing can ensure

Pupils listening to others

that this kind of in-depth thinking takes place. Look on incorrect and incomplete answers as opportunities for further instruction. Such a perspective will create an atmosphere that makes freedom of expression more likely. Constructive, corrective feedback, however, should be a part of discussion. Do not allow misconceptions to exist at the end of the discussion.

Closing a Discussion

Any discussion would be incomplete without some form of summary to bring together the ideas presented. If the discussion has been successful, you should be able to use much of what the students said during the discussion in coming to conclusions in the last half of the discussion. Remember, using students' ideas, and referring to the name of the person when doing so, is a very powerful form of reinforcement. A summary of a discussion should help students recognize instances of improved logic, corrected or additional information, and revised generalizations that may have been introduced. Through this process students should have more clearly defined positions, and they should now be better able to recognize the evidence supporting their positions.

Discussions are instructional experiences and should be designed with some objective in mind. Of course, this will not always be the case, but for purposes of most instruction, your discussions will have some instructional objective. The closing of the discussion will then include some partial assessment of students' attainment of the objective. Objectives for discussions should be thought of in terms of the students' ability to think about a topic or justify a position they may hold on an issue, not in terms of the memorization of content. Your objective should therefore be an extension of the actual discussion; that is, students should be asked to apply, analyze, synthesize, or evaluate some aspect of the discussion. While the learning of some content at the recall level may have occurred, students should be expected to do more than merely recall what they learned as a result of a discussion.

Improving Discussions

One of the purposes of having discussions, in addition to encouraging students to think more in depth about a topic, is to teach them how to interact effectively in group settings. With each successive discussion, students should improve their ability to wait to be called on to respond, to listen to what others have to say, to think about the content, and to contribute equally.

Occasionally during discussions, students will obviously not be listening to other students but will be concerned with what they want to say. To prevent this, stop the discussion momentarily and introduce an additional rule that states that before any student can respond she must repeat what the preceding student just said. The rule could be made to apply to one or a few students or the entire class. Students should be told beforehand that this will be in force to minimize any disruptions during the discussion.

Some students will seldom offer responses during a discussion; others will tend to dominate. This situation can create barriers to effective discussions. One way of helping students become more aware of their responsibility to contribute and at the same time allow others an equal opportunity to contribute is to do a post-discussion evaluation. Such an evaluation is conducted by giving the students the following criteria for effective discussions prior to the discussion:

1. all students have the right to contribute equally
2. all students have the responsibility to contribute
3. all students have the responsibility to listen to others

A small group of students can be assigned the task of observing the discussion to see how well the class meets these criteria, or the class can be told to take notes during the discussion whenever some members of the class do not conform to these criteria. When individual observers are observing a small group, make a checklist for each to complete. The checklist lists the names of the students in the group in a vertical column to the left. The things to be observed are listed across the top. The student is then to check to the right of each student's name each incident of that behavior at the time it is observed. The list across the top could include such things as

1. the student contributed an idea
2. the student asked another a question about something she said
3. the student praised someone else's idea
4. the student interrupted someone while she was talking
5. the student criticized something someone else said

Following the discussion, the observers or the entire class can critique the discussion with these criteria in mind. Those students who have not contributed or those who have dominated the discussion will be identified by the students. As a result, contributions by these students will likely be altered during subsequent discussions. With time, your students will improve in their ability to participate in a group discussion.

IMPLICATIONS FOR PLANNING

When planning questions, consider the answers you are likely to receive. If anticipated answers require one of two simple alternatives, (e.g., yes or no) or could go well beyond the topic you wish the students to think about, then rephrase your questions to focus on the intended answers. When planning lessons that involve questions, write out all key questions and include them in your plans. Rarely can a novice teacher create effective questions extemporaneously, and expecting them to possess this skill without considerable experience is unrealistic. Careful planning will prevent false starts, uncertain pauses, poor transitions between questions, and unnecessary and distracting verbal mannerisms used to fill in thinking time, all of which reduce the effectiveness of questioning (Land, 1980).

REFERENCES

Anderson, L., C. Evertson, and J. Brophy. 1979. An experimental study of effective teaching in first-grade reading groups. *Elementary School Journal* 79: 193–223.

Anderson, R.C. and G.W. Faust. 1973. *Educational psychology: The science of instruction and learning.* New York: Dodd, Mead.

Andre, T. 1979. Does answering higher-level questions while reading facilitate productive learning? *Review of Educational Research* 49(2): 280–318.

Ausubel, D. 1963. *The psychology of meaningful verbal learning.* New York: Grune and Stratton.

Bloom, B.S.(Ed.). 1956. Taxonomy of educational objectives, handbook I: Cognitive domain. New York: David McKay.

Braun, C. 1976. Teacher expectations: Sociopsychological dynamics. *Review of Educational Research* 46(2): 185–213.

Brophy, J. 1979. Teacher behavior and student learning. *Educational Leadership* 37(1): 33–38.

Centra, J.A., and D.A. Potter. 1980. School and teacher effects: An interrelational model. *Review of Educational Research* 50(2): 273–291.

Clegg, A.A. 1971. Classroom questions. In *The Encyclopedia of Education,* Vol. 2. New York: Macmillan.

Dillon, J.T. 1979. Alternatives to questioning. *High School Journal* 62: 217–222.

Dillon, J.T. 1981. Duration of response to teacher questions and statements. *Contemporary Educational Psychology* 6: 1–11.

Dillon, J.T. 1982. Cognitive correspondence between question/statement and response, *American Educational Research Journal* 19(4): 540–551.

Dunkin, M., and B. Biddle. 1974. *The study of teaching.* New York: Holt, Rinehart and Winston.

Gall, M.D. 1970. The use of questions in teaching. *Review of Educational Research* 40: 707–721.

Gall, M.D. and M. Gillett. 1980. The discussion method in classroom teaching. *Theory into Practice* 19(2): 98–102.

Good, T.L. and J.E. Brophy. 1977. *Educational psychology: A realistic approach.* New York: Holt, Rinehart and Winston.

Good, T.L. and J.E. Brophy. 1978. *Looking in classrooms.* New York: Harper and Row Publishers.

Grey, L. 1974. *Discipline without fear.* New York: Hawthorne Books.

Honea, J.M. 1982. Wait-time as an instructional variable: An influence on teacher and student. *Clearing House* 56: 167–170.

Land, M.L. 1980. Teacher clarity and cognitive level of questions: Effects on learning. *Journal of Experimental Education* 49: 48–51.

McKeown, R. 1977. Accountability in responding to classroom questions: Impact on student achievement. *Journal of Experimental Education* 45: 24–30.

Medley, D.M. 1979. The effectiveness of teachers. In *Research on teaching: Concepts, findings, and implications,* ed. P.L. Peterson and H.J. Walberg. Berkeley: McCutchan Publishing.

Redfield, D.L. and E.W. Rousseau. 1981. A meta-analysis of experimental research on teaching questioning behavior. *Review of Educational Research* 51(2): 237–245.

Rowe, M.B. 1974. Pausing phenomena: Influence on the quality of instruction. *Journal of Psycholinguistics Research* 3: 203–233.

Rowe, M.B. 1978. Wait, wait, wait. *School Science and Mathematics* 78: 207–216.

Soar, R.S. and R.M. Soar. 1979. Emotional climate and management. In *Research on teaching: Concepts, findings, and implications,* ed. P.L. Peterson and H.J. Walberg. Berkeley: McCutchan Publishing.

Tobin, K. 1984. Effects of extended wait time on discourse characteristics and achievement in middle school grades. *Journal of Research in Science Teaching* 21(8): 779–791.

Willson, I.A. 1973. Changes in the mean levels of thinking in grades 1–8 through use of an interaction analysis system based on Bloom's taxonomy. *Journal of Educational Research* 66: 423–429.

Winne, P.H. 1979. Experiments relating teachers' use of higher cognitive questions to student achievement. *Review of Educational Research* 49(1): 13–50.

CHAPTER REVIEW

Purposes of Classroom Questions

1. preassess students' knowledge prior to instruction

2. determine students' current understanding during a lesson

3. assess the attainment of objectives at the end of a lesson

4. determine students' understanding of procedural directions

5. increase student involvement in a lesson

6. provide students with opportunities to think about a topic in more depth

Openness of Questions

1. Closed question: a question with one correct answer

2. Convergent question: a question with a few correct answers

3. Divergent question: a question with a variety of correct responses

4. Open question: a question with no correct or incorrect answers

Cognitive Levels of Questions

1. Knowledge: questions that ask students to remember facts about specifics, ways of dealing with specifics, or ways of dealing with facts.

2. Comprehension: questions that ask students to translate the message, interpret the message in some fashion, or extrapolate from the message.

3. Application: questions that ask students to identify solutions to problems or demonstrate the ability to use knowledge in a novel or new circumstance

4. Analysis: questions that ask students to examine a novel or new situation and break it into its component parts, to identify the elements making the whole, to identify the possible relationships that could exist between the parts, and to recognize principles that might govern the operation of the whole.

5. Synthesis: questions that ask students to organize knowledge in order to arrive at unique (for them) solutions to problems or products of thought.

6. Evaluation: questions that ask students to make judgments about the relative values of things and to identify the bases for that judgment.

Problems in Phrasing Questions

1. Two-alternative questions: those that begin with auxiliary verbs such as **do, does, should, would, are, can,** etc. and that call for a yes or no or one of two other responses.

2. Ambiguous questions: those that begin with the words **why** and **how,** or in other ways are open to overly broad interpretations.

Properly Phrased Cognitive Questions

1. Many problems with poorly phrased cognitive questions can be avoided by beginning such questions with the words **what, which, when, who,** and **where**.
2. Properly phrased cognitive questions will
   a. be precise
   b. have a proper grammatical arrangement
   c. use easily understood terminology
3. Cognitive questions can take the form of an interrogative or declarative statement.

Kinds of Eliciting Patterns

1. Teachers should avoid eliciting responses to questions by asking a question and then letting any student or group of students answer. Teachers who follow this pattern have more disruptive behavior in the classroom than teachers who do not.

2. Teachers should avoid calling on a student by name to respond to a question and then asking the student the question. This pattern relieves all students but one from thinking about the question, and places one student in the position of possible embarrassment.

3. When eliciting responses, teachers should ask the question, pause, then indicate the student to respond by name.

When to Use Silence/Wait Time

1. immediately following a teacher's question, and before identifying the name of the student to reply

2. when having indicated a student to respond to a question and before the student's response

3. following a student's response

Kinds of Reinforcement for Correct Answers

1. The lowest levels, which should not be overused, include repeating a student's answer or categorizing an answer with an evaluative statement or phrase.

2. Pointing out to the student how knowledge of her response or the thinking that led to the response would be of benefit to the student is an effective form of reinforcement sometimes called encouragement or labeled praise.

3. Identifying something a student has said earlier by mentioning the student's name and what she said, and then using the ideas to further develop the lesson, is the highest and most effective form of reinforcement.

Responses to Incorrect Answers

1. Knowledge level questions: provide the student with the correct answer.
2. Higher cognitive levels: two possible responses:

  a. Direct corrective feedback: indicate to the student that she answered incorrectly, provide needed background information, and then provide another opportunity for the student to answer.
  b. Indirect corrective feedback: break the original question down into a sequence of simpler questions that could lead to an answer, and then ask the student to respond to each of these simpler questions. Follow this with a similar question to the same student.

Responses to Correct but Inadequate Answers

1. Probing: a question to a student about her response to a question that asks for extension, clarification, or justification of her response. Kinds of Probes
  a. Extending: asking a student to say more about her response
  b. Clarifying: asking a student to rephrase a reply or to give an example illustrating a response.
  c. Justifying: asking a student to give reasons for her reply or to provide evidence to support a reply.
  d. Redirecting: asking another student to extend, clarify, or justify a student's response.
2. Use of Silence/Wait Time: during this silence, maintain eye contact, and encourage the student nonverbally to continue.

Teacher-Directed Discussions

1. Necessary precondition: students must have had some prior experience or possess knowledge about the topic to be discussed.
2. Kinds of topics for discussion include
  a. possible positions on issues
  b. predictions or hypothesizing
  c. identification of problems that need further study
  d. interpretation of experiences
  e. exploration of beliefs or attitudes
3. Question used to initiate discussion should
  a. be stimulating
  b. focus on the topic to be discussed
  c. be in the students' vernacular
  d. be open or divergent

Criteria for Effective Discussions

Most, if not all of the students,

1. have an opportunity to respond during the discussion

2. have an opportunity to respond equal lengths of time

3. listen to what other students have to say

4. are allowed to examine their own and others' views in a nonthreatening environment

Strategies for Improving Discussions

1. Occasionally interjecting the rule that students need to repeat what the preceding student said before saying what they wish to say improves the ability of students to listen to others.

2. Having the class evaluate a discussion based on the criteria of an effective discussion can help sensitize students to their roles in group discussions.

EXERCISE 15

Preassessment Questioning

One of the preconditions for an effective discussion is prior experiences with and knowledge of the topic to be discussed. To assess students' readiness for a discussion, ask a few closed or convergent questions just before the discussion to check their understanding of the prerequisite knowledge. This exercise will provide some practice in writing appropriate questions for preassessment.

Directions

1. Write one instructional objective you would attempt to accomplish through a discussion.
2. Write one open or divergent question you would ask to begin the discussion designed to accomplish the instructional objective you wrote for item 1.
3. Write two closed or convergent questions you would ask to assess the students' understanding of prerequisite knowledge of the topic.

EXERCISE 16

Correctly Phrasing Questions Varying the Degrees of Openness

This exercise provides some experience in correctly phrasing questions that have varying degrees of openness.

Directions. Write two questions of each of the following types: closed, convergent, divergent, and open. Use the suggestions for properly phrasing questions found in this chapter when you develop these questions.

EXERCISE 17

Writing Cognitive Questions

This exercise provides some experience in writing cognitive questions at various levels of complexity. Remember, questions can be phrased at six levels of complexity: knowledge, comprehension, application, analysis, synthesis, and evaluation.

Directions. Write one classroom question on topics that could be taught in an elementary or middle school classroom at each of the six levels.

EXERCISE 18

Writing Cognitive Questions on a Topic

This exercise provides some experience in writing cognitive questions at various levels of complexity while confining the questions to a single topic. In Exercise 17 you were free to choose from any topic appropriate for elementary or middle school classrooms. In this exercise you are restricted to one topic. Writing questions at all cognitive levels about a single topic is a difficult process, but one that is a closer approximation to the task required when teaching.

Directions.   Write one classroom question on **one** topic that could appropriately be taught at the elementary or middle school level at each of the six levels of Bloom's taxonomy: knowledge, comprehension, application, analysis, synthesis, and evaluation.

EXERCISE 19

Assessing Instructional Objectives

This exercise provides some practice in writing higher-level instructional objectives that could be accomplished through discussion and in formulating the closed or convergent questions that could be used at the end of a discussion to assess the attainment of an instructional objective.

Directions
1. Write one instructional objective at a level other than knowledge that could be achieved through discussion. Choose an objective you have not included in previous exercises.
2. Write one closed or convergent question that would be used at the end of the discussion to check students' attainment of the objective listed in item 1.

EXERCISE 20

Writing Questions for Discussions

This exercise provides some practice in writing open or divergent questions that could be used when starting a discussion with students. Questions used to initiate a discussion should (1) be stimulating, (2) focus on the topic to be discussed, (3) be in the students' vernacular, and (4) be open or divergent.

Directions.   Write two open or divergent questions that could be used to begin discussion on a topic appropriate for elementary or middle school students.

OBSERVATION EXERCISE 21

Questioning Skills in the Classroom

This exercise provides some practice in analyzing the behavior of a teacher in the classroom while that teacher is using questions. This practice may help you recognize the effects when the skills of questioning are appropriately and inappropriately used.

Directions. Observe an elementary or middle school teacher teaching an activity in which questions are frequently used.

1. Identify two examples when the teacher used skills introduced in this chapter in appropriate ways. Record the skill observed, describe its use, and describe the observable effects it had on the students.

2. Identify two examples of the teacher using skills introduced in this chapter in inappropriate ways. Record the skill observed, describe its use, and describe the observable effects it had on the students. Consider such things as criticizing students, cutting off students' responses, not calling on some students, not eliciting by name, or any other behavior likely to cause students to be disappointed, uninterested, or disruptive.

3. Record three examples of the following kinds of questions asked by the teacher:
   a. knowledge level
   b. higher than knowledge level

4. Record the number of students in the class. Record the number of students responding to teacher questions during the lesson. What, if anything, did the students responding have in common? Consider gender, parts of the room, friendliness, or any other factor you think might have influenced the teacher's decision to call on them to respond.

5. What, if any, inappropriate use of questioning skills resulted in student call-outs or other misbehavior? What was (were) the skill(s), and what misbehavior resulted?

PART THREE

STRATEGIES OF TEACHING

A teaching strategy, sometimes called a lesson framework, is a sequence of teaching tasks designed to accomplish a particular kind of learning. Teaching strategies vary in both the kind and the sequence of tasks. In chapter 4 you were introduced to the sequence of tasks used in teacher directed discussions. Part Three introduces some of the strategies teachers use when teaching skills, concepts, and generalizations.

The planning and instruction skills included in earlier chapters will be applied in a variety of ways when using teaching strategies. Each teaching strategy is associated with a particular set of teaching skills. Learning when and how to apply the skills associated with each particular teaching strategy will be part of the learning required as you study the next two chapters. To the extent possible, the sequence of tasks used in these chapters with each teaching strategy are those found by research to be effective.

Skills and Strategy Teaching 5

Our lives are filled with routine activities. From the time we wake up in the morning to the time we draw up the covers at night we perform numerous voluntary physical and intellectual actions. Some require little active attention. We brush our teeth and tie our shoes without conspicuous forethought, ongoing awareness, or reflection. The same can be said of even more complex activities such as driving a car or eating a meal. For most adults these actions have become automatic and require minimal active, cognitive attention. We achieve this routine level of performance through repeated experience with the same task in similar contexts.

But there was a time when such mundane activities were not so automatic or routine, when tying our shoes was a major feat, and when getting more of the soup into our mouths than on the floor was applauded by parents. The development of routine performance is so gradual and takes so long that it is sometimes difficult to maintain perspective on the changes that have occurred. We can appreciate this development, however. For example, we can observe very young children struggling with tasks that for us seem easy (such as coloring inside of lines or putting on a sweater), we can reflect on something we are still trying to learn (like playing the piano or correctly phrasing classroom questions), or we can recall something that has been routine for us in one context but becomes less routine in another context (like brushing teeth out of a canteen cup while camping, or driving a car on the "wrong side" of the road in England).

Making physical and intellectual activities automatic is an important cognitive achievement. Automaticity frees our limited active attention to concentrate on other matters such as watching for other cars as we drive, discussing a business deal while we eat, or thinking of the next sentence as we type.

We often refer to routine or automatic performance in terms of skill: "Sue is a skilled softball player" or "Mike is a skilled gardener." For purposes of this chapter *skills* are defined as the ability to perform a voluntary physical or intellectual action. Many activities that in fact are routine, such as brushing our teeth, are not considered skills because they are simple enough for almost anyone to learn and there is no apparent advantage to achieving more refined levels of performance. But the skills involved in many other physical, and almost all of the intellectual, activities are highly valued. Higher levels of performance in these areas do result in many advantages to the individual performing the skills.

Three major influences on the development of skills are

1. frequent opportunities for learners to observe others performing the skill proficiently
2. frequent opportunities for learners to engage in practicing the skill
3. direct instruction or guidance in how to perform the skill well (Guszak and Hoffman 1980).

While each of these may vary in its effect on skill development, the first two are critical and, for some skills, sufficient. Instruction for many skills may be as simple as correctives to raise the skill to higher levels, such as demonstrating how to hold the hands when playing a piano or how to position the feet when batting. In other instances direct instruction may be much more extensive and explicit.

The development of intellectual skills, which is the focus of academics, has much in common with the development of manual skills. Simple skills must be learned to an automatic level before performance on more complex skills can be developed and refined. Skill development is influenced by observation of a model and direct application of the skill in real contexts. In the intellectual area, however, direct instruction tends to assume a more prominent role in learning because many processes associated with intellectual skills are not directly observable. Much of what we do in reading, for example, is covert. Certain aspects of writing are observable, but much occurs in the writer's mind that is skill-like but unobservable. Simply watching others perform skills of this type is not as immediately valuable in determining how to perform the skill as it is in the case of more overt physical skills.

This chapter focuses on effective teaching strategies for developing academic skills. It provides a general framework for describing academic skills and then discusses effective teaching strategies consistent with this framework.

THE CURRICULUM AND SKILLS

Typical school curriculum guides specify the major areas of study, what will be learned in these areas, and the order in which the content or processes will be taught. The areas of study represented in the curriculum are often labeled or organized by subject areas such as reading, mathematics, language arts, science, and social science. Some subject areas are considered more process oriented than content oriented; that is, some emphasize learning how to do something (a skill) and others emphasize knowing about something (a concept). Areas in the elementary curriculum that focus primarily, but not only, on skill development include reading, writing, mathematics, art, music, and physical education. In contrast, science and social studies instruction emphasizes concept development. Although some dangers exist in making such a simplistic dichotomy between skill and concept areas (e.g., the science curriculum involves important skill learning such as critical thinking, and mathematics involves important concept learning such as number and space), this approach is a functional way to introduce the teaching of skills. Because the principal focus of this chapter is on skill teaching, most examples are drawn from the reading, writing, and mathematics curricula.

BASIC, COMPLEX, AND HIGHER-ORDER SKILLS

We have organized our presentation of skill teaching around three types of skills: basic, complex, and higher order. We will define each of these types of skills and then illustrate effective teaching practices associated with each. A few caveats are in order, however, before we proceed further.

Although we present basic, complex, and higher-order skills as if they are clearly distinct and identifiable, the differences are not always clear cut in reality. It is more useful to think of these skills as ranging along a continuum from basic to higher order. We introduce the classification system merely to provide a convenient way to organize our treatment of the topic; that our treatment of skills is organized from simple to complex should not be taken to mean that we believe skill teaching and acquisition are linear. Children at all levels of the elementary grades can benefit from instruction in complex and higher-order skills. Likewise, basic skill teaching is still a common part of good instruction in the middle school.

Basic Skills

A **basic skill** can be thought of as a simple behavior necessary or useful in performing a more complex operation. "Squeezing" might be thought of as a basic skill in brushing teeth, although now "pumping" could be an alternate basic skill. For the purposes of teaching and learning, basic skills cannot be functionally divided into a set of simpler skills. Basic skills, although voluntary, are not always consciously performed. An individual who has reached an automatic level of performance of a basic skill is typically not aware of the processes being performed.

Basic skills underlie all other skill performance areas and are often taught through simple associative processes. Reading, mathematics, and writing require many skills regarded as basic. In many reading programs decoding is taught initially through the teaching of letter names and associated sounds or perhaps through sight teaching of a core set of high-frequency words. In writing programs children are taught to form letters and later to spell words. In mathematics, children are taught the basic facts of addition, subtraction, and multiplication. Each of these "basic" skill areas requires prerequisite skills that typically are not considered part of that subject area. For example, before a child can be successful in learning letter sound associations, he must achieve a level of oral language development that includes the ability to discriminate and even manipulate sounds—what some refer to as **phonemic awareness**. Phonemic awareness is a "readiness" skill for beginning reading instruction. In the same way, before a child can learn the basic number facts, he should have achieved some concept of number and one-to-one correspondences.

Complex Skills

Complex skills require the individual to coordinate two or more basic skills to achieve a specific outcome. How complex skills develop can be seen easily from an example taken from the mathematics curriculum. Learning to multiply two-digit numbers, regroup for subtraction, or reduce fractions to the lowest common denominator are all examples of mathematical procedures that require the combination of basic skills to accomplish more complex processes. Children learn to write and format a business letter or organize a newspaper article in the writing curriculum; in reading they are taught to combine strategies such as phonics and structural analysis to decode unfamiliar words. Complex skills are typically introduced in the curriculum after the students have achieved some level of automaticity with the underlying basic skills.

Higher-Order Skills

Higher-order skills are the most complex and least understood skills taught. **Higher-order skills** involve the mental processes associated with efficient reasoning and characterize advanced performance in academic areas but are not easily specified. In other words, the best readers, writers, and mathematicians perform complex mental operations in ways not readily represented as a set of basic or complex skills: The ability to read critically, including making judgments about the internal and external validity of arguments in a text, the ability to edit one's own writing to a particular audience, and the ability to problem solve in mathematics are but a few examples of the higher-order skills that are critical in advanced performance in the process-oriented subjects of the curriculum.

Like the complex skills, the higher-order skills rely on automatic processes in the basic skill areas; for example, critical reading is difficult without proficient decoding. Higher-order skills differ from complex skills in that no one way, or even any given way, to perform will ensure success. For example, a specific set of steps will lead to the successful performance of the complex skill of multiplying decimals. However, a set of specific steps to determine if one should multiply or divide to solve a particular problem cannot be specified. Executing a routine or an algorithm can enable one to complete a task involved in performing a complex skill, but selecting which complex skill among many to apply in a particular situation is a higher-order skill that cannot be represented in a series of steps or rules.

SKILLS AND STRATEGIES

Let us complicate matters a bit before moving on to a discussion of teaching skills by introducing the notion of strategies. Individuals described as skilled in reading, mathematics, and the like know more than just how to perform certain routines. They also know when and under what conditions a particular routine is appropriate; they also know when they have been successful or not and when they need to take another tack. This knowledge is sometimes referred to as procedural or conditional knowledge. Acquiring this type of knowledge in combination with proficient use of skills is strategy learning.

Knowledge of a skill without knowing when to use it or how to evaluate its success is useless. For this reason, whenever we assume responsibility for teaching any skill, we must also assume responsibility for teaching the knowledge that will enable the learner to incorporate this new skill into a set of functional strategies. We must be explicit and direct in our explanation of why the skill is important, when and under what conditions the learner might need it, and how the learner can evaluate his success with the skill (Duffy and Roehler 1986).

TEACHING BASIC SKILLS

Traditional practices associated with teaching basic skill areas such as reading, writing, and arithmetic are irksome to many. They may call forth images from our own pasts of long periods of drudgery punctuated by moments of embarrassment. This is unfortunate, because the key to successful teaching of basic skills is ensuring students' active involvement in tasks in which they can experience high levels of success.

What makes teaching basic skills often appear so difficult is that very little thinking is involved in performing the skill, and few immediate, intrinsic rewards are experienced when performing the skill well. Learning the sound associated with the letter **b** does not immediately open the world of books to a child; nor does the memorization of the multiplication tables solve many real problems facing a third grader. In teaching basic skills, the teacher must constantly remind the students that learning a letter name or multiplication facts is a means, not an end. The teacher must explain how learning this skill is important and when the student will use it. The teacher must also provide

Learning writing skills

practice in applying the skill using examples the same as or similar to those in which the student will be called on to use the skill. In this way the basic skills being learned will be better drawn into a strategic repertoire of behaviors that the learner can call on at appropriate times. The teacher must also be flexible and creative in structuring learning so that skill learning is successful, enjoyable, and fast paced.

Memorization that leads to accurate and automatic performance is a key to learning basic skills. This automatic level of response is often achieved through drill and practice. The teacher presents the association to be learned such as the sound /b/ for the letter **b** or the response twenty-four to 3×8. The students repeat the association and practice it again and again until the response is automatic. Only when the targeted response has reached an automatic level is new learning of additional associations introduced. The old learning is revisited periodically in new or novel situations to provide additional practice and to ensure retention.

Good drill and practice requires the teacher to interact with students at a fast pace with high task success and to offer corrective feedback when they make mistakes. To ensure motivation, the teacher often creates contests that use such things as flash cards and game boards. These contests typically involve competition among learners with rewards for accurate and automatic responses. Several recent research studies into methods of effectively teaching basic skills have demonstrated the power of competition between groups within the context of cooperation within groups. Groups are formed in a class, with each group representing a mix of ability levels. The groups compete with one another and the score of a group is a reflection of the individuals within groups working together (Slavin 1980; Johnson and Johnson 1987).

Teachers often create charts or graphs to record the learning of basic skills by individual students. A "letter expert" chart may be used, for example, to record each student's progress on mastery of letter names and sounds. Such charts or graphs serve several important functions: they provide children with some concrete short-term goals toward which to work; they can let learners know where they have been and how far they have to go to complete a particular area; and they can motivate students to better their own performances. As a side benefit, charts provide the teacher with an easy way of tracking the progress of individuals and the class as a whole.

Good teaching of basic skills often involves multisensory experiences. For example, many decoding programs in reading stress the importance of the children saying words, letter names, or sounds as they trace over them with their fingers (Tierney, Readence, and Dishner 1985). Spelling programs often involve the simultaneous writing and saying of letter names as a word is being recorded. Early stages of learning number facts may involve the manipulation of physical objects such as bottle caps or chips.

TEACHING COMPLEX SKILLS AND STRATEGIES

Much informative research on effective practices for teaching complex skills has been completed in the past two decades. This research clearly supports what many refer to as "direct instruction" of complex skills. In direct instruction, specific lessons are organized toward specific and verifiable learning outcomes. The teacher actively gives information by explaining and modeling to small groups of students or the whole class and provides opportunities for students to demonstrate learning under guided conditions with explicit, supportive feedback to those who need it. Following this, the teacher provides opportunities for independent practice to encourage development of automaticity and to ensure long term retention.

Recent process-product research has allowed the development of suggested guidelines for teaching complex skills in such process areas as reading, arithmetic, and writing (Rosenshine and Stevens, 1986). The following sections describe the general guidelines.

1. **Begin each lesson with a short review of previous, prerequisite learning**.   This review provides students with additional practice and overlearning of previously learned material and permits the teacher to provide corrections and reteaching when indicated. Any number of ways can be used for this review. For example, you could assign homework on the prerequisites and then have students check the homework together. You could have a verbal review with the whole class by asking a series of questions over the prerequisites. You could give a short quiz over the prerequisites and then review the test with the students, asking questions for clarification. You might engage the students in a game or drill exercise over the basic skills to be used in performing the complex skill. For example, when preparing the students for a lesson on long division, you might have a quick drill or game over basic multiplication facts. If you are preparing them for a lesson on strategies for dividing words into syllables, the review might involve a game requiring the students to identify the number of syllables in words presented orally.

2. **Make a direct, explicit statement of the objectives of the lesson**. Learning particular skills can be facilitated by telling students the important things to be learned at the beginning of the lesson (Duffy and Roehler 1986). State the objectives in terms readily understood by the students and include the reasons the skill is important and when they might need it. Learning an initial consonant through a phonics lesson, for example, is important because the students will be able to use this skill to identify many words in the stories they will read. Learning to regroup for subtraction is important because it will allow them to solve new kinds of problems that they now could not solve. This unsolvable problem provides the logical lead into the statement of the learning goal for the lesson, "In today's lesson you are going to learn to regroup for subtraction. Once you learn to regroup for subtraction, you will be able to solve problems such as this one."

3. **Present new material with clear, detailed instructions and explanations in small steps**.   At this stage in the lesson you should proceed in small steps but at a brisk pace. Visuals such as charts, overhead transparencies, manipulatives, handouts, and text material should support the presentation of the process involved in using the skill. When teaching regrouping for subtraction, for example, the teacher could demonstrate the process by using manipulatives and then outline the procedures for setting up the written problem and the steps to follow in solving the problem. Although many ways of teaching students to solve problems using regrouping exist,

teaching them one successful way of solving such problems is essential. Variations can be introduced later.

4. **Model the skill to be performed**. You should now demonstrate the processes involved in performing the skill by systematically following the steps outlined. Thinking aloud as you work through the steps can help students see how the procedure leads to success. During the modeling process, ask questions of the students to assure that each understands a given step before moving on to the next.

5. **Guide the students as a group through several practices using the skill**. The students are now to duplicate what you have demonstrated. Guide initial practice step by step until the students develop confidence and understanding. This type of practice can be organized in several ways: In mathematics, for example, have students work a small set of problems at their desks. Then call on volunteers to work problems on the chalkboard. In a reading lesson on the use of dictionary guide words, the students may work several examples on a worksheet as you ask them questions about their answers and the strategies used. The goal at this point is to check that students have the right answer, and more important, whether they followed the steps taught.

Be active in monitoring and giving corrective feedback as the students work by walking about the room, asking many questions, and evaluating the responses from all the students. Call on students with or without their hands raised so that all students have the responsibility to respond. If confusion or uncertainty is apparent, review the processes involved in performing the skill.

The feedback to a student's incorrect response should be sustaining; that is, work with that individual until he can respond correctly before you call on the next students. Do not assume that a correct response means that a student used the strategy taught. You should frequently probe correct responses by asking "What did you do to get that answer?" Remember, a process, not the answer, is being taught.

This initial guided practice should continue until you are assured that about 80 percent of the students can perform the skill independently. We will consider what must be done with the other 20 percent later.

6. **Provide a brief review of the steps used in performing the skill**. In reviewing the lesson, pull together the steps in performing the skill just learned into a few simple statements. This procedure merely reinforces and clarifies the steps in the skill being practiced.

7. **Provide the pupils with independent practice using the skill and provide corrective feedback**. The end of guided practice marks a transition in the lesson. Until this point you were actively interacting with students as a group; in the next phase, the students will be working independently.

Independent practice is important in developing automaticity with a skill as well as turning over the strategy to the students. They must become confident in their ability to know when and how to use the skill they have been taught (Duffy and Roehler, 1986).

Independent practice often takes a form referred to as seatwork. Many educators legitimately criticize the amount of time students spend doing seatwork. The rule of thumb for independent practice is to provide it for the least amount of time needed to ensure that the transfer of control of the procedure from the teacher to the student has occurred. Publishers often provide practice materials such as workbooks and ditto pages that far exceed what most students need to achieve control. This surplus of materials provides flexibility, so be selective in what you assign. Every second or third problem may be sufficient for most students. The same applies to assigning homework for independent practice.

8. **Review and reteach the skill with selected students.**   Not all of the students will learn the skill the first time you teach it. As a teacher, you may become aware during the guided practice that some students are not ready to work independently, while others are. When this occurs, divide the group and let the majority move to independent practice while the others stay with you for reteaching. Reteaching should be more than repetition of earlier instruction. Use new examples, more demonstrations, and more modeling. Provide for extended guided practice. Use peer and reciprocal teaching where possible.

You may also find after checking over the results of the independent practice that some students did not understand the steps in using the skill as clearly as you had thought. Success in independent practice should exceed 95 percent of the problems or tasks assigned. If the group does not reach this level, you will need to reteach the lesson; if some small number fall below this level, then you need to reteach that group.

TEACHING HIGHER-ORDER SKILLS AND STRATEGIES IN PROCESS CURRICULUM AREAS

One of the characteristics of complex skills is that they can be represented rather easily in terms of combined basic skills. Higher-order skills, on the other hand, are elusive and often defy simple explanation. An example of a higher-order skill in reading is the self-monitoring done by expert readers as they attempt to construct meaning with text. Expert readers constantly ask themselves whether they are making sense of text they are reading. If a breakdown in meaning occurs, the expert reader has available several strategies such as rereading sections or stopping and pondering. Poor readers who do not engage in active self-monitoring tend to plow through text word by word, content that they have "read" the words. An example of a higher-order writing skill is revision. Expert writers tend to view writing as a constructive process and constantly revise text they create to convey more effectively their meaning. In doing so, they are sensitive to the characteristics of their intended audience.

These are but two examples of higher-order skills in the process areas of the curriculum. As you might expect, higher-order skills are more difficult to teach than are basic or complex skills. Higher-order skills can be taught, but research suggests distinct differences in the approach to be used. Duffy and Roehler (1986) distinguish between direct and indirect instruction of reading skills. This distinction is useful when considering the role of the teacher in teaching higher-order skills.

Direct Teaching of Higher-Order Skills

When using the direct approach to teaching higher-order skills, the teacher must represent the higher-order skill to the students in a form that resembles a complex skill and teach it to students using the steps outlined for teaching complex skills.

For example, teaching students to find the main idea in a paragraph is a skill represented in most reading curricula, and which most reading specialists regard as a higher-order skill. This skill is important in comprehension because it appears to be the mechanism by which lengthy text is coded into long-term memory. It also requires a great deal of inferring, and it appears that expert readers are quite flexible and creative in the way they are able to determine the main idea. This skill develops in most readers from extensive reading.

In the direct approach to teaching the skill of finding the main idea, the complexity of the skill is reduced to a simple set of steps to follow. For example, the students might be instructed to (1) read the paragraph to understand what the author is trying to communicate; (2) reflect on the paragraph to determine the topic being introduced; (3) analyze the text to determine the most important thing the author

A listening center

says—sometimes called the "comment"; and (4) combine the topic and comment into a statement of the main idea. These steps can be taught following the complex skill-teaching procedures.

For students who have difficulty finding the main idea on their own, this strategy might make the difference between success and failure. The difficulty with the direct approach to teaching higher-order skills, in contrast to the direct approach to teaching complex skills, is that the formula or steps to follow do not always work in all circumstances or with all students. The steps must be regarded as a starting point or heuristic device that may provide some initial success.

Indirect Teaching of Higher-Order Skills

An alternative to the direct approach to teaching higher-order skills is the indirect approach, with an emphasis on frequent practice combined with guidance and feedback. An example of such an approach can be seen in many of the programs currently under development that employ process approaches to writing (Graves, 1982). In these programs, students are encouraged to approach writing the way professional authors do. Students select their own topics and are then guided in the process of developing drafts and the steps to a final copy. Conferencing with the teacher and peer feedback are essential in helping students become more aware of their audience. The indirect approach has an advantage over the direct approach in that the context in which the skills are developed allows students to see the relevance of basic and complex skills as they apply them. The emphasis in the indirect approach is on creating conditions under which students can experience success in using higher-order skills. The Individualized Reading Program, which places a premium on student self-selection of trade books, illustrates similar approaches in reading (Veatch 1978).

TEACHING HIGHER-ORDER SKILLS AND STRATEGIES IN CONTENT CURRICULUM AREAS

Although we generally associate the teaching of skills with the areas of reading, writing, and mathematics, skills are important in the science, social studies, and other content areas as well. The basic and complex skills of reading, writing, and mathematics, as well as higher-order skills, often referred to as thinking skills, are used in the content areas and are best learned in conjunction with the learning of the content. Some simpler thinking skills that can appropriately be taught at the elementary level include observing, inferring, looking for patterns, and classifying.

Thinking skills help children view their experiences with more clarity and accuracy. They also allow children to organize their knowledge into relationships and then use thought strategies to recall and apply knowledge to solve problems and make decisions. The less experience a child has in using thinking skills, the less likely he will be to apply them in daily life and in learning in the classroom (Travers 1977).

Higher-order thinking skills help children learn not only about things in the classroom but also about things in life.

Observing

Observing occurs when any or all of our senses perceive a stimulus. Observing is the most basic of the thinking skills, because without it you would not be able to interpret those things you detect and, hence, know anything about the world around you. Without your senses you would be unable to taste the sweetness of sugar, see the colorful sunset, hear the chirping of birds, smell a broiling steak, or feel the warmth of a campfire. It is through our senses that we learn. Mere detection with our senses, however, is an incomplete act. We must also interpret those sensory perceptions; that is, observe. Observing is learning how to use our senses in ways that lead to accurate and more complete perceptions and, hence, more accurate and complete learning. Whenever our senses are stimulated and we think about what we are perceiving, learning can take place. You as a teacher need to help students examine their perceptions and begin to refine the ways in which they interpret what they see, hear, feel, taste, and smell.

Everything observed has properties or characteristics that we sense. Sometimes we fail to think about the properties we observe and thus misinterpret what we sense. Children can be helped to observe properties by focusing their attention on them. When you provide an atmosphere that stimulates children's senses and then help them examine these perceptions, the stage is set for learning. For example, in social studies you might focus the children's attention on characteristics of maps by asking a question such as, "In what ways are colors used on this map to show different terrain features?" Repeated questions of this kind are important in helping students look for similarities and differences inherent in the things they observe.

Inferring

Quite often students will go well beyond observations when interpreting things they observe. For example, when children (and adults, for that matter) are given a sealed box with a few objects inside and asked to play with the box by tilting or shaking it and are then asked to share observations they have made, they will likely respond by telling how many objects they think are in the box. What the children actually observed were rolling or sliding sounds, impacts on the side of the box, and sounds on the side of the box concurrent with the impacts. The children then subconsciously assumed that all objects in the box could move and that all could make a sound. From their observations and these assumptions, the children then concluded that the box held some number of objects. This last conclusion is what is called an inference. An **inference** is a conclusion based on both observations and assumptions about the situation being observed. An inference will only be as accurate as the observations and assumptions used to make it. If a child thought that he heard two sounds, when in fact there were three sounds, then an inference based on that observation would be incorrect. If a child assumed that all objects could make a sound, when in fact a cotton ball was in the box, then an inference based on that assumption would be incorrect. In general then, if observations are incorrect, then an inference based on them could be incorrect; if assumptions are incorrect, then an inference based on them could be incorrect. The difference between observation and inference must be taught if children are to interpret their experiences accurately.

Children in the primary grades may not be able to learn the difference between observing and inferring. Students who have reached what is called a concrete-operational level of development (Inhelder and Piaget, 1973) may have more success in this task.

In teaching the difference between observing and inferring, a teacher could show children a drawing of two stick figures, one tall and the other short, but otherwise identical. The teacher could then ask, "What do you observe about these two figures?" A child might say, "One is the mother and the other is her little child." This is obviously an inference. The teacher could then ask, "What are your reasons for thinking the one is a mother and the other her child?" The student will probably respond that one is larger than the other, and a mother is larger than her child. The teacher then could ask something such as, "Could the larger stick figure be someone other than a mother?" "Could the smaller stick figure be someone other than a child?" Answers to these questions could then be discussed by other members of the class. Eventually the teacher would return to the original question, "What do you observe about these two figures?" "What are some different inferences we could make about the figures?" The teacher could lead a discussion on the difference between what is actually observed and what can be inferred and she could introduce the nature of observations and inferences. Additional examples of such thinking would then become a regular part of the learning experiences provided in subsequent lessons to increase the likelihood of transfer to actual situations (Travers, 1977).

It is also valuable to provide children with experience in collecting and inferring from data. For example, ask the children to predict the effect of their height and weight on the length they could jump horizontally from a standing position. Have the children measure and record their heights and weights. After each child jumps and measures the distance, have them examine the data and make inferences about the effects of height and weight on jumping distances. The children could then examine these inferences with those they predicted as well as with each individual case examined. Some will find that their predictions were wrong, which can be valuable in helping them recognize that we often make faulty predictions because we lack sufficient experience or data. They can also be lead to see that, although the inference may describe what happens in general, some exceptions can be found.

Being able to recognize when one has sufficient information to make an inference is also an important skill. Students may have a tendency to make inferences about their experiences before collecting sufficient information, thus misinterpreting many experiences. Common superstitions may result. For example, a child might see a picture fall off the wall. On the same day, someone in his family might become ill. The child might infer that when pictures fall off the wall, someone in the family will become ill. They have subconsciously assumed a cause-and-effect relationship between chance events. Drawing inferences from such limited data may result in superstition and prejudice. Only with practice in drawing inferences using sufficient data will such common tendencies be overcome.

Looking for Patterns

Much of a child's ability to feel comfortable in his surroundings is determined by his ability to predict how people and things behave. **Looking for patterns** is the process of trying to find relationships between two or more behaviors. The ability to discern patterns accurately can help children feel more comfortable in their surroundings and also be an aid to further learning. For example, the teacher could have the children attempt to memorize a long list of words. The teacher could test them on their ability to remember this list by asking the children to look at the locations on the original list of the words that they remembered. Students will find that they were more likely to remember those words at the beginning and end of the original list than those in the middle. From this, students may learn to recognize patterns, but also they will learn something about how they learn lists of things. From this, a discussion could lead them to recognize better ways of learning lists.

When introducing literature to students, a teacher may decide to focus on a particular author. The teacher could read aloud to the class each day from books by that author. Ultimately, the teacher might begin exploring the similarities of themes, characters, event structure, and plots among the different readings. Students will begin to see patterns. More important, they will begin to approach other literary works in terms of looking for patterns in writing.

Other kinds of patterns or relationships that could be studied include age with height, height with weight, length of day with time of year, length of exercise sessions with heart rate, length of cooking time with the temperature of water, shape of the moon with the days of its phases, temperature of the air with time of day, length of time studying with test scores, and the mixing of different colors with the resulting colors. The teacher might even ask students to study patterns in the behavior of people. For example, what is the distance between two people who are talking and their degree of familiarity? From the study of such patterns, upper elementary students may begin to learn about the importance and effect of nonverbal communication.

Learning to determine patterns in the ways things behave is an important step in being able to predict behaviors. The ability to predict is in turn related to a child's sense of control over his environment, an important aspect of self-concept.

Classifying

Classifying is the process of grouping entities together based on some similarity in characteristics. These groups can then be arranged in some logical fashion based on similarities and differences among the groups. For example, parts of speech can be classified into verbs, nouns, prepositions, conjunctions, and modifiers. Nouns can be divided into common, proper, and pronoun.

When given a variety of blocks that are different in size, shape, and color, most young children at Piaget's intuitive level (Inhelder and Piaget 1973) can divide the blocks into groups using one of the characteristics. In a lesson on classification using blocks, the teacher could give the children blocks and then ask, "What is one of the ways in which the blocks are different from one another?" The students will likely recognize differences in color or shape. The teacher could then ask the pupils to divide the blocks by color, after which she could ask, "In what ways are the yellow blocks different from one another?" The students will likely notice the difference in shape. The teacher could then ask the students to divide the yellow blocks into groups by shape. The same could be done with other color blocks. The teacher could then ask the children about similarities and differences between the different piles of blocks. The basic idea is to have the children focused on visual properties of the objects while they are thinking about grouping them. Children do not think in this way, of course, but the teacher can help them become aware of what they are doing while they are doing it. When this occurs, the students are learning to think about their thinking while they are thinking.

Older children at Piaget's concrete operational stage can classify objects into more than one category at the same time. For instance, upper elementary children could be expected to sort pictures of common animals into categories such as mammals, birds, reptiles, and fish while at the same time grouping each of these categories into prey and predator.

When teaching children to classify, take care that they do not lose sight of the diversity within groups of things. Perceiving a group of things as being identical can lead to forming incorrect inferences from experience. For example, students sometimes have a tendency to assume that all members of a particular group, characterized by religion, race, or occupation, for example, are identical in other characteristics, which can lead to prejudging individuals. Obviously, this is something we want our students to learn to avoid.

This process of classifying is something all humans do in the normal course of living. This process simplifies both our thinking and our communication. The next chapter, "Teaching Concepts and Generalizations," introduces more on understanding concepts.

Problem Solving

Problem solving may be defined as an ability to think patiently and analytically about complex situations in order to find answers to questions (Whimbey and Lochhead 1980). Many methods for enhancing problem solving abilities have been tried over the years (de Bono 1973; Whimbey and Lochhead 1980). As with any higher-order skill, breaking the skill into a series of complex skills is helpful for initial understanding. Problem solving is composed of five loosely defined steps.

1. **First Insight:** Examine the problem to clarify its components. This process involves an analysis of the problem and problem situation so that the relationships that exist between them can be determined.

2. **Saturation:** The problem and problem situation are examined from all angles to ensure that all relationships are well in mind and to ensure that the problem has been accurately and clearly defined.

3. **Incubation:** The problem is contemplated by the individual or discussed with a group of problem solvers to determine possible courses of action. Brainstorming, a group of two or more people generating possible solutions to the problem, can be a creative and productive activity. For an example, given the problem: "In what ways could bricks be used to build a piece of furniture on which to sit?" one person might come up with two or three ways of answering the question. On the other hand, a group of people brainstorming may be able to suggest many more ways. When brainstorming, students should be able to suggest the first thing that comes to mind, no matter how absurd it may seem on the surface. In this way problem solutions may be more creative and diverse.

4. **Illumination:** A possible solution to the problem comes to mind in its initial form.

5. **Verification:** The possible solution is run through in its entirety to check for any overlooked discrepancies that might prevent the solution from working. When this phase is completed, the student is ready to take action to solve the problem.

The example of looking for patterns in how we learn lists of things discussed earlier lends itself to a problem-solving situation. Once students have found that they tend to learn the items at the beginning and ending of lists more easily than items in the middle, they are ready to problem solve a possible solution to the question, "What are some ways of learning lists of things that could help us to learn all parts of the list equally?" If the class is divided into small groups and allowed to brainstorm possible solutions, children can learn not only some problem solving skills, but also something about how to learn. Following this brainstorming session, each group could then share its solution with the rest of the class. The class could try some of the solutions, allowing opportunities to observe and then to make inferences from the observations. When students are problem solving, the thinking skills—observing, inferring, classifying, and looking for patterns—may be part of the process.

Children enjoy problem solving not only as an activity that allows them to use thinking skills, but also as a tool to solve real problems they encounter in school, at home, and elsewhere. In establishing class rules, for example, when given the principles on which rules need to be based to protect everyone's rights, pupils are able to identify sets of reasonable rules. When given simple health problems such as cut fingers or sore throats, after having studied the characteristics of bacteria, they are capable of identifying ways of preventing infection or avoiding the spread of bacteria.

They can get excited about designing studies to determine what factors enable a plant to grow, what color of surface meal worms prefer, or what kind of food gerbils prefer.

Implications for Instruction

Practice in using thinking skills is made easier when students handle actual materials about which they are thinking or deal with life situations they are actually experiencing. Children cannot be expected to think in the abstract (Inhelder and Piaget 1973). When pupils are asked to seek answers to questions consistent with their intellectual development and that refer to direct experiences, they will more likely achieve success.

Use of questions plays a predominant role in providing instruction in thinking skills. You must not only phrase the questions clearly, but also teach students how to ask questions that they can explore with a high probability of success. Asking students to pursue questions that call for abstract reasoning will lead only to failure and frustration. You will want to avoid asking questions that ask for "yes" or "no" answers or that are ambiguous. Essentially the same criteria apply to questions calling for practice in thinking that apply to all classroom questions.

The next chapter will introduce you to an inductive strategy of teaching that is particularly effective for teaching higher-order skills in content areas. This strategy will allow the use of hands-on experiences and practice in using higher-order thinking skills. Evidence suggests that this is a particularly effective strategy for teaching these skills (Anderson 1983).

IMPLICATIONS FOR PLANNING

The teaching of skills is an important part of every elementary and middle school teacher's responsibility. Research in this area has suggested particularly effective teaching strategies. As you consider planning for instruction, you will find several important implications from the information presented in this chapter.

Consider carefully whether the skill you are expected to teach is a basic, complex, or higher-order skill. Teaching basic skills usually involves fairly simple associative processes. Teaching complex skills requires the coordination of several processes that can be represented to students as a series of steps to follow that lead to successful performance. Higher-order skills defy simple representation: many ways to achieve success may be available, but no one way seems to work for all of the students all of the time. They need flexibility and adaptation when performing higher-order skills.

In some cases categorizing a specific skill into one pure type is not possible. Don't be discouraged! Teaching is filled with gray areas. If in doubt about the skill, plan a lesson as if the skill were a complex skill. You then can adapt instruction during the lesson based on the responses of students.

Once the type of skill is determined, begin to plan the lesson according to the guidelines suggested in this chapter. If you choose the direct approach for teaching a higher-order skill, reduce the skill to a set of complex skills. If you are using the indirect approach, identify a context that will allow the practice of the skill.

Skill lessons tied to the direct instruction model should be fast paced and with success ensured. Variety in the types of activities is important in helping students stay engaged. This variety implies that your plans should include directions for transitions and reminders of starting and ending times. By including your objectives in your plans and communicating these to the students, they will come to feel a sense of success when they have reached the goals set for them.

Indirect instruction should include frequent opportunities for students and teacher to interact in solving problems and sharing solutions. Your plans should include those key questions that you intend to ask to provide these interaction opportunities. To provide students with needed encouragement, also remind yourself to refer to an individual student's name when using his idea later in the lesson.

As you plan your lessons for teaching skills, do not lose sight of the "forest for all of the trees." Skill instruction can easily become an end (e.g., "Johnny can decode words that begin with the initial consonant **f**.") rather than a means to an end (e.g., "Johnny is an independent reader."). You must remind not only yourself but also the students why they are learning a particular skill and how it fits into a bigger picture. It is this aspect of skill teaching that will enable the student to become strategic and independent in the use of skills. Writing a brief set induction into your lesson plan for use at the start of the activity may ensure that this task is accomplished.

Possessing prerequisite skills when learning sequential skills is essential for students' success; therefore, assessing those prerequisite skills is essential. Such an assessment may involve a formal testing session conducted at the beginning of an instructional unit, or it may consist of informal testing and observations as part of the daily instructional routine. No planning for the teaching of skills should take place without some information on the students' current skill level.

When planning a lesson to teach skills with which the students have had prior experience, review carefully the prior lessons before introducing guided or independent practice. Include questions in your plans that will provide the practice students need to refresh their memories on the skills introduced earlier.

REFERENCES

Anderson, R.D. 1983. A consolidation and appraisal of science meta-analysis. *Journal of research in science teaching* 20(5): 497–509.

de Bono, E. 1973. *The CORT thinking program.* Elmsford, NY: Pergamon Press.

Duffy, G.G. and L.R. Roehler. 1986. *Improving classroom reading instruction.* New York: Random House.

Guszak, F. and J.V. Hoffman. 1980. Comprehension skills. In *Teaching reading: Foundations and strategies*, 2d ed., eds. P. Lamb and R. Arnold. New York: Wadsworth.

Graves, D. 1983. *Writing: Teachers and children at work.* Exeter, NH: Heineman.

Inhelder, B. and J. Piaget. 1973. *The growth of logical thinking from childhood to adolescence.* New York: Basic Books.

Johnson, D.W. and R.T. Johnson. 1987. *Learning together and alone: Cooperative, competitive and individualistic learning.* Englewood Cliffs, NJ: Prentice-Hall.

Rosenshine, B. and R. Stevens. 1986. Teaching functions. In *Handbook of research in teaching,* 3d ed., ed. M. Wittrock. New York: Macmillan. pp. 376–391.

Slavin, R.E. 1980. Cooperative learning. *Review of educational research,* 50: 317–343.

Tierney, R.J., J.E. Readence, and E.K. Dishner. 1985. *Reading strategies and practices.* Boston: Allyn and Bacon.

Travers, R.M. 1977. *Essentials of learning.* New York: Macmillan.

Veatch, J. 1978. *Reading in the elementary school,* 2d ed. New York: John Wiley and Sons.

Whimbey, A. and J. Lochhead. 1980. *Problem solving and comprehension: A short course in analytical reasoning.* Philadelphia: The Franklin Institute Press.

CHAPTER REVIEW

Skill: An individual's ability to perform a voluntary physical or intellectual action

Types of Skills
1. Basic: simple behaviors that underly complex human activities.
2. Complex: coordinated behaviors that are integrated smoothly to perform certain tasks.
3. Higher Order: mental processes that are associated with efficient reasoning.

Suggestions for Teaching Basic Skills
1. Memorization that leads to accurate and automatic performance is needed for success in learning basic skills.
2. Use fast-paced and interactive drill and practice.
3. Provide multisensory activities.
4. Chart individual student progress to support learning.

Suggested Sequence in Teaching Complex Skills
1. Begin each lesson with a short review of previous, prerequisite learning.
2. Make a direct, explicit statement of the lesson objectives.
3. Present new material with clear, detailed instructions and explanations in small steps.
4. Model the skill to be performed.
5. Guide the students as a group through several practices using the skill.

6. Provide a brief review of the steps used in performing the skill.

7. Provide the students with independent practice using the skill and provide corrective feedback.

8. Review and reteach the skill with selected students.

Teaching Higher-Order Skills

1. Process Curriculum Areas
   a. Direct Teaching: reduce the skill to a sequence of simple skills and teach it as a complex skill.
   b. Indirect Teaching: provide students with the opportunity to use the higher-order skill in a context that emphasizes teacher modeling and peer feedback.
2. Content Curriculum Areas
   Some thinking skills
   a. Observing: interpreting sensory perceptions .
   b. Inferring: a conclusion based on observations and assumptions made about the situation being observed.
   c. Looking for patterns: finding relationships between two or more behaviors.
   d. Classifying: grouping entities together based on a set of similar characteristics and then logically arranging the groups based on similarities and differences.
   e. Problem Solving: the ability to think patiently and analytically about a situation in order to find answers to questions.

EXERCISE 22

Curriculum Analysis

This exercise is designed to provide you with practice in identifying and preparing to teach the types of skills found in the typical elementary or middle school curriculum.

Directions

1. Identify two basic skills from one of the areas commonly taught in the elementary school or from the subject you intend to teach in middle school.
2. Identify one complex skill from one of the areas commonly taught in the elementary school or from the subject you intend to teach in middle school. Define the skill and then translate the eight steps listed in the chapter into a description of what you would do specifically in teaching this complex skill.
3. Identify one higher-order skill selected from the process or content subject areas. Define the skill and then
   a. list the sequence of simpler skills that would need to be taught if using a direct approach.
   b. describe an activity that would allow students to practice the skill if taught using an indirect approach.

OBSERVATION EXERCISE 23

Skills Instruction

This exercise is designed to provide those of you working in a classroom the opportunity to analyze an actual lesson in teaching skills and apply the understanding you have gained about the strategies used to teach skills.

Directions

1. Arrange to observe your teacher teaching students a specific skill.
2. Answer the following questions.
   a. What skill was being taught? Define the skill.
   b. Classify the skill as basic, complex, or higher order.
   c. List the steps the teacher followed in teaching the skill.
   d. What are some of the similarities between what the teacher did and the strategies outlined in this chapter?
   e. What are some of the differences between what the teacher did and the strategies outlined in this chapter?
   f. Describe any observations of students that would support the effectiveness of the strategies in helping them learn skills outlined in this chapter, and describe the relationship between the strategy and the students' behavior.

Teaching Concepts and Generalizations 6

Earlier chapters introduced you to some basic teaching skills used in a variety of teaching strategies. This chapter introduces you to two additional teaching strategies that use these same basic skills. Because you probably have had limited experiences with teaching concepts and generalizations, this chapter will begin with some examples for you to analyze. This analysis may provide helpful insights into an inductive strategy, which is one of the ways of teaching concepts and generalizations. Study carefully the teaching situations presented. Look for similarities and differences between the situations being described.

LESSONS

A Spelling Lesson

A common spelling difficulty is deciding when to double the final letter of a root word when adding a suffix. For example, is the correct spelling **referred** or **refered,** or **occurring** or **occuring**? Several ways of teaching the rules governing the spelling of such words are available. Two examples follow.

Teacher A

Teacher A begins the lesson by explaining to the students that some words are difficult to spell and are therefore commonly misspelled, but that ways exist to overcome these difficulties. First, however, it is important for the teacher to determine whether the students have such difficulties, so he gives them a short spelling quiz using commonly misspelled words involving the use of suffixes (e.g., **ing, ed, al, ate, ary, ence, er**). The students then score their own papers using a transparency with the correct spellings. The students find that they have misspelled many of the words.

Teacher A then says, "Let's review some of the basic ideas we will be using in today's lesson. You will remember that we studied these in prior lessons." The teacher then asks the class the following questions and a discussion of each ensues.

"What is the definition of a root word?"

"What are some examples of root words?"

"What are some examples of consonants?"

"What are some examples of vowels?"

"What is the definition of a suffix?"

"What are some examples of suffixes?"

These questions represent an attempt to assess whether the students understand the prerequisite concepts needed to understand the lesson. If necessary, additional instruction may occur on these concepts at this time. If not, the teacher proceeds with the lesson.

Teacher A tells the students while recording the rule on the chalkboard, "Today we are going to learn the following spelling rule. You double the final letter of a root word when adding a suffix if the root word ends in a single consonant preceded by a single vowel, and if the root word is more than one syllable with the last syllable being accented. Now let's look at some examples."

Then the teacher passes out a worksheet with a list of words and possible suffixes. Students are to add suffixes to each of the words. Students complete the worksheets, and the answers are reviewed with the class. The next day the teacher gives a spelling test of the same words as those practiced in the lesson.

Teacher B

Teacher B also begins the lesson by introducing a few words that are difficult to spell and are therefore commonly misspelled. The teacher goes on to explain that students who have these difficulties can overcome them, and that a test is to be given to find out who has such difficulties. The teacher then gives the students a short spelling quiz using commonly misspelled words involving the use of suffixes, such as occurring, and offered. The students score their own papers using a transparency with the correct spellings. The students demonstrate some difficulty in correctly spelling the words.

Teacher B then says, "Let's review some of the basic ideas we will be using in today's lesson. You will remember that we studied these in prior lessons." The teacher then asks the class the following questions and a discussion of each ensues.

"What is the definition of a root word?"

"What are some examples of root words?"

"What are some examples of consonants?"

"What are some examples of vowels?"

"What is the definition of a suffix?"

"What are some examples of suffixes?"

As with teacher A, this first set of questions represents teacher B's attempt to assess whether the students possess the prerequisite concepts needed to understand the lesson. If necessary, additional instruction may be provided at this time. If not, the teacher proceeds with the lesson. Teacher B then puts up a list of similar words and then asks a series of questions about the words, including:

"Notice that all the words are composed of a root word and an attached suffix. What characteristics do those with doubled letters between the word and the suffix have in common?"

"What characteristics do those words with single letters between the root word and the suffix have in common?"

"How are the two groups of words different?"

From this discussion some patterns seem to emerge. The teacher finally writes the rule on the chalkboard while saying,

"Notice that the last letter in the root word is doubled if the word ends in a single consonant preceded by a vowel, and if the root word is more than one syllable, with the last syllable being accented. This is the rule in deciding whether or not to double the final letter."

The teacher then provides the students with practice followed by corrective feedback using new examples. The next day, the teacher administers an examination testing the students' ability to apply the rules to another set of spelling words.

A Science Lesson

One of the characteristics that is valued in science (and other fields) is curiosity. Again, let's examine how two different teachers might approach the task of teaching the role of curiosity in science.

Teacher C

Teacher C begins the lesson by telling the students that today's lesson is going to be on curiosity and the role it plays in science. The teacher then begins the lesson by asking the class, "What is a possible definition of curiosity?" The teacher then calls on several students to give their definitions of curiosity. The teacher accepts answers by students responding correctly and provides corrective feedback to students who answer incorrectly. The teacher then writes on the blackboard: "Curiosity—the desire to know something."

Teacher C then goes on to explain that curiosity is the motivation behind doing science. Without this motivation, scientists are unlikely to pursue research. Later, one of the items on a test asks the students to complete the following statement: "The desire to know something is called _____ ."

Teacher D

Teacher D begins the lesson by telling the students that they are going to be examining a small black box. The teacher goes on to say that from this experience they will learn something very important about scientists and themselves. Teacher D passes out to each student a box with some objects sealed inside. All boxes are alike, and all contain the same number of objects. The teacher tells the students to play with their boxes. They can tilt or shake their boxes, but they cannot open them. After 2 to 3 minutes of shaking the boxes, the teacher asks the students to place their boxes down on the table and asks the class, "What questions about the box came to your minds as you played with the box?" The teacher writes the questions posed by the students on the chalkboard. The teacher then says, "Let's take one of the questions and attempt to find an answer. Let's start with the question, 'How many objects are in each of the boxes?' Again take your box and tilt it, shake it, and record observations that will allow you to answer this question."

The students then write down their observations of the boxes. After a time, the teacher has the students stop the activity, asks them for their observations, and writes these observations on the chalkboard. If any students have misunderstandings about what constitutes an observation, the teacher corrects them. The teacher then asks the class, "What inference about the number of objects in each of the boxes can we make from our observations?" The students make inferences about how many objects are in each of the boxes and support their inferences with their observations. Some disagreements arise due to conflicting observations. After some discussion, the students vote on how many objects they think are in each of the boxes. The vote is used to decide the issue. The boxes are then collected without being opened. The students are upset and want to know how many objects are in the boxes. The teacher then asks the class to describe their feelings, then writes their descriptions on the chalkboard. Most center on the idea that they are upset because they don't know the answer to the question, and they want to know. The teacher then says something such as,

"This feeling you have of wanting to know is called *curiosity*. This same feeling of curiosity drives scientists to great lengths to find answers to questions. Curiosity is something all of us feel when we feel a need to know something. This feeling is not unique to scientists. Curiosity is the feeling that drives us all to find answers to questions we might have, and this curiosity is necessary if scientific research is to flourish."

Later, the teacher asks the students on a test to define curiosity in their own words and to list a recent example they have experienced outside of school.

ANALYSIS OF THE LESSONS

Lessons taught by teachers A and C are similar to those many of you have experienced as students. The teacher tells you what you are to learn. Some practice may be provided if the learning involves memorization of lists, for example. This process is then followed by a test of your ability to memorize what you had been told or practiced. This sequence describes an expository strategy that is badly used. When teachers use this pattern of teaching, memorization is often confused with understanding.

An additional example will help to illustrate how an expository strategy, when used improperly, can lead to memorization without understanding. Read the following passage carefully; then, referring to it as necessary, complete the worksheet. When you have completed the worksheet, take the examination without referring to the passage or worksheet.

Read the following passage carefully:

. . .inner retinal disease results in no change of the FRST, but does show an alteration of either the $f(s)$, $f(t)$, or both. In senile macular degeneration, for example, changes occur first in the sustained-like function, and secondly in the transient-like function. In the hard exudate stage of early diabetic retinopathy, the $f(s)$ is abnormal in the areas containing hard exudates. (Sanderson, 1983)

Complete the following worksheet:

1. Inner retinal disease results in no change of the _____.

2. What two alterations may occur from inner retinal disease?

3. In the hard exudate stage of early diabetic retinopathy, where is the f(s) abnormal?

When you have completed the worksheet, cover up the text and worksheet and take the following test:

1. Inner retinal disease results in no change of the _____.

2. List two alterations that may occur from inner retinal disease.

3. In the hard exudate stage of early diabetic retinopathy, where is the f(s) abnormal?

Did you pass the test? If so, you now know something about inner retinal disease. Do you understand what you know? For most of you, probably not. You have just learned some words and phrases that make no sense to you. Notice the similarities between this lesson and the lessons of teachers A and C. In all cases, the emphasis was on the memorization of facts, which confuses memorization with understanding.

Now, let's examine the lessons of teachers B and D. In both cases the students were presented with a situation to analyze. Teacher B presented the students with sets of words that could be used to derive a rule about spelling words. The rule then had meaning derived from direct experience with words. Teacher D provided the students with an experience with a sealed box. The experience was structured to generate feelings of wanting to know. From this, a definition of curiosity was derived. In both cases the learnings had meaning that came from the experiences provided.

Teachers A and C were using what is commonly called an **expository strategy** of teaching (Joyce and Weil, 1980); however, these teachers could have used the strategy more effectively. Essentially, the process is one of telling, followed by giving examples and then practicing. Teachers B and D were using what is commonly called an **inductive strategy**. The process is one of providing some kind of direct experience, deriving meaning from the experience, and then providing practice. An inductive strategy is one in which the confusion between memorization and understanding is less likely to occur than with an expository strategy emphasizing memorization of facts.

Teaching for understanding beyond mere memorization is crucial if students are going to be able to apply the knowledge they have learned (Ausubel, 1963). Higher levels of cognitive thinking require that students be able to think conceptually, as well as to be able to apply rules, principles, and other generalizations in appropriate ways.

CONCEPT DEVELOPMENT

A **concept** is a category or set of objects, conditions, events or processes that can be grouped together based on some similarities they have in common (Tennyson, 1980; Clark, 1971). This category of things can then be represented by some symbol. For

Pupils apply their understanding of concepts.

example, if you were asked to draw your concept of a chair, your drawing might be quite different in some respects from one drawn by someone else, but both drawings would have similar elements that we associate with "chairness." Your drawing would be similar to some generalized impression of "chair" based on your experiences with chairs. "Chair," then, is considered a concept. A chair can be defined in terms of critical characteristics and can be represented by the symbol "chair." Additional examples of other concepts include such things as: adverb, abstract art, primes, classical music, main clause, scale, density, binary numbering system, subject, living organism, animal, home, mother, marriage, teacher, or clef.

Concepts can be roughly categorized into two kinds: abstractions derived from concrete objects such as chair, animal, rain, or table, and abstractions derived from conditions or processes such as curiosity, hot, cold, freedom, density, adverb, or music. Object concepts are usually developed through a classification process of finding critical characteristics that define the concept.

A definition of a concept is composed of a list of attributes or characteristics describing the concept. No other concept would have the same list of attributes or characteristics. For example, a definition of the concept "boat" would likely include the attribute, "a mode of transportation or conveyance that has a hull and is intended to be propelled on the surface of the water." Many modes of transportation or conveyances exist, including buses, cars, airplanes, and so on. This attribute of boats is called a **variable attribute,** which is an attribute possessed by an object that is not unique to the object. A **critical attribute,** on the other hand, is one that is used to differentiate the object from other objects that have variable attributes in common. In the case of the boat, the critical attribute is "a conveyance that has a hull and is intended to be propelled on the surface of the water."

When teaching an object concept, you need to decide how sophisticated to make the concept. For example, in developing the concept of a "seat" (chair) with children, introducing all of the kinds of seats at one time would overwhelm them. Chairs or seats may take the form of kitchen chairs, barber chairs, bar stools, thrones, recliners, couches, bleachers, benches, and milking stools. All of these instruments are seats with some characteristics in common, but all differ in some characteristics.

An object concept, such as "chair," is one arrived at through the process of classification. Basically, a child sees some object (e.g., kitchen chair) being used, and asks, "What is that?" The child is then told the name of the object, "a kitchen chair." The child then remembers the appearance and name of a kitchen chair. On seeing a person sitting on a couch the child may say, "Look at Uncle Al sitting in the chair!" The child is then corrected and told, "No, that's not a chair, that's a couch." An explanation of the differences may then follow, or the child may be left to determine the differences. Eventually the child mentally develops a general representation of "seat." The child now possesses a concept of a seat that, with additional experience, can be developed to a rather sophisticated level. Without direct experiences with a variety of seats, this development would not occur. Also, recognize that after a person has had a wide variety of experiences with seats, reliance on direct experience may no longer be necessary. Pictures, models, or other representations may be used to continue development of the concept (Solomon, 1970).

Object concepts are defined through a classification process and all concepts defined from the same general concept are related. In figure 6–1 a classification system for condensation from the air is described. Notice that the definition of sleet would include the attributes that it is condensation that forms in the air, falls from the air, reaches the ground as precipitation, is formed initially as a liquid and then frozen while falling from the air, and is frozen only once and so lacks layers of ice. Other concepts in this classification system—rain, for example—share some attributes in common with sleet. The critical attribute of sleet that makes it different from rain is the fact that sleet freezes before it reaches the ground.

Introducing such a complete definition would be inappropriate for early elementary children, but would be appropriate for upper elementary and middle school students. In the middle school a more complete definition of clouds could be developed through the introduction of a classification system for clouds.

Concept formation occurs not only in the classroom, but constantly as we experience life. Although learning the attributes of chairs might be more likely to occur

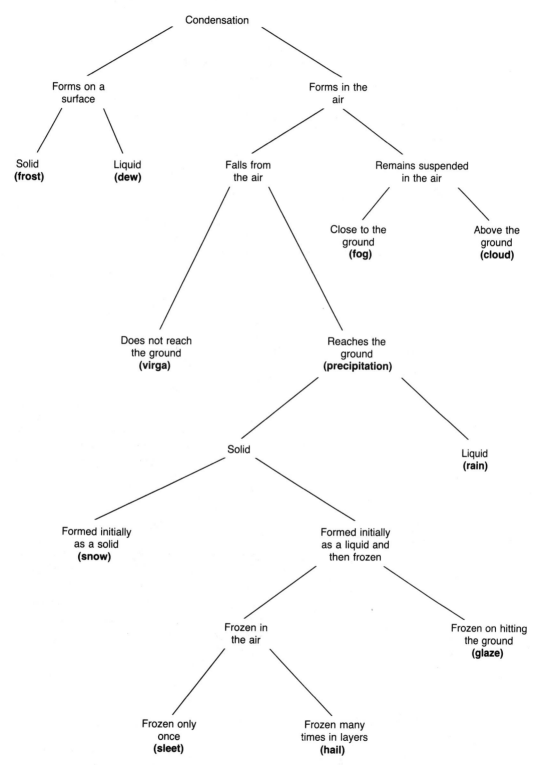

Figure 6–1 Classification of condensation

outside the school, and learning the attributes of sleet might be more likely to occur in the school, both depend on direct experience and the need to interpret that experience. Ideally, fewer misconceptions will be developed in schools than in natural settings, for once misconceptions are developed they are difficult to replace (Stepans, Beiswanger, and Dyche 1986; Carpenter, 1984).

Regardless of the concept to be introduced, the initial development of concepts is entirely dependent on direct experience. We cannot learn the meanings of concepts such as hot, cold, sleet, cloud, snow, music, noise, equilibrium, freedom, density, curiosity, and adverb by being told. Initial direct experience is necessary for understanding things conceptually. Providing direct experience for students without prior experience is essential for the development of concepts. Also, some evidence suggests that for students to change their understanding of a concept, they must be made to feel some dissatisfaction with the concept they currently hold, and the new concept must be intelligible, plausible, and have value (Posner, Strike, Hewson, and Gertzog, 1982).

When planning lessons in which concepts will be taught, the identification and assessing of prerequisite concepts is crucial. In the example in figure 7–1, students would need to have a clear understanding of the concepts of solid, liquid, vapor, and condensation. If they had not had direct experience with the different forms of condensation, then, where possible, such direct experience would need to be provided.

Direct experience should be a part of the instruction for concepts such as probability, pi, circumference, solid, gas, harmony, vanishing point, pronoun, adverb, cooperation, competition, hardware store, city council, zoo, force, lawyer, profit, and magnetism. Any concept that can be directly experienced should be taught through direct experience. When teaching concepts such as slave, starvation, virus, king, castle, shark, polar bear, heart attack, and AIDS, direct experience may not be possible. Dependence on indirect experiences such as films, photographs, stories, and other representations then becomes crucial. Some concepts such as inverse proportion, cosine, protons, electrons, decasyllabic, epenthesis, enthymeme, and other highly technical and theoretical concepts should be delayed until such time as students have undergone the cognitive development necessary for understanding. This development occurs for some students as early as middle school, but for most it occurs, if at all, in the late high school or college years (Neimark, 1975).

Teaching concepts involves the teaching of the critical attributes of a concept along with the descriptive variable attributes that define the concept. Examples are compared to nonexamples, and practice in discriminating examples from nonexamples may be provided. Concept teaching can be accomplished by either of two strategies, an expository strategy or an inductive strategy.

THE EXPOSITORY STRATEGY

The expository strategy can be effective in concept development if students have already had prior experiences with the examples and nonexamples used to illustrate and define the concept. Because an expository strategy involves the manipulation of words, symbols, or abstract ideas, this strategy is more likely to be effective with older students or those who are at the formal level of cognitive development as defined by Piaget (Inhelder and Piaget, 1973; Saunders and Shepardson, 1987). If any student, even one at the formal operational level, has not had certain concrete experiences with examples of the concept, then that student will be unable to learn the concept with understanding through an expository approach using only verbal interactions (Ausubel, 1963; Lawson, 1983). For example, imagine a teacher is teaching the concept of a "radjo." The teacher says that a radjo is a class of "semes" that smells like "quadjos" and has four "codafs" just like a "tadso." Now, if students have had no experiences with examples of semeses, quadjos, codafs, and tadsos, continued talking about them will do little to develop understanding. Even for those who have had prior concrete experiences with examples of a concept being taught, presentations using models, photographs, films, or other representations tend to result in greater understanding than instruction using purely abstract language (Solomon, 1970).

Research on concept development using expository strategies suggests what should occur during the process of instruction (Clark, 1971; Tennyson and Park, 1980).

A. Planning Phase
1. Select the concept to be taught and identify the critical attributes as well as frequently observed variable attributes of the concept needed to define it. Example: A boat is a vehicle that has a hull and is caused in some way to be moved on the surface of the water.
2. Analyze the list of attributes, and identify all of the prerequisite concepts that would need to be understood in order to grasp the concept to be taught. Assess the students on their level of understanding of the prerequisite knowledge. Example: The prerequisite concepts used to define a boat are vehicle, surface, mechanical device, and water. The notion of a hull is unique to boats, and so would be introduced in the lesson.
B. Classroom Instruction
1. Introduce the name and definition of the concept to the students at the beginning of the lesson. This can significantly reduce the number of examples that would need to be studied to master the concept (Tennyson and Park, 1980). Terminology used in the definition should be as nontechnical and easily understood as possible.
2. Introduce examples that clearly illustrate the critical attributes of the concept while limiting the number of variable attributes. Nonexamples should then be introduced. The nonexamples should differ from the examples in a minimum number of critical attributes at a time. They should also be from the same conceptual class.
   Example: In the case of boats, boats such as rowboats, outboard motor boats, monohull sailboats, and other common boats would be used for examples. Nonexamples might include rafts, ducks, and driftwood.
3. Introduce examples and nonexamples simultaneously in a random sequence with the examples having widely different variable attributes. Usually four or five examples and nonexamples will be sufficient.
   Example: Widely divergent examples might include catamarans, jet skis, jet boats, canoes, and inboard boats. Nonexamples could include such things as aircraft carriers, submarines, sea planes, and surf boards.
4. Give students some practice in distinguishing examples and nonexamples from additional cases, or in some way provide opportunities for them to apply the concept to

new situations. This practice is essential if transfer or use of the concept in new situations is expected.

Example: Give students some photographs of conveyances and ask them to separate out those that represent boats. You could also ask them to design a boat from a set of specifications. This project could be used as a class contest between small, cooperative groups. Writing a story about boats that would demonstrate knowledge of the structure and functions of different kinds of boats might also be an effective form of application.

THE INDUCTIVE STRATEGY

The purpose of an inductive strategy is to provide a common direct experience to help students understand the rule, concept, or principle being introduced. This strategy uses the well-established psychological principle that the meanings of basic words and symbols are dependent on direct experience with the phenomena that the words and symbols represent (Ausubel, 1963). When students memorize words and symbols in the abstract —that is, with little or no prior direct experience with what the words or symbols represent—they are usually learning meaningless nonsense.

In a teaching/learning context, an inductive strategy provides students with direct experiences that represent specific examples of the concept or generalization to be taught. Following the experience, the teacher helps students analyze the experience through questions, thus leading them to a statement of the generalization or concept definition (Eggen, Kauchek, and Harder, 1979). Finally, the teacher provides the formal statement or symbols representing the generalization or concept.

A suggested sequence of tasks involved in an inductive strategy is:

A. Planning Phase
   1. Select the concept to be taught and identify the critical attributes as well as frequently observed variable attributes of the concept needed to define it.
   2. Analyze the list of attributes and identify all of the prerequisite concepts that must be understood in order to learn the concept to be taught. Assess the student's understanding of the prerequisite knowledge.
B. Classroom Instruction
   1. Provide a hands-on activity or, preferably, two or three activities for the students that will provide direct experience with the critical attributes of the concept. Keep the number of variable attributes to a minimum. In the case of object concepts, provide activities that allow for experiences with nonexamples. The amount of guidance by the teacher may vary. When little guidance is provided, the inductive strategy is commonly referred to as **discovery learning**. When much guidance is provided, the inductive strategy is commonly called **guided inquiry**. Beginning teachers will likely need to follow more of a guided strategy in order to keep the management of the class within their abilities. Although a set induction is important in establishing a clear purpose for the activity, rarely as part of this set induction should students be told the actual concept to be taught or the particular objectives to be accomplished. For example, a teacher intending to teach the meaning and use of antonyms and synonyms might say something such as, "Today

Pupils have direct experience with living things.

we are going to discover two ways of using words to make our writing more lively and interesting to read," rather than something such as, "As a result of today's lesson you will be able to state the definitions of synonyms and antonyms and correctly use three examples in sentences." The latter is a statement of an appropriate objective for the inductive lesson, but stating the objective should wait until the activity is completed. This will facilitate incidental learning, which in inductive lessons may be considerable.

2. Once students have completed the activity, encourage them, through the use of questions, to talk about the experience and to examine and analyze the experience. The use of questions is of critical importance if an inductive strategy is to be used to its maximum potential. The use of questions when using this strategy will not necessarily follow any particular pattern as it does in a discussion lesson. Rather, use a sequence of questions that allows you to lead the students from the experience you provided to a point where you will be able to provide the generalization to be taught. The questions may be observational; that is, they may require the students to describe what they saw, felt, smelled, heard, or tasted. Questions may require students to identify similarities and

differences or to draw conclusions from evidence. Most questions will require thought and understanding beyond mere recall.

3. Through the questioning process, the critical attributes of the concept will be identified verbally. Some information-giving (presentation or lecture) will be needed at the end of the questioning to summarize the definition of the concept. In rare instances, students will be able to do this without being told, but expecting them to discover the definition of a concept strictly on their own is usually not reasonable. Then write the definition on the chalkboard or overhead transparency using easily understood vocabulary.
4. Introduce the name symbolizing this definition of the concept.
5. Give the students some practice in distinguishing examples from nonexamples or in some other fashion provide opportunities for them to apply the concept to new situations. This practice in applying the concept is necessary if students are to be expected to use the concept when they encounter new situations requiring that use.

The planning phases for the expository and inductive strategies are similar. In both cases, the concept must be clearly defined and a preassessment of students made. After the concept is taught, both strategies require practice in applying the concept. The differences lie in the sequence followed during the actual lessons. In the expository strategy the concept is first given and then experience with examples and nonexamples provided. In the inductive strategy an experience is first provided, the experience analyzed and the critical and variable attributes defining the concept identified, and then the name for the concept is given. With an expository strategy the words are first given and then meaning is given to the words; with an inductive strategy, an experience is first provided and then the meaning derived from the experience is put into words. An inductive strategy has been found to result in higher achievement and more cognitive development than an expository strategy when used with students who have reached the concrete operational stage (Saunders and Shepardson, 1987).

TEACHING GENERALIZATIONS

Generalizations can include statements of rules, principles, processes, or other kinds of relationships among concepts. Concepts, then, are the building blocks of rules, principles, and other generalizations (Gagne, 1977). Generalizations merely describe relationships between concepts.

A rule can be a prescribed set of regulations governing a procedure, or it can be a standard procedure to follow. Rules are important in guiding many of the tasks we do, and they usually have applicability in settings beyond those in which they are learned. Examples of rules would be:

☐ Pi is calculated by dividing the circumference of a circle by the diameter.

☐ Use quotation marks to enclose a direct quotation.

☐ A citizen of the United States must be registered in order to vote in elections.

Within each rule several concepts may be found. The rule describes the manipulation of concepts to perform a particular task. In the first rule above, for example, circumference, circle, calculate, divide, diameter, and pi are all concepts. In order to understand the rule, a student must understand each of these concepts and must also have the procedural knowledge of how the concepts are manipulated. In teaching a rule, understanding the concepts is a necessary prerequisite to understanding the rule. When teaching rules, two contextually similar rules should be taught simultaneously rather than sequentially or randomly (Tennyson and Park, 1980). The comparison of similarities and differences in juxtaposition will improve learning. The teaching strategy is the same one used to teach any concept. For example, the following steps would be used in teaching the rule for pi using an inductive strategy.

A. Planning Phase
   1. Identify the rule:
      Pi is calculated by dividing the circumference by the diameter of a circle.
   2. Identify the prerequisite concepts and assess the students:
      calculate, division, circumference, diameter, circle
B. Classroom Instruction
   1. Hands on activity:
      Give students some tin cans with the tops and bottoms removed, along with a string and a ruler. Have them measure around the tin can with the string, lay the string on the table, and then measure the length of string needed to go around the can (the circumference). Then have them measure across the end of the can at its widest point (the diameter). Students then divide the circumference by the diameter. All of the students place this value on a table prepared on the chalkboard.
   2. Students discuss the experience:
      Lead the students in a discussion on what they did to find the number they placed on the chalkboard.
   3. Analyze the results and arrive at a generalization:
      An analysis of the number leads to the conclusion that all of the numbers are very similar. The value of the number is about 3.14. This number is given the name **pi**.
   4. State the generalization:
      Lead the students to recognize that pi is found by measuring the circumference of a circle and its diameter, and then dividing the circumference by the diameter.
   5. Practice:
      Give the students some additional practice with circles in calculating pi. They then may practice finding the circumference of circles given only the diameter or finding the diameter given only the circumference. Examples should include situations the students are likely to experience, such as wheels or the path of helicopter blades.

Principles are also generalizations or combinations of concepts. In particular, they make sense out of the behavior of things in our world by describing relationships among concepts. Examples of principles would be:

□ Images in advertising have more effect than substance.

□ The higher the pressure on a gas, the less the volume occupied by the gas if the temperature of the gas remains unchanged.

□ Many common words have more than one meaning.

□ The rights of individuals are sometimes in conflict and cannot be resolved without some restrictions being placed on individuals.

Principles have wide applicability and they represent the kind of learning that is the most useful and meaningful. Principles have more use in the real world than do concepts, concepts have more use than do memorized facts, and memorized facts have very little use. Concepts should therefore be taught in relationship to other concepts. Rarely are concepts taught in isolation; to do so makes their transfer unlikely.

As stated previously, rules and principles involve two or more concepts and the relationships among them. In teaching any rule or principle, it is essential that the students have an understanding of the prerequisite concepts prior to teaching the rule or principle. Should pupils lack such understanding, then teach these concepts before introducing the rule or principle. Failure to ensure understanding of prerequisite concepts will result in an incomplete or erroneous understanding of the rule or principle. In most respects the teaching of generalizations, either through an expository or inductive strategy, does not significantly differ from the tasks involved in teaching concepts.

ASSESSMENT OF THE INDUCTIVE STRATEGY

An inductive strategy is a valuable tool in helping students learn knowledge with understanding. More students enjoy learning in this fashion than with didactic or expository methods (Renner, Abraham, and Birnie, 1985). Learning abstractions in the context of experiences makes sense to students; they are not merely memorizing symbols, but understanding experiences. When a concept is presented on a concrete level by allowing the students to have direct contact with the object, understanding as measured by student behavior appears to be high (Solomon, 1970).

If properly conducted, an inductive strategy will result in more student involvement, more intrinsic interest in the lesson, better transfer of learning, and higher achievement of more complex cognitive understandings than with other strategies teachers commonly use (Hensen, 1980; Hermann, 1969). There is also evidence that direct attempts to teach higher-order thinking skills through inductive strategies have a high probability of success (Anderson, 1983; Sadow, 1983). Additional studies suggest than an inductive strategy is particularly effective in promoting achievement and cognitive development when used with concrete operational learners (Linn and Thier, 1975; Saunders and Shepardson, 1987). An inductive strategy, on the other hand, is not an efficient strategy if your intent is to have students memorize large amounts of content taught in short periods of time (Hensen, 1980). The expository strategy, drill-and-practice, and other such strategies are more efficient in exposing students to larger amounts of content. An inductive strategy leading to conceptual understanding, along with the ability to apply that understanding, takes time. No short cuts exist.

Using an inductive process requires more planning due to the increased complexity of classroom management. If a teacher's behavioral management skills are less than adequate, more student misbehavior could result from the use of this strategy than with simpler strategies (Emmer, Evertson, Sanford, Clements, and Worsham, 1984). However, skilled teachers will find this to be a more satisfying strategy for both themselves and their students. An inductive strategy is one you will want to learn to use with skill.

IMPLICATIONS FOR PLANNING

When preparing lessons intended to teach concepts, you must develop a careful and accurate definition of the concept or concepts to be taught. Failure to define carefully the critical and variable attributes needed to define a concept can result in lack of clarity in the lesson and development of misconceptions.

The preassessment process of student understanding of prerequisite concepts is also crucial. If they lack prerequisite understandings, or if they possess misconceptions, failure to correct these deficiencies will lead to a lack of understanding of the concept being taught and the generation of misconceptions, which, once taught, are difficult to change.

As with any hands-on experiences provided in the classroom, careful management is essential. With inadequate management many problems can arise during an activity, which can be frustrating to teachers and may cause them to avoid such activities in order to avoid such problems. When planning these lessons, therefore, include specific directions to be given, the particular method to be used to communicate the directions, and the specific questions you will ask to ensure that students understand the directions before giving them a signal to begin. Before the lesson, check your directions and try to think about them in the way that students might. Will they have difficulty understanding or following directions? Try to anticipate potential problems students may experience and modify the way you give directions so as to avoid the problems. Also remember that giving clear directions to end the activity, in addition to those to begin the activity, can also do much to reduce the confusion that could result when bringing the activity to a close.

Inductive strategies commonly require student movement to pick up and return materials. You need careful planning of this movement if you wish to avoid confusion and misbehavior. Since students may be working in small groups, having one group member pick up and return materials may be helpful. Working in small groups also requires that reasonable rules be used to regulate behavior. Expecting students to remain seated with their groups and not talking between groups would be reasonable. If they have questions or need to leave their seats for some reason, ask them to raise their hands and wait until you recognize them.

Do not fall into the trap of avoiding future use of hands-on activities because you feel the activities are inappropriate for students because of problems that arose during the activity. You would be inferring that students can't do them properly when, in fact, with reasonable management skills, hands-on activities work well with any group of students.

REFERENCES

Anderson, R. D. 1983. A consolidation and appraisal of science meta-analyses. *Journal of Research in Science Teaching, 20*(5): 497–509.

Ausubel, D. 1963. *The psychology of meaningful verbal learning.* New York: Grune and Stratton.

Carpenter, E. T. 1984. Students' misconceptions interfere with science learning: Case studies of fifth-grade students. *Elementary School Journal, 84:* 365–379.

Clark, C. D. 1971. Teaching concepts in the classroom: A set of teaching prescriptions derived from experimental research. *Journal of Educational Psychology Monograph, 62*(3): 253–278.

Eggen, P. D., D. P. Kauchak, and R. J. Harder. 1979. *Strategies of teachers: Information processing in the classroom.* Englewood Cliffs, NJ: Prentice-Hall.

Emmer, E. T., C. M. Evertson, J. P. Sanford, B. S. Clements, and M. E. Worsham. 1984. *Classroom management for secondary teachers.* Englewood Cliffs, NJ: Prentice-Hall.

Gagne, R. 1977. *The conditions of learning.* 3d ed. New York: Holt, Rinehart and Winston.

Hensen, K.T. 1980. Discovery learning. *Contemporary Education 51:* 101–103.

Hermann, G. 1969. Learning by discovery: A critical review of studies. *The Journal of Experimental Education, 38:* 58–72.

Inhelder, B., and J. Piaget. 1973. *The growth of logical thinking from childhood to adolescence.* New York: Basic Books.

Joyce, B., and M. Weil. 1980. *Models of teaching* 2nd ed. Englewood Cliffs, NJ: Prentice-Hall.

Lawson, A. E. 1983. Investigating and applying developmental psychology in the science classroom. In *Learning and motivation in the classroom,* ed. G. Scott, et al. Hillsdale, NJ: Erlbaum.

Linn, M. C., and H. D. Thier. 1975. The effect of experimental science on development of logical thinking in children. *Journal of Research in Science Teaching, 12* (1): 49–62.

Neimark, E. 1975. Intellectual development during adolescence. In *Review of child development research,* ed. F. D. Horowitz. Chicago: University of Chicago Press.

Posner, G., K. Strike, K. Hewson, and W. Gertzog. 1982. Accommodation of a scientific conception: Toward a theory of conceptual change. *Science Education, 66:* 211–228.

Renner, J. W., M. R. Abraham, and H. H. Birnie. 1985. Secondary school students' beliefs about the physics laboratory. *Science Education, 69* (5): 649–663.

Sadow, S. A. 1983. Creative problem-solving for the foreign language class. *Foreign Language Annals, 16:* 115–118.

Sanderson, D. 1983, Summer. Quantitative layer-by-layer perimetry. *Optometry News.* 7–9.

Saunders, W. L., and D. Shepardson. 1987. A comparison of concrete and formal science instruction upon science achievement and reasoning ability of sixth grade students. *Journal of Research in Science Teaching, 24* (1): 39–51.

Solomon, G. O. 1970. The analysis of concrete to abstract classroom instruction patterns utilizing the TIP profile. *Journal of Research and Development in Education, 4:* 52–61.

Stepans, J. I., R. E. Beiswanger, and S. Dyche. 1986. Misconceptions die hard. *The Science Teacher, 53:* 65–69.

Tennyson, R. D., and O. Park. 1980. The teaching of concepts: A review of instructional design research literature. *Review of Educational Research, 50* (1): 55–70.

CHAPTER REVIEW

Concepts
Definition: a category or set of objects, conditions, events, or processes that can be grouped together based on common similarities, and represented by some abstract symbol.
Kinds of Concepts:

1. an abstraction derived from concrete objects

2. an abstraction derived from a condition or process

Concept Statement: composed of a list of critical attributes along with other more general attributes.
Concept Learning: involves the identification of the critical attributes of the concept along with some descriptive variable attributes, and the ability to use the definition in the context of examples and nonexamples.

Generalizations
Rule: a prescribed set of regulations that may govern a procedure or define a standard procedure to follow.
Principle: an established mode of operating or behaving.

Expository Strategy
Definition: one of providing a definition, followed by the presentation of examples and nonexamples to illustrate the definition.
Steps in Planning

1. select the concept or generalization and identify the critical attributes.

2. Identify prerequisite knowledge and assess students.

Steps in Instruction

1. introduce the definition to students

2. introduce examples and nonexamples as needed, usually three or four

3. introduce examples and nonexamples simultaneously

4. provide practice

Inductive strategy

Definition: one of providing students with some kind of direct experience, then, through using questions about the experience, leading them to a statement of the critical attributes, followed by the identification of the symbol representing the statement.

Steps in Planning

1. select the concept or generalization and identify the critical attributes
2. identify prerequisite knowledge and assess students

Steps in Instruction

1. provide a hands-on activity that gives students experience with the critical attributes
2. use questioning to analyze the experience
3. use a combination of questioning and presentation to identify the critical attributes
4. identify the symbol or symbols used to represent the concept or generalization
5. provide practice

Assessment of an Inductive Strategy

1. Students are more intrinsically interested in lessons.
2. Students achieve more at levels above the knowledge level.
3. Students are better able to transfer the learning.

Limitations of an inductive strategy compared to other strategies

1. not an efficient method for teaching large numbers of facts to be memorized
2. more misbehavior occurs when used by teachers who lack classroom and behavioral management skills

EXERCISE 24

Concept Analysis

In this exercise you will identify two concepts taught in elementary or middle school grades. Once you identify two concepts, you will then analyze each one in order to list the concepts that would be prerequisite to understanding the new ones. This is followed by a description of activities that could be used to teach one of the two concepts.

Directions. Complete the following tasks.

1. List two concepts that you think would appropriately be taught in an elementary or middle school classroom. Define each of the concepts, being sure to include all of the critical and variable attributes needed to define them.

2. For each of the two concepts identified, list the concepts that a person must already understand in order to learn each of the new concepts.

3. Choose one of the two concepts above and describe the direct experience that you would provide in your classroom as part of an inductive strategy to teach the concept.

4. List the ways that the direct experience would illustrate the attributes that define the concept.

PART FOUR

MANAGEMENT

Recent research findings have provided a wealth of valuable information about managing classrooms effectively. A teacher using this information can make the classroom a pleasant, businesslike, and enjoyable place in which to learn. In such a situation, student motivation to learn and remain on task is high. Failure to manage a classroom adequately can result in an environment replete with confusion, misbehavior, antagonism, anger, and unpleasantness. Fortunately, creating a pleasant environment for the teacher and the student is within the ability levels of most, if not all, beginning and experienced teachers.

The term **classroom management** usually refers to management of the physical environment and instructional materials. The management of the behavior of students is commonly referred to as **behavioral management**. This text accepts and uses these definitions.

Classroom management and behavioral management are often defined as separate entities, but they are actually closely related. Poor classroom management results in behavioral problems; poor behavioral management makes effective classroom management difficult. The primary purpose for both kinds of management is to increase the time students spend engaged in appropriate learning activities and, hence, achieving the teacher's goals and objectives.

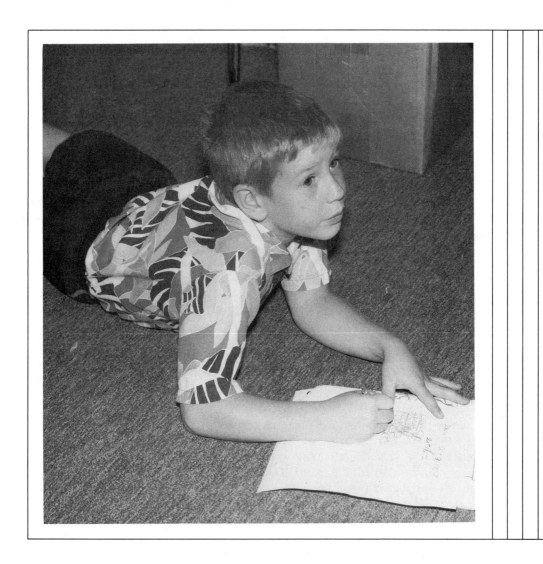

Classroom Organization and Management 7

Research has shown that failure to conduct classroom management tasks efficiently and effectively results in confusion, disruption, lost learning time, students failing to complete tasks, and lower achievement (McGarity and Butts, 1984; Sanford, 1984; Evertson and Emmer, 1982; Medley, 1979). Teachers who are poor managers of classrooms also tend to limit the learning tasks in the classroom to those that involve easy control of students, such as having them seated at their desks filling out routine worksheets (Sanford, 1984; Doyle, 1979). Teachers are heard to say, "You can't do _____ with kids. They just can't handle that kind of situation." How sad! In fact, students are able to handle almost any task if it is well managed and within their ability levels. Teachers, not students, are quite often the ones who can't handle situations.

Effective teachers tend to use similar patterns of management regardless of the subject and grade level or ability of pupils (Sanford, 1984). They tend to have high student motivation, high student achievement, high levels of student engagement and little disruptive behavior or classroom confusion. The evidence suggests that certain behaviors characterize these effective classroom managers. These teachers monitor student work closely, communicate directions clearly, make smooth transitions from one activity to the next, pace lessons consistent with the ability levels of the students, establish comprehensive, workable rules and procedures and make them routine, and deal with even minor inappropriate behavior quickly and consistently (Sanford, 1984; Emmer and Evertson, 1981; Doyle, 1980; O'Leary and O'Leary, 1977; and Kounin, 1970).

The beginning of effective classroom management takes place during the first few weeks of the school year or, for student teachers, during the first few weeks of student teaching. The planning that occurs before a teacher ever meets with a class at the start of the year directly reduces the management problems likely to occur (Evertson, Emmer, Clements, Sanford, Worsham, and Williams, 1981). Maintaining an initially well-organized classroom is far easier than regaining control over a disorganized class and teaching more appropriate behaviors. Effective classroom management is therefore a function of prior planning and careful implementation.

Guidelines for Classroom Management

Analysis of research findings relating to classroom management has led to the development of a set of critical guidelines for teachers shown to be related to increased student time on task and decreased student misbehavior (Emmer, Evertson, Sanford, Clements, and Worsham, 1984; Sanford, 1984; Evertson and Emmer, 1982; Emmer, Evertson, et al., 1981; Doyle, 1980; Brophy, 1979; Medley, 1979; Kounin, 1970). Teachers should use these guidelines when planning and implementing classroom management procedures.

1. *Make procedures simple.* Management procedures should be as simple as possible. Any procedure should include steps that are as few and as simple as possible. Less complex management procedures take less time to teach and maximize the chance that students will be successful in completing the procedure.

2. Make procedures efficient. Classroom management procedures should minimize the amount of time required for completion. Because the main purpose of any management task is to increase the amount of student on-task time, choose procedures requiring the minimum of time.

3. Avoid dead time. When students are left with little or nothing to do, they often find something to do the teacher would rather they not be doing. Minimizing the amount of time that students are idle is important in choosing any classroom management procedure.

4. Minimize student movement. Any student movement during an activity is likely to create some problems; therefore, minimize the number of students who need to move during any procedure. Also, carefully choose the kind of movement that students will need to do; avoid movements that require them to congregate around some point or require them to stand and wait. You will need to have rules governing student movement to the drinking fountain, bathroom, pencil sharpener, sink, and waste basket. Having essentially the same rule to govern all of these movements is helpful. For example, having a child raise his hand and ask for permission to leave his seat is recommended. Going to the drinking fountain, pencil sharpener, sink, and waste basket during whole-class instruction is forbidden.

5. Make procedures routine. Attempt to make classroom management procedures routine; that is, students should use the same procedures in a consistent fashion from one day to the next and from one activity to the next. When possible, avoid novel procedures, because students will lose some time in learning any new procedure. Expert teachers have been found to use routines in ways allowing them to devote attention to more important matters inherent in lessons (Hoffman and Edwards, 1986).

6. Teach procedures. Invest the time needed at the beginning of the school year to teach students classroom management procedures they will be expected to use. Spend whatever time is needed to ensure that students fully comprehend and are able to follow the classroom routines they will be using during the rest of the year. A single presentation of procedures may not be sufficient for student comprehension; be prepared to repeat and reinforce earlier instruction. This is time well spent. As each new procedure is introduced, such instruction should occur.

7. Secure attention. When ready to implement a particular procedure, do not begin giving directions for the procedure until you have the attention of all of the students; otherwise, some students will not know what to do when they begin the task assigned. This lack of understanding will result in many procedural questions or much misbehavior at the start of the assigned task.

8. Check understanding of procedures. Before giving the signal to start any procedure, check for student understanding of the procedure. Checking for understanding involves more than just asking, "Do you understand?" Before giving the students a signal to begin, you should review the task they are to accomplish. In order to ensure that all of the students can do the task, have the class run through an example together, ask a student or students to demonstrate the task, or have individual students explain the task.

9. Monitor progress. Once you have given students the signal to begin a procedure, monitor the procedure to ensure that they are doing the procedure as directed. Avoid being distracted by other tasks at the times students are in the process of carrying out management procedures. Effective teachers have been found to monitor pupils' progress much more closely than do ineffective teachers (Medley, 1979).

10. Hold students accountable. Students must be accountable for all tasks. A classroom should be a pleasant place for children to learn, but it is also a place of work. Accountability can take the form of some product to be turned in, or the demonstration of some behavior during the activity. Rewards or negative consequences are then attached to successful completion of the task—rewards being much more effective in modifying and maintaining appropriate behavior (Madsen and Madsen, 1981; Walker and Shea, 1980).

SOME COMMON TASKS TO BE MANAGED

Applications of the guidelines just described are found in the following examples. Although the examples may seem complex, the processes involved are relatively simple. Once you become acquainted with these processes, their application will become natural and logical.

Starting the Day or Class

When students enter the classroom at the start of the day or, in the case of middle school grades, the start of class, they should be expected to be in their seats and ready for the start of instruction. Begin school or class each day with the same productive routine. This routine, usually lasting approximately five minutes, should allow you sufficient time to take attendance, pass back papers, and conduct other tasks prior to formal instruction.

Prior to the start of school or the class, write a daily agenda and announcements on the chalkboard. The agenda would include a list of the day's activities and the approximate times. The announcements could include such things as homework assignments and due dates, special TV shows that are going to be shown, PTA meeting times and dates, or due dates for projects. If you are teaching in the primary grades, have a riddle or some other puzzle ready for the students. If teaching in the intermediate or middle school grades, in addition to the agenda and announcements, have one or two questions already on the overhead projector that review the previous day's work or cause students to start to think about some topic to be introduced that day. When the bell for the start of the day or period rings, turn on the overhead projector. Primary students would be responsible for trying to solve the riddle or puzzle; intermediate elementary or middle school students would be responsible for copying the agenda and the announcements into their notebooks. They would then proceed to answer the questions. The students should be expected to turn in the paper with their answers to the questions, or record the questions and answers in a notebook, so that they will know they are accountable for answering them. Have a system of points to be awarded to students who make an honest attempt at answering the questions. At the end of a grading period, you could give them a grade, credit, or extra credit if they have a minimum of a predetermined number of points. Whenever possible, try to reward students who work on tasks assigned rather than punish those who do not (Madsen and Madsen, 1981; Walker and Shea, 1980).

When the bell first rings to start the day or class, monitor the students to ensure that all are doing the assigned tasks. If any are not, go to the student's desk and determine the cause of the delay. After ascertaining that the students are on task, check attendance from a seating chart and complete any other administrative chores while keeping an eye on the students.

If you follow these procedures each day, and if you take the time needed at the start of the year to teach these procedures, the students will eventually know what to expect and will not need to be told what to do each day. The tasks you ask the students to do will benefit them. They will know from the agenda what to expect in class that day; thus readiness will be fostered. The puzzles or questions will cause the students to think about learning. While they are involved in these tasks, you can accomplish mundane administrative tasks, reducing the time students will be left idle.

Student Seating

For most classrooms, assigning seats for whole-class instruction is preferable to allowing students to choose their own seats. For example, a student with a visual impairment needs to be placed in a location of optimum viewing; a pupil with a hearing impairment needs to be placed in a location of optimum hearing. Such differences must be accommodated in any seating arrangement. Allowing students to choose their own seats usually will not allow for such accommodations. Students are easily distracted. Allowing them to sit where they choose usually means they will sit near friends, with resulting distractions.

Regardless of how classroom seating is determined, you should expect students to stay in the same seats. This enables you to make up a seating chart to ease the taking of roll and the learning of student names.

Grouping Students

Many instructional activities will require the grouping of students in pairs or other small groups. When forming such pairs or groups, you would be well advised to make the pairs or groups as heterogeneous in ability as possible. The evidence is clear that such grouping benefits the lower achievers without any sacrifice to higher achievers (Johnson and Johnson, 1987; Emmer, et al., 1984; Bondi, 1982) because it allows a great deal of peer tutoring to occur. On the surface, the benefit to the underachiever of getting some help beyond that which the teacher can provide is more easily recognized by teachers; the benefit derived by more able students may not be so apparent. The need of the higher achiever to explain what he knows about something apparently helps him to better master the material. For example, most teachers recognize how much they themselves learn about what they are teaching as a result of planning and teaching lessons. The same sort of thing apparently occurs when one student teaches another.

Heterogeneous groups can be used as opportunities to teach students how to work together cooperatively, which is part of learning to function outside of school. When students are placed in situations requiring interdependence to complete a task, and then taught how to work in such a situation, many positive things can happen (Johnson and Johnson, 1987), one of the most important of which is that it may help students overcome stereotyped images they may have about people who are different. They also can learn how to communicate and adjust to a variety of kinds of people. These are significant learnings.

If you expect students to learn to work together cooperatively, then you must teach them the skills involved. Students in the elementary and middle school grades have not yet learned the skills of accepting others' ideas, disagreeing constructively, sharing materials, listening to what others have to say, encouraging others to participate, making eye contact while listening, praising others, presenting their own ideas, probing others' responses, giving directions, identifying tasks to be completed and assigning responsibilities, assuming individual responsibility, and coordinating tasks. These skills are important, but they cannot be taught simultaneously; rather, they need to be taught throughout the elementary and middle school years. Teachers therefore need to plan activities that require groups to work together on common tasks and evaluate not only the academic product resulting from the activity, but also each individual's ability to perform the cooperative skills being practiced. Vast differences exist between the practices of merely assigning students to groups to complete tasks and assigning them to groups in order to learn skills of cooperation in addition to the assigned tasks. The latter practice results in increased achievement and improved student attitudes toward others, school, and learning (Johnson and Johnson, 1987).

Grouping students in heterogeneous groups has the added advantage of cutting down on the difference in the time it takes different groups to finish a task. Dealing with students who finish tasks long before others is a common problem most teachers face. Heterogeneous grouping diminishes this difficulty.

When forming such groups, make the procedure appear random. This can be accomplished by placing the name of each student on a separate card and arranging the cards into two stacks. Each of the two stacks is compiled by alternating low and high achievers, with the first card of one stack being a high achiever and the first card of the second stack being a low achiever. You then pick up one card from the first stack and one card from the second stack, pairing a high achiever with a low achiever. Without telling the class how you arrived at the stacks, begin turning over cards, alternating between each stack. If forming groups of two, then take one card from each of two stacks, one a high achiever, and the other a low achiever. For groups of four, take two cards from each stack. If you are forming groups of three, make three stacks, each stack alternating between high achievers, middle achievers, and low achievers.

Students will perceive such a process as random, and publicly categorizing students based on achievement is thus avoided.

Transitions

Much time can be lost in moving from one activity to the next. Effective management can considerably reduce this lost time.

When you are about to close an activity, stop the students and tell them to put away the materials on which they are currently working. If the procedures involved are complex (for example, they may need to leave their seats and return materials to some location), be sure they understand what they are to do. Check their understanding by asking some students to repeat the directions. Then review the directions for the start of the next activity. Again check for understanding. Do not allow the students to finish the one task and start the next until you know they all understand what they are to do. Then give them a signal to go ahead with the tasks.

When the students begin the procedures, monitor their progress closely. Do not do other things that could distract you from this monitoring. If possible, praise those students who are following through on the task. This will tend to encourage others. If some students do not start the tasks immediately, go to the students and make sure they do start. Monitoring the students' progress is essential if transitions are to occur smoothly and efficiently. Considerable instructional time can be gained each year through effective management of transitions.

Seatwork

When giving students individual seatwork to do, establish rules about talking and movement. Students should be instructed to raise their hands if they have any questions, but not to leave their seats. You should go to them and stand in a position so that all or most of the class is visible.

Before giving the students a signal to begin, review the task they are to accomplish. In order to ensure that all of the students can do the task, have the class run through an example together, ask a student to demonstrate the task to be accomplished, or have individual students explain the task.

Students should know they are accountable for some product as a result of the seatwork. Rather than have students merely study or read some assignment, assign some specific written report such as answering a series of questions. Then check these papers for completion and, if possible, accuracy. Grades, point rewards, or some other method of accountability should be attached to the assignment. To the extent possible, try to implement a system of rewards to encourage students to complete tasks. When necessary, you may also need to institute a system of consequences for not completing tasks. For example, if students fail to complete the assignment in the allotted time, they may be required to complete the assignment at home, after school, or during recess. Time limits should rarely be extended unless it is obvious that you have allowed too little time. Such extensions merely encourage students to expect additional time even when they may not have extended sufficient effort.

Effective teachers have been found to supervise students engaged in seatwork more closely than do ineffective teachers (Medley, 1979). Therefore, monitor the students' progress with the assignment. Praise those who start immediately. If a student delays starting the assignment, immediately go to his desk and ascertain the reasons for delay, and remain near the student until he begins the assignment. No student should be allowed not to do the task assigned. You may not need to move about the class continually as they work on the assignment, but at the very least you should keep good eye contact and immediately go to any student who raises his hand or who is not doing the assignment.

As mentioned earlier, you can introduce occasional variation in seatwork by having students do the work in heterogeneous pairs. This sharing of seatwork can be particularly valuable when students are practicing something that is presenting some difficulty for lower achieving students (Bondi, 1982). Allowing the students to talk quietly when doing shared work also allows some chance for them to talk in a constructive way rather than sit silently and passively.

Collecting and Returning Materials

Much instructional time can be lost by inefficient handling of classroom materials and assignments. Using the same procedures each day for collecting homework or other assignments will save time because explanations of procedures will be unnecessary. In self-contained classrooms a "mailbox" for each student may be set up. Students then know to place homework in the box and pick up returned homework from the box on arrival to the classroom in the morning. They may then be expected to correct any errors made in homework assignments and have their parents sign the corrected papers for return the next day. In middle school, you may use the first few minutes of class to collect and return homework assignments. If the students are completing the routine copying of the daily agenda and answering the daily question, you are provided an opportunity to talk briefly to individual students.

When passing out instructional materials at the start of activities, avoid having every student go to one central place to pick up the materials. When students are waiting with nothing to do, they will have a tendency to be disruptive. Alternatives include having one of every four or five students pick up the materials for the others; placing all materials for small groups in containers and dispensing the containers, one for each group; having the student at the front of each row pass out materials to the students in that row; or placing the materials on the students' desks before the beginning of class. The last option should be used only when you want the students to start working with the materials immediately at the start of class.

Pacing Lessons

Because student off-task behavior tends to increase during long periods of teacher-talk, you will want to enhance student on-task time by planning different kinds of activities of short duration to follow one another. Breaking the instructional time into shorter segments, each involving a different kind of activity, will help students concentrate on the class activities. For example, the class day may start with students working quietly in their seats copying the daily agenda and doing other assigned tasks. The next activity could be a review of homework requiring interactions between the teacher and the students. The next activity could involve a change of pace, such as a small group activity involving interactions among the students. The next activity could be devoted to quiet, individual assignments. No general agreement exists for the proper number, sequence, or duration of activities for variety (Sanford, 1984; Brophy, 1979), but avoid activities requiring students to be passive for extended periods. In middle school classrooms, breaking the period into three activities can usually be helpful. During the middle of the class period, students tend to let down and lose concentration, so an activity requiring student-to-student interactions working in pairs or small groups could alleviate the problem.

Homework Assignments

The three basic reasons for assigning homework are remediation, practice, and enrichment. If students have demonstrated some difficulty in learning content or skills, then remedial homework for only those students would be indicated. If the whole class is having a problem learning something, then the best approach would be to provide further classroom instruction. Enrichment and practice, on the other hand, may be appropriate for entire classes. For example, if some particularly informative television program is going to be shown after school hours, an enrichment assignment—watch and be prepared to discuss the program—may be given to the whole class.

All homework should be directly related to class lessons. Assigning homework just to keep students busy or as punishment is inappropriate. Because homework will be directly related to class lessons, and will therefore have some effect on achievement, monitoring homework assignments is necessary. Students should produce some product from the assignment; to ask them to read or study something without also requiring a product is to ensure that most students will not do the reading or studying. Younger students have not yet been taught how to study. Many will not read unless they are reading under supervision or are asked to answer questions about the reading and turn in their answers. Students should be required to turn in some product, and the product should be graded or rewarded. Providing rewards in the form of extra credit can be a more effective strategy than punishment in motivating students to complete assignments. Another recommended practice is to display homework that is well done. You will want to establish high expectations for the products that students produce, but do not set standards so stringent that some are unable to meet them.

Keep careful records of students' progress on homework, and talk with those who fail to complete homework to determine the cause. If a student does not turn in two consecutive assignments, a call or note to the parents is recommended to ensure that the student completes homework. In upper elementary and middle school grades, students can be expected to keep records of their completed assignments and grades received in a notebook. A master notebook can be kept in an easily accessible location so that if a student is uncertain about past assignments the master notebook is available. The student may go to the master notebook before or after class and check the list. A complete list of daily schedules, homework assignments, and announcements of other kinds may also be kept in the master notebook. If a child has been absent, he can check the notebook and then request any papers needed to complete missing assignments. This will considerably reduce the time spent dealing with questions about assignments.

When assigning homework, make sure students are able to do the homework by following the same processes used when giving directions for seatwork. Examples should be worked, or students should demonstrate that they understand the directions before they leave the classroom with the assignment. Forming heterogeneous pairs, and then allowing them to do homework cooperatively, can occasionally be beneficial when the task is procedurally complex (Bondi, 1982).

Reviewing homework and correcting errors the day the homework is returned can have a direct effect on achievement (Good, Grouws, and Ebmeier, 1983). Such a review is highly recommended as a regular practice (Rosenshine and Stevens, 1986) and should be done just following the opening activities for the start of school or class.

Movements Outside the Classroom

In the elementary grades students are expected to leave the classroom to go to other classes such as music, art, or physical education; for recess; to go to lunch; to go to the bathroom; and to leave for the day. Ask students to form lines when they are to leave as a group. When lining up the students, have them go to the line by rows or some other small groups. Consider the behavior you expect them to exhibit while in line and establish appropriate rules. What should they be doing with their hands and feet? Which direction should they face? Should they be talking? When a student breaks one of the established rules, have him return to his seat; when the line is completely formed and ready to move, the offending student may then go to the end of the line.

If the line is to move through the building during school hours, talking should be discouraged. One way to help students move quietly through the school is to reward a student who was well behaved the last time you moved through the school by making him the line leader. He will go at the head of the line and keep the line moving at a reasonable pace; this leaves the teacher free to follow at the end of the line and monitor the behavior of students in the line.

Ending Class or the School Day

Scheduling quiet, individual seatwork as the last activity makes bringing the class or day to a close easier. Insist on being able to dismiss the class rather than relying on the school bell for that purpose. By having the students wait to be dismissed by you, the class or day can be brought to a more orderly ending with less lost time. If all papers have not been turned in, time can be used for that purpose. If all instructional materials are not yet turned in, having the students waiting in an orderly fashion until all are turned in ensures that none will be lost. Try to make the ending of school or class periods as routine as possible.

The last minutes of a day or period should usually involve some scheduled activity. Students should not begin to put materials away until signaled by you to do so. Allow sufficient time, however, for students to return materials before the end of the day or period. Making students stay well beyond expected times may be perceived as an undeserved punishment or may cause them to miss a waiting bus. Avoid telling them they have the last few minutes to sit and relax and talk. Such a practice may be appropriate on occasion, but allowing such a practice to become the norm is undesirable.

IMPLICATIONS FOR PLANNING

A classroom is a crowded place with many activities going on simultaneously. Many students have different preferences about the things they would like to experience in the classroom. If activities are to proceed with minimal confusion, then careful planning is necessary. Anticipating problems and planning ways to avoid them is crucial. Events sometimes occur in unpredictable fashion; have alternatives in mind for such events. Careful planning ensures that activities flow smoothly.

Much of management planning occurs before students begin the school year or enter the classroom on a given day. Think all routines through before introducing them in the classroom. Plan in advance such things as starting class, moving students, dispensing and collecting materials, and student seating. Include anything in your lesson plans that will help you to use efficient management procedures. Student on-task behavior and subsequent achievement are essentially by-products of well-managed activities (Kounin, 1970; Gump, 1982).

Daily lesson plans should include detailed lists of directions to be given. If the directions are at all complex, place them on an overhead transparency or provide copies for each student. Specific questions to ask the class to check the essential steps in each set of directions should be a part of your plans. Reminders to yourself to wait until you have the attention of all students before giving directions and to monitor them when they first start the task are also helpful.

When planning activities, refer to the guidelines for management procedures referred to earlier in this chapter. Check each procedure with the guidelines in mind to assure yourself that each of your procedures meets the guidelines. In this way you will avoid many problems that might otherwise occur.

REFERENCES

Bondi, E. F. 1982. Two heads are better than one: Peer tutoring makes a difference. *Academic Therapy, 17*(4): 401–405.

Brophy, J. 1979. Teacher behavior and student learning. *Educational Leadership, 37*(1): 33–38.

Doyle, W. 1979. Making managerial decisions in classrooms. In *Classroom management,* ed. D. L. Duke. 78th Yearbook of the National Society for the Study of Education (Part 2). Chicago: The University of Chicago Press.

Doyle, W. 1980. *Classroom Management.* West Lafayette, IN: Kappa Delta Pi.

Emmer, E. T., and C. M. Evertson. 1981. Synthesis of research on classroom management. *Educational Leadership, 38:* 342–347.

Emmer, E. T., C. M. Evertson, J. P. Sanford, B. S. Clements, and M. E. Worsham. 1984. *Classroom management for secondary teachers.* Englewood Cliffs, NJ: Prentice-Hall.

Evertson, C. M., and E. T. Emmer. 1982. Effective management at the beginning of the year in junior high classes. *Journal of Educational Psychology, 74*(4): 485–498.

Evertson, C. M., E. T. Emmer, B. S. Clements, J. P. Sanford, M. E. Worsham, and E. L. Williams. 1981. *Organizing and managing the elementary school classroom.* Austin, TX: The Research and Development Center for Teacher Education.

Good, T. L., D. A. Grouws, and H. Ebmeier. 1983. *Active mathematics teaching.* New York: Longman.

Gump, P. V. 1982. School settings and their keeping. In *Helping teachers manage classrooms,* ed. D. L. Duke. Alexandria, VA: Association for Supervision and Curriculum Development.

Hoffman, J. V., and S. A. Edwards. 1986. *Reality and reform in clinical teacher education.* New York: Random House.

Johnson, D. W., and R. T. Johnson. 1987. *Learning together and alone: Cooperative, competitive, and individualistic learning.* Englewood Cliffs, NJ: Prentice-Hall.

Kounin, J. S. 1970. *Discipline and group management in classrooms.* New York: Holt, Rinehart and Winston.

Madsen, C. H., and C. K. Madsen. 1981. *Teaching discipline: A positive approach for educational development.* Boston: Allyn and Bacon.

McGarity, J. R., and D. P. Butts. 1984. The relationship among teacher classroom management, behavior, student engagement, and student achievement of middle school and high school science students of varying aptitude. *Journal of Research in Science Teaching, 21*(1): 55–62.

Medley, D. M. 1979. The effectiveness of teachers. In *Research on teaching: Concepts, findings, and implications,* ed. P. L. Peterson and H. J. Walberg. Berkeley, CA: McCutchan Publishing.

O'Leary, K. D., and S. G. O'Leary, eds. 1977. *Classroom management: The successful use of behavior modification.* Elmsland, NY: Pergamon Press.

Rosenshine, B., and R. Stevens. 1986. Teaching functions. *Handbook of research on teaching,* 3d ed., ed. M. C. Wittrock. New York: Macmillan.

Sanford, J. 1984. Science classroom management and organization. In *Observing science classrooms: Perspectives from research and practice,* ed. C. W. Anderson, AETS Yearbook. Columbus, OH: ERIC.

Walker, J. E., and T. M. Shea. 1980. *Behavior modification: A practical approach for education.* St Louis: C. V. Mosby.

CHAPTER REVIEW

Management is not an end in itself. Management serves the ultimate purpose of helping the teacher achieve goals and objectives.

1. **Classroom Management** is the management of the physical environment and the instructional materials in the classroom.
2. **Behavioral Management** is the management of the behavior of students in the classroom.

Guidelines for Utilizing Classroom Management Procedures

1. make procedures simple
2. make procedures efficient
3. avoid dead time
4. minimize student movement
5. make procedures routine
6. teach procedures
7. secure attention
8. check understanding of procedures
9. monitor progress
10. hold students accountable

Some Common Tasks That Need to be Managed

1. starting the day or class
2. student seating
3. grouping students
4. transitions
5. seatwork
6. collecting and returning materials
7. pacing lessons
8. homework assignments
9. movements outside the classroom
10. ending class or school day

EXERCISE 25

Using Positive Reinforcement

This exercise provides some experience in identifying positive reinforcement that could be effective in motivating students to complete homework assignments, bring needed materials to class, and be in their seats at the start of the class.

Directions. Briefly describe one positive reinforcement strategy you could use to encourage students to

1. complete and turn in homework assignments on time
2. bring needed materials to class
3. be in their seats at the start of the class period

Do **not** use any of the examples already discussed in the textbook.

OBSERVATION EXERCISE 26

A Study of Classroom Management

This exercise provides an opportunity to observe a teacher managing a classroom and then to analyze those observations to gain valuable insights.

Directions. Record the following observations, and then answer the corresponding questions related to each.

1. What does the teacher do or say during the first minute to begin the class at the start of the day in an elementary school or the beginning of the period in a middle school?
   a. In what ways was this behavior effective?
   b. In what ways, if any, could this behavior be changed in order to start the class more effectively?

2. What are the students doing during the first five minutes of class or the school day? Record the number of students who are quietly off task during the first five minutes. Record the number of disruptions.
   a. What could the teacher have done differently to minimize the number of students who were off task or disruptive?
   b. If the students were all on task during this period, what did the teacher do that caused them to be on task?

3. Record the length of time needed for the class to make the transition from the end of one activity to the productive beginning of the next.
   a. If you feel the time was held to a minimum, what steps did the teacher take, and what did the teacher do at each of these steps, that resulted in the time being held to a minimum?
   b. If you feel that the time was excessive, what changes in what the teacher said or did could have resulted in a more efficient use of the time?

Discipline 8

When beginning teachers are asked to identify problems they experience in the classroom, discipline ranks the highest of the 24 most frequently mentioned problems (Veenman, 1984). Novices may easily perceive the management of student behavior as an end in itself, the end being self-survival. Effective management is not, however, an end in itself. A teacher does not manage a classroom solely to control students, but to make it possible to use activities that will motivate students to learn and thereby promote the achievement of goals and objectives. When students are off task, little learning can occur. Some degree of control is necessary. Whether or not students learn while on task is determined by other factors such as appropriate choice of objectives and activities to accomplish those objectives. Effective management is thus necessary, but not sufficient, for learning to occur.

Another goal of any effective behavioral management system is helping children develop self-discipline. The use of the system, therefore, is not only for control, but for educating students to recognize and accept behaviors more likely to help them function more effectively in the classroom and elsewhere as learners and as social beings.

All teachers are expected to provide a classroom environment conducive to learning. All students should have an equal opportunity to learn, and no student should be allowed to deprive others of their right to learn. A teacher is responsible for ensuring that the rights of all students are preserved. This requires some reasonable level of orderliness. Effective teachers are found to have a learning environment that is orderly and psychologically supportive (Medley, 1979).

Perceiving teaching as the process of transferring knowledge of content and developing basic skills only is too narrow. Teaching also involves helping students learn ways of behaving that make them more effective human beings, which includes learning how to effectively conduct oneself in group settings. Fundamentally, individuals are not born humane; they are not born, for example, with communication and socialization skills. These skills are learned behaviors, and it is one of your responsibilities as a teacher to teach them. Good discipline, or encouraging appropriate student behavior, should not be perceived as a punitive process, but rather as one of education. You should be no more upset about a child demonstrating inappropriate behavior than you are about a child who is unable to answer a question correctly. Both behaviors identify opportunities for instruction and, hence, learning.

When thinking of educating students about behavior, effective teachers tend to make certain assumptions:

1. All students are capable of learning and have a desire to learn, if we teach meaningful things that are consistent with their levels of ability.

2. All students, with few exceptions, can be taught to stay on task and not disrupt lessons.

3. Almost all student misbehavior that is allowed to continue is the result of something the teacher has done or has failed to do.

CAUSES OF PUPIL MISBEHAVIOR

Teacher Causes

Most student misbehavior results from things that teachers do or do not do. Inappropriate behaviors by teachers cause or allow students to wander off task or exhibit disruptive behavior (Emmer, Evertson, Sanford, Clements, and Worsham, 1984; Wayson and Pinnell, 1982; Grantham and Harris, 1976; Kounin, 1970). Any system of behavioral management will be ineffective if the teacher assumes that the students are the cause of misbehavior (Wayson and Pinnell, 1982). Such a perception on the part of a teacher likely will result in the teacher dealing with symptoms of misbehavior rather than causes. If basic causes of misbehavior are not altered, then misbehavior is likely to persist. When teachers recognize that they are part of the problem, improved discipline results (Grantham and Harris, 1976).

Beginning teachers, and some experienced teachers as well, tend to feel anxiety and fear from lack of confidence in their ability to control a situation. Teachers will then do things to reduce the anxiety and fear associated with this insecurity by using inappropriate behaviors. For example, teachers may:

- □ turn their back on the class
- □ maintain poor eye contact with the class
- □ ignore problems in the hope that the problems will go away
- □ threaten students
- □ bluff when they don't know what to do
- □ lack body and voice expression
- □ behave like a dictator
- □ reject student comments when they are unexpected
- □ restrict interaction with certain students
- □ "hide" behind the desk and not move about the classroom
- □ adopt verbal, facial, and body mannerisms
- □ use sarcasm or be defensive

Some of these behaviors seem to be subconscious attempts to put distance between the teacher and the students in order to relieve teacher anxiety. Others are attempts to intimidate or embarrass students in order to control them. None of these behaviors relieves anxiety, nor do they control students; they are counterproductive (Howell and Howell, 1979; Kounin, 1970) and, in fact, may contribute to student misbehavior.

Other things that teachers do may also cause problems. Ineffective instructional practices are some of the major causes of disruptive behavior. These include, but are not limited to:

- □ using poor eliciting patterns
- □ being unconcerned about student motivation
- □ teaching too much content in the time available
- □ not using students' names
- □ being unconcerned about student learning during a lesson
- □ overusing presentation (lecture) or other methods that require a great deal of pupil passivity
- □ praising or criticizing some students more than others
- □ utilizing inadequate classroom management
- □ failing to provide a variety of activities
- □ failing to enforce rules consistently
- □ teaching skills and content beyond the students' ability levels
- □ teaching skills and content that seem irrelevant to students

Notice that most of these behaviors represent an unconcern for student motivation and learning. When teachers become unconcerned about student motivation they tend to adopt such ineffective teaching behaviors. These behaviors result in students feeling no need to be involved in lessons. Disruptive behavior is likely to result.

These lists of inappropriate teacher behaviors are not exhaustive. Teachers may also demonstrate many other behaviors that cause problems for themselves and children. The important fact is that much misbehavior results from what teachers do or fail to do. If you want your classroom to be a pleasant place where learning can and does occur, then the place to start making needed improvements is with yourself. You are not merely a passive victim of anything students decide to do in your classroom. You have control. If you recognize that fact, you are more likely to do something about it. This recognition is the first step in effective behavioral management.

Student Causes

Not all inappropriate student behavior results from things teachers do or fail to do. Although continued misbehavior is due solely to the teacher, students do try to misbehave for a variety of reasons, some caused by the teacher and others not, including:

- □ an attempt to escape the reality of failure (by misbehaving, some students believe that they can create an excuse for failure such as "the teacher doesn't like me")
- □ the need for attention from the teacher and/or peers
- □ retaliation because of some earlier embarrassment from the teacher or peers
- □ excitement due to some external event
- □ boredom over tasks that are too easy

□ frustration from attempting tasks that are too difficult

□ frustration or uncertainty from not understanding directions for doing a task

□ being emotionally disturbed

□ lack of interest in the ongoing activity

PREVENTING DISRUPTIVE BEHAVIOR

If teachers can recognize some of the causes of misbehavior that result from their instructional practices, then they can do the following kinds of things that will reduce the amount of student-initiated misbehavior:

1. **Keep good eye contact with the entire class.** Walking around the perimeter of the classroom allows you to keep visual contact with all students. When talking to small groups or individuals, looking up occasionally at the entire class can help you maintain visual contact. Once students are aware that you maintain visual contact, they will tend to stay on task. Looking at them will also allow you to become aware when individuals might be having difficulties with a task. A prompt response will reduce the tendency of students to turn to others for help.

2. **Do not threaten or bluff students.** Threatening students tends to raise the level of tension in a classroom by creating feelings of resentment. When you attempt to bluff students by using threats, the students will usually test you (Kounin, 1970).

3. **Treat students with respect and avoid arbitrariness.** Expecting the same behavior from all of the students by responding consistently creates a sense of fairness and ensures that a teacher will not be arbitrary. Respecting students implies that a teacher does not embarrass them, talk to them sarcastically, and in other ways treat them as less than important human beings.

4. **Accept sincere student comments even when they are unexpected.** Students frequently say things that are unexpected. Most times these comments or questions are sincerely stated. In their innocence, students may misinterpret something you have said. Accepting these unexpected comments reduces the risk that a child will be embarrassed by the teacher. Embarrassment can lead students to try to recover their self-esteem at the expense of the teacher.

5. **Interact equally with all students.** When you fail to call on a student for an extended period of time, that student may begin to feel left out, which may result in the student losing interest in the activity or feeling that you are unconcerned about her. Such feelings can cause a student to do something to get the attention of peers or you.

6. **Move around the classroom, particularly in the vicinity of students becoming restless.** When you change the proximity between you and a student, the student will tend to become more attentive. This increases the student's tendency to stay on task. By moving about the room, you are also more likely to become aware when students are having difficulty or becoming bored with tasks. When in close

proximity, you have more opportunities to interact personally with students, which can be useful in developing feelings of mutual respect and making disruptive behavior less likely.

7. **Use an eliciting pattern of accepting no responses from students not called on to respond (Q—N—R).** When you allow students to call out questions or answers without being called on by you to respond, you are allowing them to talk without permission. This practice increases the incidence of further call outs and unsolicited student talking. Following the pattern of requiring students to raise their hands and wait to respond until called on to do so reduces the tendency for misbehavior. This way also allows you to use their names more frequently, which makes interactions more personal and communicates the fact that you recognize them as individuals. This helps develop better relationships with students and results in more feelings of respect.

8. **Plan the start of lessons with student motivation in mind.** How you start a lesson can have a dramatic impact on the willingness of students to be motivated to learn and not disrupt the lesson. When doing a set induction, or anticipatory set, try to place the lesson in an interesting context. Students will tend to stay on task more if the lesson to follow has some interest to them related to things outside the school setting.

9. **Use students' names.** When you use students' names you are letting them know that you recognize them as individuals. If you do not use their names they may feel that you are unaware of them and don't care about them; those feelings may cause them to go off task more easily.

10. **Do not extend activities past the students' attention span.** Students can maintain attention to a task only as long as interest is high. Stopping activities when interest begins to wane can reduce the tendency of students to misbehave out of boredom.

11. **Give clear directions and plan the management of transitions with great care.** When directions are not clear to students, confusion and misbehavior may result when they are then told to do the task directed. Transitions are more complicated to manage than other situations; therefore, the directions must be planned with care. Smooth transition will help you keep instructional momentum with fewer disruptions (Kounin, 1970).

12. **Monitor the level of difficulty for individual and small group activities.** When tasks are too easily completed, students tend to become bored. Boredom is then relieved through misbehavior. On the other hand, when students are unable to complete tasks because they are too difficult, they may become frustrated. Feelings of frustration may result in withdrawal and other off-task behavior. At the first signs of boredom or frustration, respond by stopping the activity or determining the source of frustration and then doing something about it.

13. **Praise good behavior.** Children who are in Piaget's preoperational stage of development tend to accept praise for good behavior in a literal and concrete way. They do not analyze such praise to see if it makes sense. Therefore, praising students for good behavior in the primary grades can result in reduced misbehavior. When

students reach the concrete operational stage sometime during the elementary grades they are more likely to reduce misbehavior when praise is specific, credible, and provides information about the value of that behavior in terms of the effect it might have on classmates rather than the teacher (Brophy, 1981). Whenever possible use appropriate praise rather than criticism to help students stay on task.

While many other suggestions could be listed to help you avoid the causes of student misbehavior, those just listed and in the preceding chapter, "Classroom Organization and Management," have resulted in significant differences for many teachers (Emmer, et al., 1984; Sanford, 1984; Evertson and Emmer, 1982; Kounin, 1970). Obviously, not all teachers experiencing problems with misbehavior need to change their behavior in the same ways to solve their problems. You need to analyze, or have someone else help you to analyze, what you are doing or not doing that contributes to behavior problems. Such an analysis can then be used to identify and change particular behaviors in ways likely to prevent the problems.

A SYSTEM OF BEHAVIORAL MANAGEMENT

In addition to using instructional behaviors that reduce misbehavior in the classroom, teachers will also need to use a system of behavioral management. The purpose of such a system is to allow teachers to minimize the effect of misbehavior on the learning of students when it occurs (Duke and Meckel, 1984). Many systems of behavioral management exist, and no attempt will be made to discuss all of them (Alschuler, 1980; Canter, 1979; Gordon and Burch, 1974; Dreikurs, Grunwald and Pepper, 1971; Glasser, 1969; Glasser, 1965). Each has its advantages and disadvantages. Each is built on sets of philosophical premises about learners and teaching that differ somewhat from one system to the next. The system introduced here is composed of the best elements of several different systems put together into what, it is hoped, is a coherent whole.

When adopting a behavioral management system, carefully consider the plan you decide to adopt. First, choose a plan consistent with your level of skill. Second, adopt a complete systematic plan that deals with more than the immediate symptoms and does not treat every incidence of misbehavior as a unique event. That is, you will want a system that enables you to deal with misbehavior as a matter of education. Ineffective teachers have been found to simply react to problems as they arise. When teachers use a planned, systematic approach, they find it easier to deal with problems more consistently and with less emotion. Teachers who are effective in behavioral management have been found to use such systematic long-term strategies (Brophy, 1982; Medley, 1979).

Also recognize that having a plan to deal with disruptive behavior before it occurs is important (Duke and Meckel, 1984). Having no plan ensures continued difficulty with misbehavior in your classroom. Your classroom likely would be constantly under tension. Considerable time would be spent in calling down students, venting anger, threatening students, and other nonproductive activities. Under such conditions, your classroom would not be a pleasant place in which to teach or learn.

Regardless of the system you choose, a rare student may not respond to the system as expected. Some students may be emotionally disturbed or incorrigible and need trained counselors or psychologists. Dealing with them may be beyond the expertise of most teachers. These students are the exception and are not found in most classroom.

The system of behavioral management being recommended here is a total system, and as such, the essential elements of the total system must be used to achieve the desired results—a pleasant classroom for both the teacher and students and one devoid of misbehavior. Consider this system as you would a car: a car works fine when all of its parts are working; if one or more parts are removed or modified by someone not understanding the system, then the car may run poorly or not at all. Some parts may be removed or modified by a person familiar with cars, and the car may run as well or better. But the likelihood of a person who knows little about cars being able to make such modifications successfully is slim. The same is true of any system of behavioral management. If you remove or modify some part of the system, you could inadvertently cause it to work poorly or not at all. This plan has been used successfully by teachers, so if it doesn't work for you, make sure you have not modified an essential part of the system that should have been left alone.

Establishing Rules

Before students can be comfortable in a classroom, the classroom must have predictability; that is, students need to know what you are going to expect from them. Effective teachers have been found to be those who establish and consistently enforce reasonable rules (Emmer, et al., 1984; Charles, 1981; Gnagney, 1981; Bloom, 1980; Clarizio, 1980; O'Leary and O'Leary, 1977). When students walk into your classroom, they know that rules defining acceptable behavior will be used, but they will not know exactly what you will expect. If rules are reasonable and consistently enforced, students will have no difficulty in accepting them and, in fact, usually prefer that such rules be established (Fisher and Fraser, 1983).

If rules are reasonable, every student in the classroom should be expected to abide by them. Some teachers have the mistaken notion that some students (e.g., minorities or special pupils) cannot be expected to abide by rules. For any system of behavioral management to be effective, all students must abide by the same set of rules.

Students will accept rules more easily if they understand the reasons for them and if they have had some role in defining them. Starting with acceptable principles on which rules are based removes arbitrariness from the process and makes acceptance more likely. When discussing these principles, be businesslike, but do not project feelings of hostility. Remember, teaching effective behavior is the same as teaching content. Both are educational processes, and neither requires feelings of anger or hostility.

Although the specific wording will vary depending on the grade level, the basic principles on which classroom rules could be based include:

1. Every student has the right to learn as well as the responsibility not to deprive others of their right to learn.

2. Every student has the right to a safe environment as well as the responsibility not to deprive others of a safe environment.

3. Every student has the right to an environment of mutual respect of persons and property as well as the responsibility not to deprive others of an environment of mutual respect of persons and property.

4. Every student is accountable for his or her actions.

Next, these principles must be translated into language appropriate for the grade level in which they will be used. Some general rules of behavior corresponding to these principles then need to be developed by you or in conjunction with the students. The principles, along with their corresponding rules, then are discussed with the students. Statements of rules should be presented in a positive form rather than as "do nots." The number of general rules should be relatively short (Brophy and Evertson, 1976). **Include no rules unless you actually expect students to follow them, the rules are enforceable, and you are willing to do whatever it takes to enforce them consistently**. Stating rules you do not intend to enforce will result in the loss of your credibility with students (Smith and Smith, 1978).

Discuss illustrations of specific behaviors reflecting the rules with the students. The number of rules, and the number of specific examples that illustrate rules, may need to vary with grade level. When first introducing the rules, include only obvious examples or examples of things the students will be expected to do immediately. Other examples may then be introduced as the need arises.

Recognize that the specific rules may vary with the nature of the activities being used. For some activities you will want the students to talk freely; for others you will want highly controlled student-talk. For example, during whole-class instruction you would want students to raise their hands and wait to be called on to respond, but during small group activities you would want them to talk freely but only to students in the same group. While you are working with one group of students and others are to work independently, you would not want those working independently to come to you with questions or get out of their seats for other reasons. Students in learning centers would be expected to work quietly and put away materials when finished and clean up the area without being told. Students will understand all of these variations of rules if they learn them in relationship to general principles.

Some general rules that would logically follow from these principles would include:

1. Students will come to class prepared to learn.
   Specific Rules:
   a. Students will come to class with only the materials necessary for that class. This includes having notebooks, pencils, paper, books, and assignments with

them. They will not bring things to class that are likely to distract them from the work of the class.

   b. Students will participate in classroom activities by responding to teacher questions and following directions.

2. Pupils will not distract others from learning.

  Specific Rules:

   a. Students will remain in their seats unless given permission to move about.

   b. Students will refrain from talking when this would distract others.

   c. Students will be in their seats and silent when the bell rings to start class.

   d. Students will make no distracting noises during lessons.

   e. When sharing ideas during a small group activity, students will talk in low tones and will talk only to members of their group.

3. Students will respect others and their property.

  Specific Rules:

   a. Students will raise their hands and wait to be called on to respond and will not interrupt others who are talking.

   b. Students will ask permission to use the property of others, and they will return such property in good condition.

   c. When an activity has been completed, the students will clean up the area in which they worked.

   d. Students will not deface or deliberately damage school property or the property of others.

   e. Students will refrain from insults and name calling.

   f. Students will not copy others' work.

4. Students will respect the safety of others.

   a. Students will refrain from striking others.

   b. Students will throw nothing in the classroom.

   c. Students will handle classroom materials in a way that will not threaten the safety of others.

In upper elementary and middle school classrooms, once the rules are identified and discussed, pass out a list of the principles and the rules and have them signed by the students (and, maybe, by the parents) and returned. Giving the students a copy of the rules is probably unnecessary at the primary level. Regardless of the level, posting the general rules in a conspicuous place in the classroom is advised.

Students need to be informed of the procedures you intend to use when there are infractions of the rules. Each part of the procedures to be followed needs to be explained fully. This explanation will help you respond more consistently and simply when you deal with infractions. Responding more consistently will help you maintain credibility and save valuable instructional time.

Procedures for Responding to Misbehavior

Your responses to disruptive behavior should be based on the following premises:

   1. At the first indication of misbehavior on the first day of class and every day following, the teacher must respond. **To wait any period of time (even a few**

seconds or minutes) will significantly diminish the effectiveness of this system, or most other systems (Sanford, 1984; Smith and Smith, 1978; Brophy and Evertson, 1976). When misbehavior first begins, you must do whatever is necessary to ensure that the misbehavior stops and does not begin again. Waiting any significant period of time to respond gives that student permission to misbehave. Later attempts to stop the misbehavior are then perceived by the students as unfair and will cause resentment.

2.   When indicating to students that you recognize their misbehavior and that they are to stop, interact with individuals. Rarely, if ever, should you direct comments to the whole class when attempting to stop misbehavior. You will on occasion ask for the attention of the class, but if some students do not respond, then warn individuals to stop, not the class. Admonishing and preaching to the whole class is ineffective.

3.   Ignore no misbehavior during the first few weeks with a new class. Later, after students have accepted your rules, then you may overlook minor infractions when you know that the infraction is not likely to continue. Allow minor violations only after you have established your predictability.

4.   When considering your response to student misbehavior, you should expect the same behaviors from all students. If your limits on behavior are reasonable, then expect all students to operate within these limits.

5.   You should respond initially in the least overt way necessary to cause the behavior to cease.

6.   With each continued infraction of the rules by an individual, your response should escalate in strength until the behavior is stopped.

7.   Do not send a student to anyone else to solve problems of misbehavior in your classroom unless **absolutely** necessary. To do so tells the student that you are either unable or unwilling to deal with students who do not follow your rules. Both messages are detrimental to your future ability to deal with that student's misbehavior. Teachers effective in behavioral management follow this practice (Brophy, 1982).

A Plan for Responding to Disruptions

The following plan can be followed step by step, but, with practice, you can and should modify the plan to fit your circumstances. If you change the specifics of any part of the plan to suit your situation, be sure that any change is consistent with the basic premises already introduced. The sequence of your responses to misbehavior must make clear that continued misbehavior is unacceptable and that any individual who persists in such behavior cannot be allowed to continue to deprive others of their rights.

Step 1—first disruption by an individual.
The response will be a low key, unobtrusive nonverbal response such as a frown, a stern look, a movement placing the teacher in close proximity to the student, or some simple verbal response such as mentioning the student's name. In the primary grades, at the first sign that a student is beginning to disrupt, praising those who are on task nearby that student sometimes will stop the misbehavior. If this fails, then some other response directed toward the specific student is needed. Moving near the student or asking her a question about the lesson may then help her to get more involved in the

lesson and discourage further attempts at misbehavior. Whatever the signal you plan to use to let students know they are noticed should be made clear and then used consistently. You will have no need to think about the nature of your response and will likely be able to be more consistent in signaling students. This first step may be difficult for the novice teacher to manage. If that is the case, then starting with the second step may be more effective.

Step 2—second disruption (regardless of the kind) by the same individual.

Call the person by name and remind her that she is not abiding by the rules. Tell her to stop the misbehavior. Demonstrate no hostility, but be calm and insistent. Widespread agreement exists on keeping your responses as mild as possible (Weber, Crawford, Roff, and Robinson, 1983; Howell and Howell, 1979; Soar and Soar, 1979; Tanner, 1978; O'Leary and O'Leary, 1977; and Harris, 1972). Again, use a consistent signal to let students know that they are to stop the misbehavior. A simple signal such as, "Alice, you are being warned," if used consistently, would be sufficient. Avoid any lengthy response, and do not attempt to explain your response. If a student questions this warning, move directly to the next step calling for the removal of the student without discussion. Be sure that students know before the situation arises that questioning a warning will result in their removal. This should not be presented as a threat, but merely as a reasonable step to ensure that misbehavior does not interrupt the flow of lessons. Taking time during lessons for disruptive students deprives others of the right to learn. If you have been inconsistent in enforcing rules, and many students are attempting to misbehave, then you may need to start with warnings rather than unobtrusive signals until you establish your consistency.

Step 3—third offense by the same individual.

Send the person to a seat set off from the rest of the class; that is, remove the student from the ongoing activity. (The seat should be placed in the rear of the classroom, or in some other location not in view of other students, but in view of the teacher.) Again, show no hostility, but be calmly resolved. Anger or hostility on your part may merely breed a hostile, defiant reaction from the student (Howell and Howell, 1979; Kounin, 1970). Use the same signal each time this response is used regardless of the infraction or the particular student committing the infraction. This will allow you to use less emotion when responding and will make it easier to respond more consistently. Removal of a student who persists in misbehavior after being asked to stop has widespread support as an effective strategy (Charles, 1981; Gnagney, 1981; Brodinsky, 1980; Curwin and Mendler, 1980; Wolfgang and Glickman, 1980).

The student removed from the activity takes nothing back to the seat with her and does nothing while seated there. The student also may not take part in the ongoing activity. This removal from the activity is a direct consequence of the misbehavior. Since the student has persisted in depriving others of their right to learn, she cannot continue as a participating member of the group. The student will remain in the seat for a predetermined period of time (e.g., 10 minutes) or until the teacher directs that she may return to the ongoing activity.

A student who needs to be removed from an activity in this fashion should be required to see you for a conference after school that day or before school the next day. This conference is an important part of helping the student modify her behavior in more effective ways (Jones, 1980; Tanner, 1978; Wallen and Wallen, 1978; Gordon and Burch, 1974; Glasser, 1965).

When students break the rules on one day, but not to the point of needing to be removed, and then do the same thing the next day and the next, you may need to modify this system. The usual modification would include telling the student after about the third day to stop, and then adding that you would like to see her after school or after that class. Arrange a conference time and then conduct a conference either after school or before school the next day. Students should not be allowed to continue misbehavior without experiencing some consequence.

Description of the Conference

The purpose of this conference is to help the student come to recognize more appropriate behaviors when in the classroom setting. Students must learn ways of accomplishing their purposes without depriving others of their right to learn. This learning can be accomplished by having the student think about and respond to a series of questions. If the student responds, "I don't know," or remains silent after the question is asked, wait until the student does respond. Explain that the purpose of the conference is to "help you solve your problem; if I answer the questions for you, you will not benefit from the conference." Tell the student you are willing to wait until she is able to answer your question, and then wait silently. Approach the conference as an opportunity to help the student with her difficulties. Feelings of hostility or defensiveness on your part are inappropriate and should be avoided. A typical conference will follow the steps listed. Modify the suggested wording depending on the grade level and maturity of the student.

Step 1—Pupil Identifies the Misbehavior

"What (not why) were you doing that you were not supposed to do that resulted in this conference?"

This question is not to provide the student with the opportunity to make excuses but to help the student recognize her misbehavior. No excuses for depriving others of their right to learn are acceptable.

Step 2—Pupil Identifies the Consequences

"What harmful effects did your behavior have on the other students and yourself?"

The purpose of this question is to help the student associate her action with the effects of that action—the consequences of that misbehavior. The student needs to recognize that there were consequences other than, or in addition to, those she may have intended. She needs to decide the ways her behavior was detrimental to herself or others. The student needs to see that her acts can have detrimental effects on others if continued.

Step 3—Student Formulates a Plan

"What could you do the next class period to prevent yourself from doing the same thing, but still achieve your purposes?"

The student should be encouraged to identify several possible alternative plans to accomplish her purposes without misbehaving. If the student is reluctant, then be patient and wait until she can formulate reasonable alternatives. Telling the student what she should do would defeat the purpose of the conference. Do not accept an answer such as, "I'll try harder." The student must be specific about what she will do to prevent the misbehavior and still accomplish her purpose.

Step 4—Secure a Commitment to a Plan

"Which one of the alternatives you suggested would be the one you will try during the next class period?"

Do not accept a vague commitment such as, "I don't know which one to try, but maybe the first idea will be OK." Have the student give reasons why she thinks a particular plan will work. Encourage her to make a definite commitment to actually follow through on one of the plans discussed.

Step 5—Consequences for Not Following the Plan

"What should the consequences be if you do not follow your plan in the next class period?"

Do not let the student choose additional academic work as a consequence. Avoid punishment. Removal from the activity for a longer duration than the time for this last infraction, changing her seating, staying after school and helping the teacher or helping another student with an assignment, or sending a note or calling the parents could be some possible options. The consequence must be more severe than the initial consequence. Also, the consequence must escalate for each succeeding conference if more than one conference is necessary. If this is the second conference and parents have not yet been called, they should be called following this conference. If a student persists in misbehavior, then a parent conference should be held.

Step 6—Offer Help

"Is their anything I can do to help you follow your plan or accomplish your purposes?"

This is a teaching/learning situation, and should not be punitive in nature. You are here to help the student with her problem. You should sincerely want to help. Also recognize that you may be part of the cause of the student's misbehavior. To that extent, you will want to modify your practices in order to help that student and others remain on task.

On the surface, having conferences may seem to be a burden on the teacher if many students need them. Conferences would indeed be a burden if that were the case. If, on the other hand, the teacher begins this plan on the very first day of classes, and is consistent in following the plan, then there will very quickly be little or no need for conferences. Students will have ceased their misbehavior. In fact, in most classes, the conferences are unnecessary after the first two or three weeks.

When first implementing your plan, explain the steps of this conference to the students. The reasons for each step, along with examples of appropriate and inappropriate responses, should be discussed. The time necessary to teach the students the steps of this conference will pay off when the time comes to actually conduct a conference. If they understand each step, then the process will be of short duration. Your willingness to invest this amount of time in explaining the conference will convince the students that you intend to follow through on acts of misbehavior, thus discouraging misbehavior.

Appropriate Consequences

Providing incentives for appropriate behavior is a more effective use of consequences than is trying to stop misbehavior after it occurs through the use of punishments or deterrents. Students as a class or individually should be encouraged to maintain appropriate behavior. Such incentives as award certificates, stick-on smiling faces, or "warm fuzzies," posting an honor roll, allowing a student or small group to sit with the teacher at lunch, calling parents or sending a note with favorable reports, and labeled praise all can be effective in helping students maintain good behavior.

When students misbehave, the consequences should be reasonable and closely related to the infraction. Some examples of appropriate consequences for infractions of rules are:

1. removing a student from an activity for disrupting the work of others
2. having a student come in for a conference after she has been removed from an activity for continued disruptions
3. calling a parent or having the parents come in for a conference when a student has failed to comply with an agreement arrived at during a conference
4. having a student return to her seat and then take a place at the end of the line for being disruptive while a line is being formed in the classroom
5. keeping a student in from recess or having her come after school to finish incomplete work.

Whatever consequences you choose to influence the students' behavior, apply the consequences at the time of, or soon after, the misbehavior. Students must be aware of the relationship between the misbehavior and consequence. Consequences should be related to the effects the student's misbehavior had on herself and others. An infraction should never be interpreted as a personal offense against the teacher, nor should consequences be used as a power struggle between the teacher and students.

Carry out consequences in a consistent fashion; that is, every infraction by every student must result in a consequence consistent with the infraction. Students see everything a teacher does or does not do; if you fail to stop the misbehavior of one, others see this as permission to misbehave in the same way. When you stop one student for an infraction and not another for the same infraction, students perceive this as showing favoritism. When you do not stop misbehavior, you are giving permission to misbehave; later if you stop the same misbehavior, students see this as being arbitrary and unfair. If you do not stop misbehavior until things get almost out of hand and then get angry with the students for misbehaving, they feel resentment. Consistently enforcing your rules and implementing appropriate consequences is not being "mean and nasty," as many beginning teachers think; actually, you are being fair, kind, and helpful.

When reinforcing classroom behavior try to keep a positive climate. When it becomes necessary to stop misbehavior, follow that response as soon as possible with some praise directed toward the same student for good behavior. Look for students who are doing things right and then let them know. The more encouragement can replace negatives in your classroom, the more pleasant the classroom climate becomes.

PREVENTING AND RESPONDING TO OTHER INFRACTIONS OF RULES

When students do not turn in work on time, do not arrive to class on time, do not bring necessary materials to class, or in some other way fail to abide by class rules, then this behavior should also be modified. The most effective method for motivating students to complete assignments, bring materials to class, and so on, is to use a positive reinforcement (Charles, 1981; Gnagney, 1981; Madsen and Madsen, 1981; Walker and Shea, 1980). For example, you could check the students at the start of the class for bringing necessary materials. Tell them that such unannounced checking will occur. All students who bring the required material for that day will get an "A" for effort. A similar strategy for homework also could be applied, but check all homework. With a little imagination, you undoubtedly could come up with some other forms of positive reinforcement for these and similar tasks.

When reward systems still do not result in students meeting responsibilities, then other methods need to be used to deal with infractions. The same basic premises apply to these infractions as to those used in dealing with disruptive behavior; that is, you should respond immediately to each infraction and escalate your response with repeated infractions. For example, if the student did not turn in homework on time, then you may choose to give her a reminder, have her complete the work, and turn it in the next day without penalty. If the student failed to bring necessary materials to class, then give her a reminder and give her the materials. With the first infraction, little or no penalty needs to be levied. A reminder to the student should suffice.

The student may have legitimate reasons for certain infractions. For example, if the student needed to care for a sick mother in a one-parent family, the student may have been unable to complete the assignment. Penalizing a student by expecting the impossible is not reasonable. When dealing with infractions over which the student may not have complete control, use some compassion and understanding.

If a student has not turned in homework for a second time, then the student may be asked to stay after school (assuming she did not come to school by bus) to complete the work and the parents notified. If a student arrives late to class for a second time, then the teacher may have a seat set off from the rest to which the student can go without disrupting others. If the student has failed to bring needed materials for a second time, then she may not take part in the activity. These are but a few examples of escalating responses to continued infractions.

SPECIAL PROBLEMS

When teaching children in the early years of elementary school, some special problems arise that are not considered as misbehavior, but still can be disruptive, such as crying or wetting. Some forms of misbehavior in the primary grades may be rather extreme and involve biting, hitting, rolling on the floor, and other evidences of violent anger. Responses to such special situations may fall outside the usual responses to misbehavior.

Wetting

Wetting is one of the most embarrassing things that can happen to children in school. Since children are already going to be embarrassed, try not to add to their embarrassment by calling attention to the accident any more than necessary. Having a small washcloth and towel for such incidents can reduce the reaction time. Tell the child privately to go to the washroom and clean up. At the same time, contact the office and have someone from home bring a change of clothes if possible. If this seems to be a continuing problem for an individual, you might have the parents send a change of clothes that can be kept at the school for use when needed.

Arrange a quiet time alone with the student and try to determine the reason for the accident. Some students may be afraid or be embarrassed to ask permission to go to the bathroom. Having regularly scheduled times for all to go to the bathroom may eliminate that reason for the problem. Do not be overly sympathetic to the child, but do respond considerately. Showing too much concern and attention may increase the incidence of such behavior in students who are in need of attention.

Crying

Some young children may begin crying in your classroom without apparent cause. They may have been teased by a fellow student, be fearful of some activity, or merely be afraid of the classroom setting. When crying occurs, be understanding but avoid reinforcing crying behavior by excessive attention or sympathy. Approach the child and give her permission to cry by saying something such as, "It's all right to cry, but would you stop for just a moment and tell me what is causing you to cry. After you have told me you can then go on and cry." Usually, you can talk a child into telling you what is wrong. Often, when children have had a chance to tell the problem, many will stop crying. If they continue to cry after telling you the problem, then instruct them to cry quietly and when finished crying to go wash up and then come join the class. If the child continues to cry in a disruptive fashion, someone may need to be summoned from the office to remove the child. In extreme cases, a parent may need to be contacted and asked to come to the school.

Assigning pairs of students to act as "buddies" at the start of the year in kindergarten and first grade can be effective in helping children overcome their fears and reduce incidences of crying. Each student is to work with his or her buddy and also move about the building and go to recess together. In this fashion no child has the sense of being alone.

Tantrums

Sometimes a pupil may suddenly get very angry and seem to explode. When this occurs, remove the child from the classroom or isolate the child within the classroom. Allow the child time to calm down, but do not allow the child to continue to disrupt the rest of the class. If the child cannot be calmed enough to allow the class activity to continue, then she may need to be removed from the classroom. After the child has calmed down, talk quietly to the child about the cause of the outburst. Help the child realize that alternative ways of dealing with frustration and anger are available that do not disrupt the rest of the class. Help the child recognize that violent disruptive behavior is unacceptable and that there are alternatives.

IMPLICATIONS FOR PLANNING

Plan to have a note pad and pencil available during lessons to jot down the names of students who receive warnings or who have been told to come in for a conference. This will enable you to follow through more consistently when working with individuals.

Obviously, the careful planning and management of instruction can contribute significantly to the reduction of disruptive behavior. When planning lessons, try to anticipate when students may likely become disruptive and then plan what you will do to avoid the disruptions. For example, if you know that you are going to be asking a series of questions and you want the students to raise their hands and wait to be called on, then plan to remind them of the rule at the start of the activity. This will remind the students to follow the rule.

A continuing concern for motivating students at the beginning of activities can also reduce the incidences of misbehavior. Plan set inductions carefully with this in mind. Motivating students involves much more than just the beginnings of lessons, however. When planning lessons, think of the things teachers can do to improve motivation, and plan accordingly. Such careful thought can do much to reduce off-task behavior.

DEALING WITH MISBEHAVIOR: SOME REMINDERS

1.   Misbehavior, or attempted misbehavior, is an opportunity to teach students more effective behavior. Don't perceive misbehavior as a personal threat—it is not.

2.   Misbehavior can be a signal to you for some possible needed change in your teaching. Examine the reasons why students might be disruptive to determine what you are doing that may be causing students to misbehave, and change them accordingly.

3.   Be calm and clinical. You are essentially involved in teaching, so treat misbehavior the same way you would treat the teaching of content. If students lack some knowledge or skills, then that lack is an opportunity to help them learn new knowledge or skills.

4.   Do not ignore misbehavior when beginning your work with a new class. Respond to each act of misbehavior. Ignoring misbehavior can be interpreted by students to mean you were not sincere when you set your rules for behavior, you don't care how students behave, or you are afraid to deal with the misbehavior. Students expect you to respond. When you don't, you lose credibility. Later, when your limits are well established and students no longer attempt to misbehave, then some incidents of misbehavior can be ignored without consequence. However, you will always need to respond to any significant infractions.

5.   React to individuals; that is, do not respond to misbehavior by directing your remarks to the whole class. However, if several members of the class frequently attempt to misbehave, then it may be necessary to discuss your rules with the whole class. The class may need to be reminded of the rules, the reasons for each, and the responses you intend to make when there is misbehavior.

6.   Avoid being vindictive about student misbehavior.

7.   Avoid feeling hurt by such behavior and communicating to them that you feel hurt. Students are not to behave for your benefit but for their own benefit. If they misbehave, it is not a threat to you, but it is detrimental to the students and to others.

8.   Do not send a student to anyone else to solve problems of misbehavior. To do so tells the student that you are either unable or unwilling to deal with the misbehavior. Both messages are detrimental to your future ability to deal with that student's misbehavior. However, recognize that on some rare occasions when a student becomes totally belligerent and will not respond to your directions, the principal or assistant principal responsible for discipline in the building may need to be called on.

9.   Avoid feelings of anger or displays of anger. Both are indications to students that their misbehavior is a problem to you. Signs of anger on your part could cause

students to react in anger or encourage them to further acts of misbehavior whenever they feel a need to upset you.

10. The basic purpose of responding to misbehavior is to help students recognize when they are depriving others of their rights, to recognize more effective ways of letting the teacher know when something is bothering them, and to accept more effective ways of behaving in order to accomplish their purposes. Remember, students are misbehaving for some purpose; try to help them learn more effective ways of accomplishing that purpose.

11. Never use additional work in the subject being taught as a punishment. Doing so tells the student that learning your subject is something repulsive or undesirable.

12. Never punish a whole class. Mass punishment is basically unfair because not all students are responsible for the misbehavior that occurs. If misbehavior reaches the point where large numbers of students are involved, then you have been grossly deficient in your behavioral management.

13. Consequences students experience from misbehavior should be logically related to the infraction; that is, the consequences chosen in dealing with misbehavior should be directed toward helping students discontinue the misbehavior and adopt more effective behaviors. Punishment for the sake of retaliation has no place in this process.

14. Students are responsible for their behavior in the classroom as well as the consequences of that behavior. You are responsible for protecting the rights of all of the students to learn. You have no option but to respond when students try to violate other's rights. Students are responsible for avoiding behavior that violates others' rights, and they are responsible for anything that you are called on to do to prevent that violation from occurring.

15. If an individual decides not to learn, a teacher can do little other than try to encourage that student to learn. Whether a teacher should ignore nondisruptive, off-task behavior depends in part on the maturity of the student as well as the possible effect such behavior could have on other students if allowed to continue. Usually, if a student is quietly off task, a teacher should at least have a conference with the student to find out if the teacher can be of help. If a student persists in not getting involved in the classroom activities, then a parent conference could be helpful. Ultimately, such a student should either be removed from the classroom or separated in some way from the other students.

REFERENCES

Alschuler, A. S. 1980. *School discipline: A socially literate solution.* New York: McGraw-Hill.

Bloom, R. B. 1980. Teachers and students in conflict: The CREED approach. *Phi Delta Kappan, 61:* 624–626.

Brodinsky, B. 1980. *Student discipline: Problems and solutions.* Arlington, VA: American Association of School Administrators.

Brophy, J. and C. M. Evertson. 1976. *Learning from teaching: A developmental perspective.* Boston: Allyn and Bacon.

Brophy, J. 1981. A functional analysis of praise. *Review of Educational Research, 51*: 5–12.

Brophy, J. 1982. Supplemental group management techniques. In *Helping teachers manage classrooms,* ed. D. L. Duke. Alexandria, VA: Association for Supervision and Curriculum Development.

Canter, L. 1979. *Assertive discipline.* Los Angeles: Canter and Associates.

Charles, C. M. 1981. *Building classroom discipline.* New York: John Wiley and Sons.

Clarizio, H. F. 1980. *Toward positive classroom discipline.* 2d ed. New York: John Wiley & Sons.

Curwin, R. L. and A. N. Mendler. 1980. *The discipline book: A complete guide to school and classroom management.* Reston, VA: Reston Publishing.

Dreikurs, R., B. Grunwald, and F. Pepper. 1971. *Maintaining sanity in the classroom: Illustrated teaching techniques.* New York: Harper & Row.

Duke, D. L. and A. M. Meckel. 1984. *Teachers guide to classroom management.* New York: Random House.

Emmer, E. T., C. M. Evertson, J. P. Sanford, B. S. Clements, and M. E. Worsham. 1984. *Classroom management for secondary teachers.* Englewood Cliffs, NJ: Prentice-Hall.

Evertson, C. M. and E. T. Emmer. 1982. Effective management at the beginning of the year in junior high classes. *Journal of Educational Psychology, 74*(4): 485–498.

Fisher, D. L. and B. J. Fraser. 1983. A comparison of actual and preferred classroom environments as perceived by science teachers and students. *Journal of Research in Science Teaching, 20*(1): 55–61.

Glasser, W. 1965. *Reality therapy.* New York: Harper & Row.

Glasser, W. 1969. *Schools without failure.* New York: Harper & Row.

Gnagney, W. J. 1981. *Motivating classroom discipline.* New York: Macmillan Co.

Gordon, T. and N. Burch. 1974. *Teacher effectiveness training.* New York: Peter H. Wyden Publisher.

Grantham, M. L. and C. S. Harris. 1976. A faculty trains itself to improve student discipline. *Phi Delta Kappan, 57*: 661–664.

Harris, M. B., ed. 1972. *Classroom uses of behavior modification.* Columbus, OH: Merrill.

Howell, R. G. and P. L. Howell. 1980. *Discipline in the classroom: Solving the teaching puzzle.* Reston, VA: Reston Publishing.

Jones, V. F. 1980. *Adolescents with behavioral problems: Strategies for teaching, counseling, and parent involvement.* Boston: Allyn and Bacon.

Kounin, J. S. 1970. *Discipline and group management in classrooms.* New York: Holt, Rinehart and Winston.

Madsen, C. H. and C. K. Madsen. 1981. *Teaching discipline: A positive approach for educational development.* Boston: Allyn and Bacon.

Medley, D. M. 1979. The effectiveness of teachers. *Research on teaching: Concepts, findings, and implications,* ed. P. L. Peterson and H. J. Walberg. Berkeley, CA: McCutchan Publishing.

O'Leary, K. D., and S. G. O'Leary, eds. 1977. *Classroom management: The successful use of behavior modification.* Elmsland, NY: Pergamon Press.

Sanford, J. 1984. Science classroom management and organization. In *Observing science classrooms: Perspectives from research and practice,* ed. C. W. Anderson, AETS Yearbook. Columbus, OH: ERIC.

Smith, D. and J. Smith. 1978. *Child management: A program for parents and teachers.* Champaign, IL: Research Press.

Soar, R. S. and R. M. Soar. 1979. Emotional climate and management. In *Research on teaching: Concepts, findings, and implications,* eds. P. L. Peterson and H. J. Walberg. Berkeley, CA: McCutchan Publishing.

Tanner, L. N. 1978. *Classroom discipline for effective teaching and learning.* New York: Holt, Rinehart and Winston.

Veenman, S. 1984. Perceived problems of beginning teachers. *Review of Educational Research, 54*(2): 143–178.

Walker, J. E. and T. M. Shea. 1980. *Behavior modification: A practical approach for educators.* St. Louis, MO: C. V. Mosby.

Wallen, C. J. and L. L. Wallen. 1978. *Effective classroom management.* Boston: Allyn and Bacon.

Wayson, W. W. and G. S. Pinnell. 1982. Creating a living curriculum for teaching self-discipline. In *Helping teachers manage classrooms,* ed. D. L. Duke. Alexandria, VA: Association for Supervision and Curriculum Development.

Weber, W. A., J. Crawford, L. A. Roff, and C. Robinson. 1983. *Classroom management: Reviews of the teacher education and research literature.* Princeton, NJ: Educational Testing Service.

Wolfgang, C. H. and C. D. Glickman. 1980. *Solving discipline problems: Strategies for classroom teachers.* Boston: Allyn and Bacon.

CHAPTER REVIEW

Assumptions on Which Effective Behavioral Management Depends

1. All students are capable of learning and have the desire to learn when taught appropriate content with effective methodology.
2. Students can be taught to stay on task.
3. Most student misbehavior that is allowed to continue is the result of something the teacher has done or failed to do.

Some Reasons Students Attempt to Misbehave

1. attempt to escape the reality of failure
2. need for attention from the teacher or peers
3. retaliation for earlier embarrassment
4. excitement due to some external event
5. boredom over tasks that are too easy
6. frustration over tasks that are too difficult
7. frustration or uncertainty from not understanding directions for doing the task

8. being emotionally disturbed
9. lack of interest in the ongoing activity

Things a Teacher Can Do to Prevent Disruptive Behavior

1. keeping good eye contact with the entire class
2. not threatening or bluffing
3. treating students with respect and avoiding arbitrariness
4. accepting sincere student comments even when unexpected
5. interacting equally with all students
6. moving around the classroom
7. using an eliciting pattern of accepting no responses from those not called on to respond
8. planning the start of lessons with student motivation in mind
9. using students' names
10. not extending activities past the attention span of students
11. giving clear directions and planning the management of transitions with great care
12. monitoring the level of difficulty for individual and small group activities
13. praising good behavior

Principles on Which to Establish Rules

1. Every student has the right to learn and the responsibility not to deprive others of that right.
2. Every student has the right to a safe environment and the responsibility not to deprive others of that right.
3. Every student has the right to an environment of mutual respect of persons and property and the responsibility not to deprive others of that right.
4. Every student is accountable for his or her actions.

Reasonable General Rules

1. Students will come to class prepared to learn.
2. Students will not distract others from learning.
3. Students will respect others and their property.
4. Students will respect the safety of others.

Guidelines for Rules

1. Include no rules unless you are willing to enforce them.
2. State rules in a positive manner if possible.
3. Keep the list of rules short and to the point.

4. Each rule should be based on valid and reasonable principles.

5. Be clear on the specific behaviors you feel would violate the rules and be able to communicate these to the students in a consistent fashion.

6. Expect every student to abide by the rules.

Guidelines for Dealing with Misbehavior

1. Respond to all misbehavior immediately, beginning the first day of class and every day following until rules are firmly established.

2. Ignore no misbehavior until rules are firmly established.

3. Expect the same behaviors from all students.

4. The initial response to misbehavior should be in the least overt way necessary to stop the behavior.

5. With each continued infraction of the rules by an individual, escalate your response until the misbehavior ceases.

6. Do not send a student to anyone else to solve problems of misbehavior unless absolutely necessary.

Guidelines for the Conference on Misbehavior

1. student identifies misbehavior

2. student identifies the consequences to self and others

3. student formulates a plan

4. student makes a commitment to a plan

5. student identifies consequences for not following the plan

6. offer to help the student achieve the plan

Some Reminders

1. Misbehavior is an opportunity to teach more effective behavior.

2. Be calm and clinical when dealing with misbehavior.

3. Never use additional work in the subject being taught as a punishment.

4. Never punish a whole class.

OBSERVATION EXERCISE 27

On-task/Off-task Student Behavior

This exercise provides some experience in observing and analyzing the behavior of students in the classroom. You will study the relationship of the students' behavior to the things the teacher is doing or not doing. From this exercise you should learn some methods of systematically observing student behavior in addition to what you learn about on-task and off-task behavior.

Directions

1. Draw a blank seating chart, providing small blank squares approximately 1 to 2 inches square at the location where each child is seated.
2. Sit in a location to the side and front that will allow you to see the faces of all the students.
3. You will now look at a student for approximately 2 to 3 seconds. At the end of that time you will record one of a set of possible symbols on the seating chart that will represent what the student was doing. The symbols are:

   E—engaged or on task (If in doubt, record an E.)
   OQ—off task, but quiet
   OT—off task, talking
   OM—off task, moving from seat

   If the teacher corrects and off-task behavior, circle the symbol. This will allow you later to determine the number of off-task events that went corrected or uncorrected.
4. You now will look at each student in this same fashion using some kind of systematic order until you have viewed each student in the class, after which you will repeat the same pattern until you have collected data for a period of 15–20 minutes.
5. Along with this data, record the nature of the activity being conducted and any other comments that will help you respond to the questions listed below.
6. Answer the following questions:

   a. Calculate the percent of time the students were
      (1) on task
      (2) talking
      (3) quietly off task
      (4) moving about the classroom

   To do this, count all of the on-task and off-task symbols, count the number of on-task symbols, count each of the off-task symbols. Then use the following formula:

   $$\text{Percent} = \frac{\text{\# of symbols of the behavior} \times 100}{\text{total number of all symbols}}$$

   For example, percentage of off-task talking would be calculated as follows:

   $$\frac{20 \text{ off-task talking symbols} \times 100}{80 \text{ total symbols}} = \frac{2000}{80} = 25\%$$

b. What fraction of the off-task talking and off-task movement was corrected by the teacher? Did the teacher ask some students to stop their disruptive behavior and not others? If so, what observable effects did this have?

c. What kinds of things seemed to be causing the off-task behavior? Were students in particular parts of the class engaged in off-task behavior?

d. What things could the teacher have done or not done to reduce the amount of off-task behavior?

e. If there was little or no off-task behavior, what did the teacher do or not do that seemed to limit off-task behavior?

f. In what ways were you comfortable with the teacher's behavioral management? In what ways were you uncomfortable with his behavioral management?

PART FIVE

EVALUATING STUDENT LEARNING

Ultimately, the teacher is accountable for student learning. Growth in student learning is viewed by parents and educators as an important criterion by which to judge the success of schools. Teachers are constantly assessing learning not only for purposes of accountability, but also to help them make instructional decisions that will promote learning. Teachers also assess student learning to evaluate the performance of students in order to communicate their progress to parents and other interested parties.

The chapters in this part of the text focus on the measurement of learning and the interpretation of these measurements. Better measurements and interpretations should result in more valid evaluations and, hence, better instructional decisions, better communication with parents, and, ultimately, better student learning.

Assessment **9**

One of the recurring themes in this book is that effective teachers are active decision makers. Teachers are constantly assessing the instructional situation and shaping their actions to make their teaching more effective and their students' learning more efficient. **Assessment is the systematic collection of data that reveal information about students' abilities, capacities, needs, and interests.** Good assessment is the basis for good decision making. All of the assessments done by a teacher should contribute in some real and direct way to decisions made about students.

Evaluation is the use of assessment information to make decisions. All decision making involves the process of assessing a situation before making a decision. For example, a parent will observe a child's behavior during a meal to decide if the child should be given more food based on certain values about how much a child should eat. Some parents overfeed their children because they believe that a chubby baby is a healthy baby. Some parents may leave their children hungry because they believe that children are more active when not overfed, and they value an active child. The same kind of process of decision making, or evaluation, is continually used by a teacher.

When making decisions prior to instruction (**preactive decision making**), the teacher's assessment of the instructional situation is considerate and systematic. During this planning phase, teachers use assessment information to guide decisions about the course and content of future instruction. On the other hand, when teachers make decisions during instruction (**interactive decision making**), the assessment of the instructional situation tends to be more fluid and dynamic. During instruction the teacher relies on subtle cues such as student body language or the responses of one or two "key" students as a means of assessing how well a particular lesson is going. The skills of assessment used in interactive decision making are best nurtured and developed through hands-on practice and coaching by example. This chapter focuses on the development of the skills of assessment that are conducive to good preactive decision making.

TYPES OF EVALUATION

Making instructional decisions that have direct and immediate effects on the learner being assessed may be called **formative evaluation.** Some examples of uses for formative evaluation follow.

- ☐ to assess students' abilities in order to decide on grouping for or pacing the instruction
- ☐ to assess the appropriate level of instructional materials to use with an individual child, such as a particular book in a basal reader system
- ☐ to assess at the end of a lesson or unit to determine the areas that may need reteaching or which students are now ready to move on

□ to preassess before beginning a unit of instruction to determine if any areas might need more attention than others, or even which areas may be skipped altogether

□ to assess, perhaps with a specialist, whether any students are in need of some special instructional services, materials, or programs.

When a teacher collects data on students that will have little or no effect on subsequent instruction provided those students being assessed, then the evaluation may be referred to as **summative evaluation.** An example of this is using assessment to assign final grades at the end of grading periods. These grades are the basis for communication about learning between the teacher and the students, their parents, and other professionals. Grading is such an important function in teaching that an entire chapter in this text is devoted to the subject (see chapter 10, "Grading"). Teachers or specialists may use summative evaluation to determine whether students are to graduate with a diploma or continue participation in school programs such as a bilingual program.

Formative and summative evaluations are also used in the process of designing and developing curriculum materials. When commercial publishers or funded projects develop curriculum materials, this development goes through stages. During the early stages of development, the materials may be written and then used with students to determine what changes need to be made to ensure the materials' effectiveness. These materials may also be reviewed by other educators and their feedback used to improve the materials. The evaluation done during the development of these materials is a type of formative evaluation.

Once materials have been developed, they may then be evaluated to determine if students achieve the goals for which the materials were designed. The evaluation following the development of the materials is a type of summative evaluation. Teachers who design their own materials are continually engaged in formative evaluation of those materials; seldom does a teacher get involved in summative evaluation of materials. If a teacher is to ever determine the ultimate worth of materials she has prepared, then she must clearly identify the goals she wants to achieve with the materials, and then find out if the materials help students accomplish those goals.

ASSESSMENT PROCEDURES

The key to successful assessment is the same as with any other aspect of teaching: you must be thoughtful, adaptive, flexible, and, as often as not, creative. Assessment in education is too often approached so formally and rigidly or so haphazardly and unthinkingly as to make it ill-suited for productive decision making.

A common and unfortunate misconception is to think of assessment as synonymous with testing. Testing is merely one method of assessment. Although in this chapter on assessment considerable attention is given to testing, recognize that other

Some assessment requires written responses.

important means for "the systematic collection of data that reveal information about students' abilities, capacities, needs, and interests" are commonly used. This chapter also introduces you to the use of interviews, inventories, and observations as means of assessment in addition to the use of tests.

QUALITY OF TESTS

A test is designed to sample a student's performance under controlled conditions in order to permit inferences about his general level of knowledge and skills. A test is a means to gather data systematically and assign a numerical value to the performance. **Measurement** is the assignment of a numerical value to assessment. For example, when we use a yardstick to determine how much carpet will be needed to cover a floor, we count the number of standard measurements that fit along each dimension of the room, and record numerical values. Measuring a room would not be considered testing. Measuring is not synonymous with testing, and testing is only one form of measuring. All tests, however, involve measurement because all tests yield a score of some type that represents the student's performance.

At least three important criteria are used to evaluate the quality and appropriateness of tests: efficiency, reliability, and validity. These three criteria are also important in other areas of assessment, but their importance may be easier to appreciate in relation to testing.

Efficiency

Efficiency in testing is related to the least-effort principle; that is, a test should be as simple and as easy to administer as possible without sacrificing reliability or validity. Efficiency in testing typically requires that we sample behavior in a way that is representative of the student's overall skill or knowledge, without sampling more than needed. For example, if you are interested in assessing spelling skills, you would not create a test that included every word introduced during an entire school year. Rather, you would develop a list of words that is long enough to be representative of the words introduced, but short enough to be easily administered. The function of assessment is to provide enough data to make an appropriate decision. No more data than necessary to make the decision needs to be collected when giving tests.

Reliability

In theory, a student taking the same test repeatedly should perform at a constant level on the test as long as no intervening learning occurs. Such a test would measure consistently. This is what is meant by **reliability.** When the domain is fairly small and well defined, it is easy to design a test with a high degree of reliability. For example, if students are being assessed on their knowledge of simple addition facts, a test could easily be constructed of items of representative difficulty. If you had only a few items of addition facts on the test, you could erroneously interpret good luck or carelessness as evidence of ability and skill. You could not have confidence that a score was accurately measuring the students' overall knowledge of addition facts. By increasing the number of items on the test, you could be increasingly confident that the test was measuring accurately the students' overall knowledge of addition facts. You eventually reach a point, however, when the increased reliability may be beyond that which you need to make a decision and so you are asking children to perform tasks unnecessarily. You may also make the test so long that student fatigue may become a factor, thus lowering reliability. A test should be no longer than needed to be reliable.

Examining a situation taken from a nonacademic area may help to clarify this relationship between reliability and efficiency. Imagine that you had the goal of assessing children's running ability in short sprints and you wanted to measure (i.e., assign a numerical value) their skill. You could simply take your class outside and have them take turns timing each other running a one-hundred-yard dash. This sounds efficient, but how reliable are the measurements (i.e., the times) taken? In other words, if they ran the same distance again, how likely is it that their time would be the same? To answer this question, you must consider all of the possible factors that may have influenced the children's times that are not related to their ability to run the one-hundred-yard dash. For example, how accurate and precise are the stopwatches being used? How skilled are the students who did the timing? How might the weather or wind have affected performance? What effect would the changing surface of the track with use have on the times? What effect would the time of day have on the abilities of different students to run? Some ways of increasing the reliability of this test of running ability come to mind from such an analysis: You could have only one well-trained individual time each student, and each could be timed at several different times over a period of several days. Testing could be restricted to those days with no wind, or testing could be done inside under controlled climatic conditions. The addition of each of these modifications would be done at the cost of reduced efficiency. No right or wrong answers exist here, but a direction is suggested by considering the decisions that will be made as a result of the assessment. If the decision you are facing is the selection of Olympic participants, then you probably want as much reliability as possible. This would require extensive testing. If you are simply searching to identify skill levels in order to group for a week-long series of lessons on sprinting, then lower levels of reliability could be tolerated, and the original measurement may well be adequate.

Validity

Validity in testing refers to the degree to which a test measures what is intended to be measured. Good decisions must be based on valid tests. Validity is at the heart of good testing, and it is much more elusive than reliability. Developing a reliable test is easy compared with developing a valid one. For example, assume that you wanted to develop a test to measure student knowledge of letter names. You randomly sample eight letters, print them on cards, and then show the card to the students on a one-to-one basis. Is this a reliable and valid test? You could measure the reliability of the test by comparing the scores (i.e., the number correct) on the even numbered items with the equivalent scores on the odd numbered items. If the scores are similar for each student, then the test has demonstrated one kind of reliability. You could also test the students again on a different day and compare each student's score for consistency from one test to the other. You could create alternative forms of the test by randomly selecting a different set of eight letters for each of two tests. You could then administer these two forms on different days, and compare each individual's scores. If reliability levels are low, you would increase the number of letter names on each test until you are satisfied with the test's reliability.

Having established a satisfactory reliability, you now need to ask, Is this test valid? How confident are you that this test measures a student's overall ability in recognizing letter names? One way to determine this would be to find another widely recognized test that purports to measure the same thing and administer both tests to your students.

If the relative performance of each student is similar on both tests (i.e., those who score high on your test also score high on the recognized test, etc.), then you have some evidence that the two tests are measuring the same thing. This kind of validity is referred to as **concurrent validity.**

Another indication of validity available to most teachers is that of **construct validity,** which indicates the degree to which your test conforms to some theoretical relationship you might create. For example, assuming that the students who score high on a reading readiness test would also score high on your letter recognition test would be reasonable. You would then administer both tests and compare the relative performances of your students on the two tests. If the performances of individuals in relationship to the other students is similar, then your test has construct validity.

The examples presented here are fairly simple, and the issues, straightforward. When it comes to measuring more complex knowledge and skills such as mathematics problem solving, demonstrating reliability is not much more difficult, in theory. Demonstrating validity, however, is much more problematic. Reliable tests can be easily constructed, and for this reason, consumers of tests must examine the validity of tests carefully before making judgments on their value. Many examples of tests with high reliability and low validity can be envisioned. For example, suppose that I were to argue that a good measure of intelligence is the ability to tap rapidly on a computer touch screen with an index finger. I suspect that I could demonstrate good reliability on such a task, but would you accept the test as a valid measure of intelligence? Probably not. The relationship between the two characteristics is questionable. The same distinction can be seen in the earlier example with sprinting ability. In that example high reliability could be achieved. What if we wanted to argue that the sprinting test was a test of physical coordination? We could show the test to be invalid by demonstrating that someone who scored high on the sprinting test also scored low on a test that purports to measure coordination.

Efficiency, reliability, and validity are three important characteristics of tests you must consider when assessing students' abilities. Any test that is weak in any of these areas will hamper your success in making good instructional decisions.

TYPES OF TESTS

Let us now consider some basic distinctions in the types of tests used in elementary and middle school grades. These distinctions will become the basis for an in-depth discussion of the role of testing in a comprehensive assessment plan.

Informal tests are constructed, administered, and interpreted by the classroom teacher. The teacher typically has some objectives that she wants to assess through the use of such a test. **Formal** tests are standardized; that is, the procedures for administering and scoring them and interpreting the scores of individual students are prescribed by the publisher of the test.

Qualitative tests are designed to provide specific information on the skills and strategies over which the student has control, or how much or how little knowledge about a topic he possesses. For example, these tests are used to measure mastery learning when diagnosing students during individualized instruction to determine when a student is ready for the next instructional experience. Such a test would measure minimal prerequisite understandings required for the next step in the instruction. Most, if not all, students who were successful in completing the prior lesson would be successful on such a test.

Quantitative tests are designed to provide a score that can be used to assign a student a rank or relative ability level. An example of such a test would be an achievement test administered for the purpose of ranking students and then assigning grades to those rankings.

The resulting four types of tests—formal quantitative, formal qualitative, informal quantitative, and informal qualitative—are used with regularity by teachers. Some examples of each of these kinds of tests will be introduced to illustrate their particular uses and strengths.

Formal Qualitative Tests

Formal qualitative tests are often referred to as **criterion-referenced** tests, because a student's performance on such a test is judged not in terms of how well he scored in relation to other students, but rather in relation to a criterion level of performance (i.e., mastery) on a representative task. Mastery performance on criterion-referenced assessments is often set at a 75 percent or higher success rate.

Elementary and middle school teachers are involved on a regular basis with criterion-referenced tests. These tests are often used in conjunction with commercially prepared instructional materials. Most basal reader systems, for example, provide the teacher with criterion-referenced "end-of-the-unit" or "end-of-book" tests that are used to determine whether students have acquired mastery over the skills that have been taught. The results of criterion-referenced tests can be used to make decisions about special attention for students who have not responded as expected to instruction.

Student performance on criterion-referenced tests is fairly easy to interpret: mastery is either demonstrated or it isn't. On a criterion-referenced test, a passing score is what matters; the degree of success above or failure below that level is relatively unimportant.

Other commonly used formal qualitative tests are statewide minimum competency tests that assess performance in such basic skill areas as reading, writing, and mathematics. These tests are used by states to gain some measure of statewide, district, and individual school success. The results of these tests are of little use to the teacher as the basis for diagnostic teaching because the scores are typically not even reported at the student level or in a timely manner. States and districts use such tests primarily to evaluate the quality of instructional programs and to plan program revisions. Reporting of scores to districts and schools typically takes the form of the percentage of students at a particular grade level who achieve mastery levels in each specific skill area covered in the test.

Formal Quantitative Tests

You have had frequent experience with formal quantitative tests throughout your school experiences. These tests, commonly called **norm-referenced** tests, are produced by commercial test makers. The name comes from the fact that the tests are carefully developed through many trial administrations and are then given to a representative sample of the population, called the **norming sample,** that would be expected to use the test. Thus, the performance of a third-grade student taking a norm-referenced reading test is interpreted by comparing the student's performance with that of the representative group of third graders who took the test as part of the developmental process.

Some norm-referenced tests, reading and mathematics achievement tests, for example, are subject specific. Other norm-referenced tests cover several subject areas and are merely called **standardized achievement tests** (e.g., California Achievement Test or CAT, Iowa Test of Basic Skills or ITBS, and the Metropolitan).

Several different types of scores are typically given for each student on each domain tested. Sometimes, scores of each part of the test are combined into a composite score. Commercial tests come with a manual to guide the teacher in the appropriate use of the test and the correct interpretation of the test scores to ensure better decision making when using the results. Scores commonly provided by these tests include raw scores, percentile scores, and grade level equivalent scores.

Raw Scores

Raw scores typically represent the number of items to which a student responds correctly on sections of a test or on the total test. A raw score is not directly interpretable; however, by comparing the student's total raw score to the total number of items on the test, the appropriateness of the test can be determined. Sometimes a student will "top out" a test; that is, he gets most, if not all, of the items correct. This is not a good test for that student because it does not offer items at a level of difficulty that could be used for reliably determining his actual achievement level. Similarly, a test that allows a student to receive a raw score close to chance level (e.g., with four-choice multiple-choice items, a chance score should lead to 25 percent correct responses) is also not a reliable measure of this student's ability. The difficulty level of the items on this test are too great for the student to respond in a way to demonstrate his actual ability. An achievement test should have an average score of approximately 60 percent for the students to whom it is being administered. If a test average varies significantly from that percent, then you should not consider using it for measuring achievement.

Percentile Scores

A percentile score is calculated by comparing a student's raw score to the scores of those in the norming sample. The percentile score represents the percentage of students in the norming sample that the student outperformed. A percentile score of 55 percent means that the student did better than 55 percent of the students to whom he is being compared in the norming sample.

Often, commercial test publishers will report more than one percentile score by comparing the individual's score to different norming samples. Publishers will distinguish these percentile scores in relation to national, state, or local norms that form the bases for the comparison. In schools serving students from an economically disadvantaged area of the country, for example, the percentile score for local norms (i.e., scores compared to a group of students from the same area) may be considerably higher than the percentile score for the national norm.

One problem in interpreting percentile scores lies with interpreting those scores that fall in the middle range of scores. On a well-designed norm-referenced test, most of the students tend to score near the middle. As the raw scores move out to the extremes, the frequency of students earning a particular score decreases. This means that a very small difference in a student's raw score in the middle ranges can result in a fairly dramatic increase in the percentile score. A substantial change in a raw score at the extremes may result in a small change of the percentile score. For example, imagine that two students of comparable ability take a mathematics achievement test in which the sample achieved an average score of 44. One of the two scores a 43, and the other, a 45. This hardly represents a significant difference in their abilities, and yet the student who scored 45 will have a considerably higher percentile score than the one who scored 43, because a large number of students in the norming sample would have a raw score of 44. Percentile scores, therefore, must be interpreted with caution.

Recently, test developers have begun to report what are called **Normal Curve Equivalent Scores** (NCEs). These scores look like and can be interpreted very much like percentile scores, but they have been statistically adjusted (transformed) to minimize the effects of changes in raw scores on percentile changes. A difference in one or two points in an NCE score can be interpreted the same whether it occurs near the middle or at one of the extremes of the distribution of scores.

Grade-Equivalent Scores

Grade-equivalent scores attempt to represent the level at which a student is achieving based on a comparison of his performance with that of a sample of students at the grade level for which the test was designed. These scores are difficult to interpret because they involve a statistical extrapolation from the raw score. They are not direct measures of the score being reported.

For example, a second grade student who receives a grade-equivalent score of 5.3 is said to have a grade-equivalent score of fifth grade, third month. Does this mean that this student is scoring at the same level as a typical fifth grader in the third month of school? Does this mean that he is achieving at the fifth grade level? The answer to both questions is no. The second grade test is quite different from the fifth grade test. The second grader who scores high on the second grade test is operating at the upper limits of that test, which may represent a high level of achievement for a second grader, but it does not mean that he knows as much or can perform at the same level as fifth graders. To find out if this second grader can perform at the fifth grade level, he would need to take a fifth grade achievement test.

Because such scores are so widely misinterpreted by teachers, parents, and others, most educators have come to the conclusion that such scores should not be used at all. As a result, you may or may not be called on to interpret such scores.

Informal Quantitative Tests

Teacher-made tests that yield a score or rating of a student's performance on a particular task are called informal quantitative tests. In reading programs, for example, wide use is made of the assessment technique commonly referred to as an informal reading inventory (IRI). This type of assessment has many purposes, one of the most important of which is the information it provides about the student's reading ability in relation to the difficulty level of the text. IRIs are often used to determine the placement of students in a basal reading series. To do this, the teacher identifies one passage for the student to read aloud and another to read silently. The teacher monitors oral accuracy and the rate, and then assesses comprehension through questioning. In this process errors are merely counted, and a numerical value determined by adding up the errors made. Based on the student's performance, the teacher decides whether the text is too easy (at the child's independent level), too difficult (at the child's frustration level), or optimal (at the child's instructional level). The test may be repeated with other samples of text from the same level or different levels to ensure greater reliability of results.

Teachers may also use informal quantitative tests to determine the child's achievement on the content or skills studied during a grading period as one of many criteria to be used in determining grades. The purpose of such tests, called **teacher-made achievement tests,** is to assign a number that reflects the level of learning that was achieved. In this case, the teacher is not concerned with precisely determining achievement of basic objectives for diagnostic purposes as would be done with a criterion-referenced test.

Informal quantitative tests typically are composed of items that sample what the child has learned compared with other pupils or a predetermined standard. No attempt is made to test everything that a child is expected to have learned. The overall intent is to get a score in a reliable and efficient manner that indicates what a child has learned.

Informal Qualitative Tests

While informal quantitative tests such as an IRI provide useful information, a teacher can learn far more through qualitative assessment about what a student knows or does not know, or can or cannot do. One dramatic illustration of the rich information that can be gained from qualitative tests has been the use of what is termed "miscue analysis in reading assessment" (Goodman, Watson, and Burke, 1987). The principle focus for miscue analysis is, as with IRI, oral reading. In miscue analysis though, an effort is made to capture the way(s) in which the learner is demonstrating control over reading through strategic processes; in an IRI, errors are simply counted. Patterns in miscues are analyzed and interpreted for what they reveal about the reader's reliance on graphophonic, syntactic and semantic cues in contextual reading.

Just as with informal quantitative tests, teachers use informal qualitative tests to assess cognitive understandings. When administering qualitative tests, the teacher is concerned with the particular things the student has or has not mastered. Such information is valuable as part of preassessment and may be useful when making instructional decisions about whether students have learned those things they need to know in order to move on to the next step in a learning sequence.

CONSTRUCTING INFORMAL COGNITIVE TESTS

The process of constructing tests to determine cognitive understandings tends to be complex and subject to error. Learning the fundamentals of constructing teacher-made quantitative (achievement) tests and qualitative (criterion-referenced) tests can help reduce the frequency of measurement errors, and, thus, lead to more effective decision making. Tests used to measure complex skills may best be learned in the context of the methods courses in reading, language arts, and mathematics, so will not be treated here.

The initial task in test construction is choosing or writing the test items that will measure the instructional objectives. Developing the objectives and the test items concurrently is advisable. Regardless of whether the objectives are determined prior to or concurrent with the test items, once the objectives are identified, the items on a test are specified. Both the objectives and the resultant test items should also be concerned with significant learning, because many students perceive tests as measuring important things to be learned. This perception dictates what students attempt to learn (Medley, 1979).

If a test measures cognitive learnings, the next task in constructing the test will be to group together like kinds of items; that is, short essay questions will be placed together, multiple-choice questions will be placed together, and so on. Do not mix different kinds of test items on a test. On a test measuring cognitive understandings, you will use several different kinds of items, including essay and multiple-choice. Avoid constructing a test composed solely of true-false, matching, and completion items. Such tests place a premium on low-level understanding, and encourage students to do that kind of learning (Medley, 1979).

Once items are grouped, provide directions for students to follow in answering each kind of question. For example, students need to be told when answering an essay question to confine their answer to the space provided or to write their answer on a separate answer sheet. In the case of multiple-choice questions, they need to be told that there is only one best answer and to circle their choice, place an "X" through the answer, or respond on an answer sheet in some fashion. They must be told what to do, how to do it, and where to do it. Nothing is left for their interpretation. In the early elementary grades, keep the complexity of tests and the accompanying directions as simple as possible.

When using achievement tests in the upper elementary and middle school grades, inform the students of the relative values of items. For example, if a test is composed of true-false and essay items, and the essay items have twice the value of the true-false items, then the relative values should be indicated either in the directions at the beginning of the test or in the directions for each item type. If different essay questions will be assigned different values, then indicate the value of each essay question at the left of the number for each item.

In middle school grades a teacher can expect to administer tests to a large number of students. Ease of scoring then becomes an important consideration. Many middle schools now have computer scoring available for use by teachers. The answer sheets provided with the computer system will dictate the nature of your answer sheets. If such a system is not available, you will need to design your own answer sheets. If most or all of your test is composed of objective test items, or if you are going to be scoring a large number or very lengthy tests, you should consider the use of a separate answer sheet. For most objective items, scoring a separate answer sheet is easier than scoring answers spread all over the test itself. Finally, the test should have overall directions listed at the beginning of the test. For example, you should provide a place for the student's name and direct the student to place his name in that space before proceeding to answer questions on the examination. If the test has a time limit, you should state this.

SAMPLE FORMAT FOR TESTS

The formats of tests can vary, depending on several factors, including:

1. Will a separate answer sheet be used?
2. Will students need to confine answers of essay questions to the space provided, or will they respond on a separate sheet of paper?
3. Will different kinds of items be scored differently?

Figures 9–1 and 9–2 illustrate a commonly used arrangement that involves the use of a separate answer sheet.

In upper elementary and middle school grades, students can begin to be taught to take tests with answer sheets. When an answer sheet is first used with a group of students, explain to them the care needed in recording answers. Students may even be provided some practice using answer sheets on short examinations before using answer sheets on major tests. When first using separate answer sheets, students may make many errors in recording answers, even with this practice. To minimize these errors, use the same format for all examinations so that the examination procedures become routine. Routine formats, learned through practice, may help reduce the errors students make when recording answers on a separate answer sheet.

Much variation in scores on achievement examinations may result because some students are "test wise" and others are not. Students need to be taught how to take examinations. They should be told to go through the examination and answer only questions for which they know the answers before proceeding to answer others for which the answer is uncertain. Sometimes they will pick up clues for answering

NAME _____

Read these directions before starting.

1. Place your name in the space provided above and also on the answer sheet before continuing with this examination.
2. All answers should be placed on the answer sheet.
3. You have fifty minutes to complete this examination.
4. Should you complete the examination before others, quietly turn it over and be silent until all examinations are collected.

I.   Multiple-choice (1 point each.)
Each question has only one best answer. Place an "X" through the letter on the answer sheet to indicate your answer.

1. The stem of the question will go here
   a. the alternatives from which to choose go here
   b. alternative
   c. alternative
   d. alternative

2. The next item stem
   a. alternative
   b. alternative
   c. alternative
   d. alternative

II. True-False (1 point each).
Place an "X" through the T (true) or F (false) on the answer sheet to indicate your answer.

3. First statement

4. Second statement

III. Essay (5 points each).
Write your answers on the answer sheet in the space provided for each question. Do not exceed that space.

5. First essay question

6. Second essay question

Figure 9–1. Sample Examination (Using An Answer Sheet)

Name _____

I.   Multiple-choice Answers (Place an "X" Through your answer.)

   1. a b c d

   2. a b c d

                              (etc.)

II.   True-False Answers (Place an "X" Through your answer)

   3. T F

   4. T F

                              (etc.)

III. Essay Answers (Confine your answers to the space provided.)

   1.

   2.

Figure 9–2. Sample Examination Answer Sheet

questions they initially did not know. If taking a multiple-choice examination, they should answer all questions for which there is a strong likelihood they will be correct. For the rest of the questions that would require strictly guessing, students should choose the same alternative, usually (c) or (3), for each question. Before responding to essay questions, students should underline key words. If there is doubt about the meaning intended for these key words, they should ask the teacher to clarify meanings. Such guidance, with time, will enable students to improve their achievement test scores.

COGNITIVE LEVELS OF QUESTIONS

An achievement test should measure a variety of cognitive understandings. Some teachers tend to write test items measuring only simple memorization, which is not a recommended practice because, as stated previously, students perceive tests as indicators of the important things to remember (Medley, 1979). The kinds of items on tests will ultimately determine the kinds of learning on which students will focus. Therefore, testing for outcomes beyond memory is advisable. Students must understand the content beyond the knowledge level if the content is to be of any use to them in situations other than merely responding to items on tests. Benjamin Bloom's taxonomy of educational objectives (Bloom, 1956) is a useful guide not only for determining instructional objectives and classroom questions, but also for determining the nature of test questions. Questions can be classified by degree of complexity as follows:

1. Knowledge: questions asking the student to remember specific
   a. facts
   b. definitions
   c. rules
   d. past trends
   e. sequences
   f. criteria
   g. classifications
   h. generalizations
   i. methodologies
   j. theories
   k. structures
   l. principles
2. Comprehension: questions asking the student to
   a. translate a message
   b. interpret a message
   c. extrapolate from a message
3. Application: questions asking the student to use knowledge in particular situations. The problem situation should be new or in some way different from the situations used in the instruction. These questions might ask students to

    a. determine which principles or generalizations are relevant in dealing with a new problem situation

    b. restate a problem so as to determine which principles are necessary for a solution

    c. specify the limits within which a particular principle or generalization is true

    d. recognize the exceptions to a particular rule or generalization, and be able to identify the reasons for the exceptions

    e. explain new phenomena or situations in terms of known principles, generalizations, or rules

    f. predict what would happen in new situations

    g. determine a particular course of action in a new situation

4. Analysis: questions asking the student to examine a novel problem situation and break it into component parts, identify the elements, identify the relationships between the parts, and/or recognize organizational principles that might govern the whole. The situation to be analyzed should be different from any used in the instruction. A description of the situation should be provided and it should be available for reference as the student answers the question. These questions might ask students to

    a. classify words, phrases, and statements according to given criteria

    b. infer particular qualities not directly stated from clues available in the description

    c. infer from data or information what underlying qualities, assumptions, or conditions must be implicit or necessary

    d. use criteria such as relevance or causation to determine an order in data or in a document

    e. recognize organizational principles or patterns on which an experiment or work is based

    f. infer the framework, purpose, or point of view on which a position or experiment is based

5. Synthesis: Questions asking a student to respond to a problem, task, or situation that is new or different from those experienced during instruction. When scoring synthesis questions, judge either the adequacy with which the task was accomplished or the adequacy of the process used in accomplishing the task. Synthesis questions may ask students to

    a. develop a new communication

    b. produce a plan or organization

    c. invent a set of relations

    d. produce a solution to a problem

6. Evaluation: questions asking a student to make judgments about the relative value or worth of things and recognize the evidence and criteria used in those judgments. The material to be evaluated must be new or unfamiliar, but available to the student in the testing situation. These questions may ask students to

    a. judge the accuracy or precision used in conducting an experiment, writing a document, or creating a work of art

    b. judge internal consistency of arguments used in a document or experiment

c. list the reasons supporting or refuting a position on an issue
d. make judgments of a created work by comparing it with other relevant works

Using this classification scheme merely to classify existing questions is of little value to a teacher constructing a testing instrument. As with any classification scheme, actual items do not fall easily into distinct categories. This scheme is useful, however, in helping you identify possible instructional objectives that might otherwise be overlooked. Also, using this classification scheme to generate test items will help you write items that will test beyond mere memorization. If you seldom ask questions on tests from all of these categories, then you need to put more emphasis in your planning on increasing the frequency with which you teach and test for more complex levels of understanding.

KINDS OF TEST ITEMS

Essay Questions

Essay questions are meant to allow students to answer questions in their own words. Students are asked to recall from memory that knowledge referred to in the question and then to structure or use that knowledge in a response.

1. Suggestions
   a. For the sake of efficiency, essay questions should generally be used to measure more complex understandings that require students to synthesize, organize, or solve unusual or novel problems. Objective items can usually be used to test for other understandings.
   b. The question should be phrased in a way to delimit the area being covered.
   c. The question should usually require short answers. Questions calling for lengthy responses are prone to scoring errors as well as to the introduction of additional criteria unrelated to the understandings being tested (Chase, 1968; Klein, 1968). If the teacher wishes to provide opportunities for students to write essays on a topic, then these opportunities usually should be provided outside an achievement testing situation. If longer responses are required to assess an objective, then the criteria for the students' responses to the item must be listed as part of the question. The absence of these criteria for longer answers will significantly reduce the reliability and validity of the item. Essay questions calling for lengthy responses have the added disadvantage of limiting the number of kinds of learning that can be sampled. This results in an advantage to some students and a disadvantage to others, depending on whether they guessed the topics to be examined. A broader sampling of learnings reduces the probability of this disparity occurring on an achievement examination.

d. The reliability of an essay test can be improved by using a relatively large number of questions requiring short answers rather than a few questions with long answers.

e. Measure only one kind of understanding within one question. Do not try to measure two quite different kinds of understanding with the same question. Making two separate questions from a question with two parts is better for purposes of reliability than keeping the parts together in the same question.

f. The criteria used to score the question should be implied in the question itself. Avoid the use of words or phrases such as "tell how," "describe," "explain," "what would happen," or "discuss." It is preferable to use such phrases as "list three reasons," "record two factors," "what are three products," "what two things could happen if," "list three similarities," or "what are two differences."

g. Use time and care in writing essay questions. The idea that essay tests take less time to prepare than other forms of tests is a misconception and can lead to poorly constructed essay tests. Removing ambiguity from essay questions can be a difficult and time-consuming task. Although less time may be needed to write an essay question than to construct a multiple-choice question, the time differential is not large.

h. The reliability of scoring an essay test can be improved by scoring the same item for all students before going to the next item to be scored. The scores will more likely be the same or similar for comparable answers.

i. Prepare a key for scoring the test before it is administered. Using a key will ensure that you will not introduce additional criteria after having read some of the students' replies. The key will also ensure more consistency in your scoring. If you cannot prepare a key before you see any replies, then the item is undoubtedly too ambiguous to use on an examination.

2. Some faulty items. An analysis of some essay items may provide insights into common errors found in essay questions and help you avoid some of these undesirable practices.

a. Ambiguous items: items that poorly define the task the student is asked to perform. The student is left to guess the criteria to be used in grading or scoring the item.
   Item A: Tell how to take care of your teeth.
   Item B: What was important about George Washington?
   Item C: How are North America and Central America different?
   Item D: Describe how to write a good paragraph.

b. Testing for details: items that involve fragments of information that, if important, would be better tested through the use of objective items.
   Item A: Who was the father of our country, when was he born, and when did he serve as President of our country?
   Item B: When and where did the first battle of the Civil War occur?
   Item C: What is the difference between a pentagon and an octagon?
   Item D: How, when, and where was America discovered?

    c. Unreasonable: items that ask for extensive discussions of topics are usually both ambiguous and unreasonable. Efforts to find out the extent to which students understand a topic may lead to questions that a well-informed person could write on for days.

      Item A: How are animals important to people?

      Item B: What are the principles on which our nation was founded?

      Item C: What are the parts of speech and how is each used?

3. Some examples of good essay questions

    a. Knowledge of structures

      Item A: What are two differences in the structure of the bodies of insects and spiders?

      Item B: What are the two essential parts of a complete sentence?

    b. Applications

      Item A: What is one thing that would happen in your life if you could not add and subtract?

      Item B: Write two sentences using the past tense of the verb "to write."

    c. Analysis

      Item A: What is one thing that might cause someone who felt stealing was wrong to steal from another person?

      Item B: What is one conclusion that can be reached from the fact that not all legislators are honest with the public?

    d. Evaluations

      Item A: Some people have proposed making the use of mind-altering drugs legal. What are two reasons for opposing making such drugs legal?

      Item B: You have been taught that you should not litter, and, in fact, many states have passed laws against littering. What are two reasons that states have passed laws against littering?

4. Advantages of essay questions

    a. Essay questions can measure students' organizational skills better than other kinds of items.

    b. Essay questions allow the testing of all cognitive levels of understanding.

    c. Somewhat less time is required to write essay questions than multiple-choice and matching items.

5. Disadvantages of essay questions

    a. Scoring is more unreliable than with objective items.

    b. Writing unambiguous questions is extremely difficult, and teachers in haste tend not to do this task well.

    c. Essay tests are burdensome to score.

    d. Communication skills, in addition to the knowledge being tested, can affect the scoring of essay items. To the extent that this bias is allowed to occur, the scores on tests may not indicate the students' understanding of the content as much as their ability to communicate. Some teachers would argue that this is acceptable because students should learn how to communicate, and therefore the assessment of communication skills on tests should motivate them to learn these skills. A contrary view holds that if the objectives of learning to communicate are important, then specific tests on these skills should be given. From a testing point of view, measuring two distinctly different abilities within one item should be avoided when possible because this practice lowers the validity and reliability of items.

e. Because answers to essay questions must be written out, students will be spending more time responding to questions rather than thinking about answers. This means that the amount of student learning that can be sampled will be more limited with essay questions than with other kinds of questions because fewer questions can be completed in a specified time.

Multiple-choice Questions

Multiple-choice items are designed to ask a student to examine a question and recognize a correct choice by matching the alternatives to a correct answer that already exists in memory, generating a correct answer and comparing the alternatives to it, or evaluating each alternative as a potential answer and trying to reason from the question to that answer.

1. Suggestions
    a. Make the number of alternatives, usually four or five, the same for all multiple-choice questions on a particular test. If the number of alternatives needs to vary between four and five, then group those with the same number of alternatives together. Then caution students on the test when they reach the point where the number of alternatives per item changes. This caution will help reduce errors they make when inadvertently checking an unintended alternative.
    b. Phrase the item stem in the form of a question or an incomplete statement. Avoid using one-word or short-phrase stems. If the stem is an incomplete statement to be completed by the choice of one of the alternatives, then the alternatives listed should:
    (1) be grammatically consistent with the stem
    (2) complete the statement so as to make a complete sentence
    (3) be short phrases or sentences rather than one or two words
    c. State item stems positively. Avoid the use of "not" and "least." The use of negatives in the stem will lower the reliability of the responses because such stems create confusion. If using "not" is unavoidable, then use capital letters for the word "NOT" so that it will be clearly visible.
    d. Avoid ambiguity in the stem. While ambiguity may be less a problem in multiple-choice questions than in essay questions, avoid using words having different meanings to different individuals.
    e. Avoid giving clues to the correct answer in the stem.
    f. The alternatives listed should be approximately the same length. Different length alternatives can give clues to the correct answer; longer alternatives usually indicate the correct response.

g. Present the alternatives in a single column. Presenting the alternatives in linear sequence, in a paragraph form, or in multiple columns to save space on the paper will cause students to make more errors by inadvertently checking an unintended alternative.

h. Avoid using the alternative "all of the above." "None of the above" can be used as an alternative if it is a plausible **distractor,** and is used occasionally as a correct answer.

i. If you are testing for the understanding of a definition, it is better to place the word for the definition in the stem, and then list possible alternative definitions. Avoid stating the definition in the stem and then listing alternative words representing the definition. Such a practice encourages guessing and, more important, encourages a trivial form of learning.

j. Make all distractors plausible. Avoid using any nonfunctioning distractors—that is, distractors that all students know are incorrect. Avoid distractors that are the exact opposite of the correct response. Such a practice eliminates all other distractors as possible alternatives. Avoid two distractors having the same meaning. This eliminates them as possible correct answers. The use of nonfunctioning distractors will lower the reliability of the test.

k. Avoid using the same words and phrases for the correct alternative as those used in the textbook. Such a practice encourages trivial learning—that is, memorization without meaning.

l. Make sure all alternatives are logically related to the stem, and similar in character. The alternatives should not be an unrelated collection of true and false statements.

m. Because multiple-choice questions involve more reading than other forms of test items, use reasonable vocabulary. To do otherwise is to test both reading ability and the content being tested. The validity of a test is then suspect. Also, avoid wordiness. Extraneous words increase the time needed to answer questions and can also introduce confusion.

n. Avoid placing part of a question at the end of one page and continuing it on the next page. Dividing questions in this fashion is an especially poor practice.

2. Some faulty items. An examination of some common errors used when constructing multiple-choice questions, and comparing them with the suggestions given, may help you avoid similar errors.

Item A: The Frenchman who developed a vaccine for rabies was
1. Fleming
2. Salk
3. Pasteur
4. Schroedinger
5. Whiting

Explanation: The stem gives a clue to the answer. Pasteur is the only French name.

Improvement: The stem can be modified to read:

A Frenchman by the name of Pasteur is noted for the development of:
1. a vaccine for rabies
2. a cure for tuberculosis
3. a disinfectant against bacteria
4. a new strain of virus

Item B: Abraham Lincoln was born in the year
1. 1950
2. 1909
3. 1809
4. 1920

Explanation: Inconsequential subject matter and nonfunctioning distractors are being used. The only date related to time of the event is 1809.

Improvement: The practice of testing for this kind of knowledge is not recommended. This item cannot be improved, and should not be included in a test.

Item C: An eight-sided figure is called an
1. octagon
2. rectangle
3. triangle
4. hexagon
5. pentagon

Explanation: The stem leads grammatically to the answer. Also, using a list of names promotes guessing and tends to lower the reliability.

Improvement: Start with a stem such as: Which one of the following figures is an octagon? Then list five drawings of figures. Another alternative could be: How many sides does a shape called an octagon have?
1. four sides
2. five sides
3. six sides
4. seven sides
5. eight sides

Item D: The total surface of an object is called its
1. volume
2. area
3. circumference
4. length times width

Explanation: Using a list of names promotes guessing and tends to promote trivial kinds of learning.

Improvement: Reverse stem and responses to read: Area can best be defined as:
1. length times width
2. the space occupied by matter
3. an amount of surface
4. displacement times displacement
5. an interval between two lines

Item E: If the radius of the earth were increased by three feet, the circumference of the earth at the equator would be increased by approximately: (1) 28 feet, (2) 16 feet, (3) 9 feet, (4) 12 feet, (5) 3 feet.

Explanation: The alternatives are arranged so as to create confusion.

Improvement: Arrange the responses vertically and in descending or ascending order. If the radius of the earth were increased by three feet, the circumference of the earth at the equator would be increased by approximately:

1. 3 feet
2. 9 feet
3. 12 feet
4. 16 feet
5. 28 feet

3. Advantages of multiple-choice questions
   a. The amount of testing time spent on thinking about the question will be considerably greater than the amount of time spent on responding to the question.
   b. Because little time is needed to respond to multiple-choice questions, the reliability of tests can be improved by including a larger number of questions on an examination than would be possible with essay items.
   c. Multiple-choice questions lend themselves to statistical analysis for purposes of improvement. The ability to apply a statistical analysis allows the teacher constructing a test to improve the items on subsequent tests both by revising existing items and by developing her ability to write such items. The revision of items can lead to more reliability and more appropriate levels of difficulty.
   d. The scoring of multiple-choice items is simple and fast.
   e. Multiple-choice items can measure a wide variety of cognitive levels, as do essay questions, with the exception of synthesis.

4. Disadvantages of multiple-choice questions
   a. The construction of good multiple-choice tests is very time consuming.
   b. Without some training, teachers will usually test for trivial content and focus only on memory/recognition items. The ability to construct items measuring for higher cognitive levels of understanding takes some training and practice.
   c. More paper and typing are required to prepare the testing instruments.
   d. Scores are likely to be distorted by reading and test-taking ability.

Because multiple-choice questions have so many advantages, some authorities suggest that teachers should try to construct multiple-choice questions first. They should switch to other forms only if the type of objective makes an alternate form more desirable (Gronlund, 1977). For most teachers, however, such a practice may not be practical due to the inordinate amount of time required.

True-False Questions

True-false questions require a student to judge the accuracy of a statement. The student essentially compares the statement as written with his recollection of facts.

1. Suggestions
   a. Avoid the use of "all," "no," "always," "never," or other absolutes. Writing a valid true statement using absolutes is difficult, and the use of absolutes usually indicates a false answer.
   b. Check each item very carefully for ambiguity in words or phrases.
   c. Tell students to circle or place an "X" through the words "true" and "false" on an answer sheet. Because the first letters of the two words when capitalized can look similar, having the students write out the words or the first letter can result in scoring errors.
   d. Use an approximately equal number of true and false items.
   e. Do not mix a true statement and false statement within the same item.
   f. Avoid negative statements if possible. They will tend to have low reliability.
   g. Avoid very long statements. They will tend to have low reliability.
   h. Avoid using phrases taken directly from the textbook, because such items encourage memorization without understanding.
2. Some faulty items. In an attempt to make simple statements true or false, teachers sometimes inadvertently introduce trick questions. Writing unambiguous statements that are clearly true or false to a well-informed individual is also difficult. Examining some simple examples of such errors may be helpful.
   Item A: The battle of the Alamo was fought in 1836 B.C.
   Explanation: This is a trick question. The choice of B.C. makes the question false.
   Item B: The value of pi is 3.14.
   Explanation: This is not the exact value of pi, but one commonly used. The question could be either true or false, depending on one's interpretation. This problem is common whenever measured quantities are involved in a true/false question.
   Item C: All dogs have a sharp sense of smell.
   Explanation: Use of "all" makes the question false because obviously at least one dog exists, if not more, that has lost its sense of smell by accident or disease.
   Item D: Not beginning the first word in a sentence with a capital is incorrect.
   Explanation: Using a double negative creates confusion.
3. Advantages of true-false items
   a. Testing a broad range of topics in a fairly short period of time is possible.
   b. Answer sheets are very easily scored.
4. Disadvantages of true-false items
   a. Many of the understandings that can be measured with this kind of item are trivial.
   b. Writing a statement that is clearly either true or false without giving the answer away is very difficult.

c. Students have an even chance of guessing the correct answer. This reduces the range of scores and increases the amount of random error, making tests composed of these items susceptible to unreliability.

d. Unless statements are carefully worded, those students who actually know more tend to score lower because they are able to read more into the statements. Those with superficial understandings are more likely to take the statement at face value and respond correctly.

Matching Questions

Matching questions are designed to allow a student to identify pairs of matching statements, words, phrases, or other facts from separate lists of each.

1. Suggestions
    a. The list of numbered stems should be placed to the left. The stems can be incomplete sentences, statements, words, or phrases. Place the choices to the right, each identified with a letter.
    b. The stems and the choices should be homogeneous; that is, they should test logically related content.
    c. The number of choices should exceed the number of stems to reduce the effect of guessing.
    d. The total number of items in the stems should be limited to no more than 10–12 items.
    e. The items composing the stems should be longer than the items composing the choices if there is any difference in length. People tend to read from left to right, so such a placement reduces the reading time needed to complete the item.
    f. If names of people are used in either the stem or the choices, then complete names should be used to avoid confusion.
    g. Stems or choices composed of one or two words should be alphabetized to reduce reading time.
    h. The directions for the item should include descriptions of the columns to be matched, along with telling the students where to place the answers.
2. A faulty item

a. Carter	1. First astronaut on the moon
b. King	2. Long-time president of the coal miners
c. Nixon	3. Inventors
d. Armstrong	4. President at the time of the Watergate affair
e. Bell	5. Civil rights leader
f. Lewis	6. President in the last 50 years

Explanation: This item violates almost every one of the suggestions made. Also, the names "Carter" and "Nixon" both match choice (6). Improving this item is not possible due to the heterogeneity of the choices.

Improvement: Arrange longer stems to the left, alphabetize choices, include directions, and make the choices homogeneous.

Directions: Column A lists some processes that occur in the human body during digestion, and Column B lists parts of the digestive system. Match the process on the left with the part on the right by placing the appropriate letter for the part in the space to the left of numbers in Column A. The name of each part can be used only once.

Column A	Column B
_____ 1. most digested food passes into the blood in the	a. bile duct
_____ 2. body acid dissolves food primarily in the	b. colon
	c. esophagus
	d. gall bladder
_____ 3. undigested food passes from the stomach into the	e. mouth
	f. small intestine
_____ 4. mechanical digestion occurs primarily in the	g. stomach

3. Advantages of matching questions
   1. A large number of specific understandings can be tested in a short period of time.
   2. These items are easy to score reliably.
4. Disadvantages of matching questions
   1. The level of learning tested is restricted to the recognition of simple relationships. Matching questions are unable to measure understandings beyond this rather low level of understanding.
   2. Giving clues within the items is difficult to avoid. This lowers the reliability of the items.

Completion Questions

Completion questions require the student to associate some incomplete statement with some word or words recalled from memory.

1. Suggestions
   a. Avoid varying the length of spaces to be filled in. This practice will give clues to the answers and will promote guessing.
   b. Avoid statements to be completed by inserting measured quantities. Students would usually not know the degree of accuracy required for a correct answer.
   c. Study each question carefully for ambiguity.
   d. Avoid more than one blank for each question, and place the blank toward the end of the sentence.
2. Some faulty items. Writing completion items that are not faulty in some way is difficult. The following examples will illustrate some of the difficulties.
   Item A: The capital city of Ohio is _____.

Explanation: Possible answers include "large," "clean," "in the middle of the state," and "Columbus."

Improved Item:

The name of the capital city of Ohio is _____.

Explanation: Even here, the purist could insist that the answer "composed of eight letters" would also be correct, which merely illustrates the difficulty of writing such questions without ambiguity.

Item B: _____ was the first President of _____.

Explanation: So many parts of the sentence have been omitted that numerous answers are possible. In addition, the lengths of the blanks vary and may encourage students to guess.

Improved Item

The name of the first President of the Confederacy was _____.

3. Advantages of completion questions
   a. Items can usually be constructed rather easily.
   b. Many different memorized words can be tested in a short period of time.
4. Disadvantages of completion questions
   a. Completion items can test for only the ability to associate words or phrases with incomplete statements at the knowledge or comprehension levels.
   b. The items must be scored by reading the responses, which increases scoring time and may involve more error than other types of objective questions.
   c. Writing unambiguous items is difficult.
   d. Questions usually test for specific wording in a textbook. Testing for the recall of specific words trivializes the content being tested to the point that these questions are almost better left unused.

ADMINISTERING TESTS

When administering informal tests to whole classes, you should make procedures as simple and routine as possible. The more predictable the procedures, the less thought students need to give them and the more they can concentrate on the task at hand. Several things must be considered in order to reduce the amount of confusion.

1. The copies of the tests to be administered should be readily available and arranged in a way to minimize the time needed to distribute them.

2. All students should be silent before the tests are distributed, while they are being distributed, and while the tests are being completed.

3. The teacher should ensure that all students have the needed materials before the tests are distributed.

4. Students should remove all materials, except those needed to take the test, from the surfaces of their desks or tables.

An effective test question requires thinking.

5. All tests should remain face down when distributed, and should remain face down until the teacher gives the students a signal to turn them over.

6. Before students begin the test, they should read the directions, and the teacher should check for understanding by asking them to repeat the directions.

7. Students should be told what to do when they finish the test so as not to disturb those still completing the test.

8. When tests are completed, they should be collected in a way that reduces confusion.

DIFFICULTY LEVEL OF TEACHER-MADE TESTS

Tests designed to measure the cognitive understandings of students are usually administered for two quite different purposes. First, tests may be used to measure mastery learning; that is, they are criterion-referenced. Second, tests are commonly given to rank students in relation to one another for assigning grades or placement. These two different purposes require tests with different characteristics.

For example, if a test is going to be used to decide whether students are ready for the next instructional experience, it would be composed of items measuring minimal prerequisite understandings required for the next instructional experience. Most, if not all, of the students who were successful in completing the instructional lesson would answer the questions successfully. The same could be said for a test used to evaluate the effectiveness of some curriculum materials or method of instruction. If the materials or method of instruction were successful, most students should be able to answer the items on the test. As stated earlier, tests designed to measure minimum understanding are referred to as criterion-referenced tests. Such tests would be expected to produce very high scores. Ideally, most students would get all of the items correct. Criterion-referenced tests, or diagnostic tests, are designed so that the average scores will be approximately 80 to 100 percent.

Tests designed to assess student achievement for purposes of ranking students and then assigning grades to those rankings are called norm-referenced tests. Such tests must be reliable; that is, they need to measure accurately and consistently. If an achievement test has a low reliability, then students could have positions in the ranking that are higher or lower than other students, not because of some real difference in their knowledge, but because of errors in the measurement. Such measurement error differences would result in inaccurate grades; therefore, the scores for achievement tests should extend over a wide range in order to maximize their reliability. The range of scores on achievement tests will be from 30 to 95 percent with an average of approximately 50 to 60 percent.

Trying to measure mastery and achievement with the same instrument will lower the reliability or usefulness of the instrument and ensure that neither task is done well. Including mastery items on an achievement test would be counterproductive for reliably measuring achievement. Including difficult items on a mastery test reduces the usefulness of information acquired to help make decisions. These tasks, therefore, should be accomplished with different tests.

Each item on a test will present its own challenge to students. If an item is too easy, almost all students will answer it correctly. If an item is too difficult, almost all will answer it incorrectly. On mastery or criterion-referenced tests, students should answer most, if not all, items correctly. On the other hand, items on an achievement test should be answered correctly by approximately 60 percent of the students. Studies have found that the precision of an achievement is highest when all of the items possess approximately the same level of difficulty, with the average level between 60 to 70 percent correct responses (Diederich, 1969). Such an unvarying level of difficulty for all items is almost impossible to achieve, but teachers should at least try to avoid the usual practice of deliberately varying the item difficulty on achievement tests from easy to difficult.

CHARACTERISTICS OF EFFECTIVE TESTS

We can summarize the characteristics of good tests, regardless of type, in the following manner:

1.   The test should measure what is intended to be measured; that is, it should be **valid**. The sum total of the items on the test should be a complete, or at least a representative, sample of the objectives to be tested. Further, the actual task to be completed by the student in answering the item should correspond to the task that the test maker intended. Therefore, each item must be carefully analyzed to determine the kind of thinking the student will use to answer the question successfully and to compare that thinking with the kind of thinking the test is intended to measure.

2.   A test should be **reliable;** each individual should perform the same with repeated administrations of the same instrument. Just as you would not want to measure some critical distance with an inaccurate ruler, you should not want to measure a student's understanding with an inaccurate or inconsistent test.

3.   The items on a test, in total, should be **reasonably difficult**. If a test is designed to measure achievement for the purpose of ranking students, then it would not be reasonable to have items on the test that all students could answer. The difficulty level of items on a test should be chosen so that the range of scores will be the range desired.

4.   The cognitive levels of the questions should vary from those requiring memory to those requiring more complex understanding. Any one test will not necessarily include questions from all categories of Bloom's taxonomy, but at least some variety, consistent with the objectives, should be present.

5.   The test should be efficient. Enough data should be collected to ensure reliability, but not so much that time is wasted responding to an excessive number of items.

OTHER METHODS OF ASSESSMENT

Teachers use many forms of assessments other than tests. Any tasks that we ask students to complete, and for which we then examine the students' performance, are forms of assessments. For example, we frequently have students complete homework assignments, complete worksheets, do practice problems, build models, draw pictures, write stories, collect specimens, role-play, give oral reports, and perform mechanical tasks. During lessons, a teacher asks students questions to assess their learning during lessons. Teachers may have informal conversations with students to find out those things they are interested in learning. Teachers meet a child after school to discuss some difficulties the child may be experiencing. All of these are forms of assessments that are frequently used in elementary and middle school classrooms.

In addition to these, there are other less commonly used forms of assessment that may help you expand the list of things you choose to assess and thus help you make better decisions about your students.

Inventories and Interviews

Often, teachers are interested in gathering data that cannot be achieved through testing. For example, students' study habits, reading interests, social networks, motivation, and self-esteem can be assessed through interviews conducted with individuals or groups, or, with older children, through the use of questionnaires that focus on key issues. Consider two examples from the area of reading. A teacher may be interested in examining a particular student's conception of what good reading is and also that student's conception of himself as a reader. The teacher may set aside a time for a conversation with the student that would be guided by such probes as the following:

1. Whom do you know who is a good reader?
2. Why do you think they are good at reading?
3. How did they get to be good readers?
4. Do they ever have problems reading? What kind of problems? What do you think they do to solve these problems?
5. Do you ever have problems in your reading? What do you do when faced with these problems?
6. Are you a good reader? What makes you think that?
7. How are you learning to become a better reader?
8. Do you like to read? What do you like to read? When do you like to read? Where do you like to read?

These kinds of questions will yield an enormous amount of data that can contribute to some important decisions about appropriate instruction.

In a different situation, a teacher might be interested in assessing how well students have understood books they are reading as part of an independent reading program. Rather than develop a test, the teacher may decide to have a conversation with the student about the book he read. The teacher may ask the student to summarize the text and then probe for clarification and extensions. These data are compared with the text in order to make judgments about the quality of the child's reading skills. A good structured interview or questionnaire can provide an enormous amount of data on children that is no less reliable or valid than a test.

Informal conversations with students can provide much information about their interest in different topics of the curriculum. Continuing conversations with children on how they feel about those things occurring in the classroom can be very helpful when planning subsequent lessons. Informal conversations with individual students can also provide helpful information about difficulties they are experiencing both in and outside the classroom. Use care, however, not to pry into those things that the child either does not wish to talk about or that you need not know about for educational purposes.

Observations

Much can be learned about children by watching them interact with other children and pursue academic tasks. This kind of assessment is often done on a case-by-case basis because it can be time consuming. The preferred method of observing is to write a "running narrative" of classroom behavior, sometimes called an **anecdotal record**. These typically describe instances of behavior that are outside of what is normally being assessed by other means. Anecdotal records of behavior should be nonjudgmental descriptions of what occurs. They are dated and retained. Such records should be collected systematically on each student in comparable situations. A typical anecdotal record would involve a record of the child's on-task and off-task behavior, which could then be used to prepare reporting forms on student conduct. Such records can be a data base for developing a program than will assist a child in establishing positive social relations and for learning to get academic work done efficiently.

Shadowing is another observational technique that is quite useful in gathering data. Here, the observer follows or accompanies the child for a portion of the instructional day (e.g., to different classes, to different learning activities, to lunch, or to recess) to see how he responds and interacts in different situations. This kind of assessment can be powerful in revealing how context influences behavior.

Performance sampling is an observational technique used to gather data on how well a new set of instructional materials or grouping pattern, for example, is working in the classroom. For example, for a new literature corner, the teacher may take notes each day on how students interact with each other, the books they choose to read during free time, and the time they spend reading different kinds of books. If the teacher is attempting to incorporate more small group work in science activities, she would use performance sampling as students work in these small groups. Such things as the length of time each student talks, how well each student listens to others, and the amount of off-task behavior may provide data needed to make decisions about modifications in the directions given prior to these small group activities, the number of students assigned to each group, and other important decisions that help the small groups function more effectively.

FACTORS TO CONSIDER WHEN ASSESSING

Assessment involves the systematic collection of data. By now you see that assessment is more than just testing. Good assessment is judged by how well the assessment helps in making instructional decisions. In the effective classroom, all of the types of assessment combine to form a comprehensive array of options and opportunities.

In deciding which forms of assessment to use, you must consider several factors, including the domain being assessed, the purpose of the assessment, and economy of time. Consider, first, the domain you are assessing. Skills are often amenable to testing or observation of performance. Attitudes, values, and beliefs are perhaps best assessed through observation and interview. Cognitive learnings are usually assessed through the use of tests and written assignments. Second, consider the purpose of the assessment; if it is to help you make decisions about the curriculum or the instruction, then qualitative tests are often most appropriate. If the purpose is to systematically document student achievement in specific subject areas, then quantitative tests may be more in order. Consider, finally, economy. Time devoted to assessment is time taken away from instruction. The optimum amount of assessment is the minimum needed to acquire the information necessary for good decision making. An enormous amount of time is spent assessing children through the use of tests. The value of these tests in helping to make better decisions about the child and his instructional program is not always clear. Basing your decisions on systematic observations rather than tests is not only acceptable but, at times, more reasonable and defensible. Although tests have a valuable role in assessment, other forms of assessment are also necessary if you expect to know enough about your students to make effective decisions about their instruction.

ASSESSING SPECIAL STUDENTS

Usually, the teacher bears the primary responsibility for student assessment. In some cases, however, the teacher may need the skills and expertise of specialists to conduct in-depth assessments of children who have special learning needs. Most school districts provide such services. Your role as a teacher is one of early identification of special learning needs through informal testing and observations. When students demonstrate difficulties in learning beyond the normal, then referral to specialists for in-depth assessment is recommended. Some areas for which specialists may be needed include physical problems (e.g., vision, hearing, motor control), psychological problems (e.g., emotional disorders, specific learning disabilities), and language problems (e.g., speech impediments). Your sensitivity to these special needs will make it more likely that students will be referred when needed.

CAVEATS AND CONCERNS

Some educators have voiced concerns that the status of testing in schools represents a serious case of the proverbial tail wagging the dog. In other words, what we test has become the primary determinant of what is taught. This is unfortunate for several reasons. Numerous educational outcomes or goals such as appreciations and values are not amenable to testing. In a world where testing determines the curriculum, time may not be devoted to these untestable areas. When tests drive the curriculum, the teacher is often in the position of making a decision to work on those areas being tested rather than working on those things that are at the ability levels of the learners. When minimum competency tests are used, performance is reported as a percentage of students mastering the objectives. Teachers in this situation may feel a need to raise the percentage of students passing a competency test. As a result, they may devote more time to the students who have not yet mastered the minimum levels than to those who have. The overall achievement of higher-ability students may then suffer.

The same tail-wagging-the-dog syndrome can be seen to affect instruction at a different level. Consider the problems associated with the use of student achievement tests as a measure of teacher effectiveness. Some seem to believe that the best teachers are those able to raise test scores to the highest level. The logic is flawed because much more must be taught than the content and skills being tested. Such a narrow view overlooks the importance of teaching children the attitudes and behaviors needed to function as human beings. The implementation of programs of teacher evaluation based on the premise that achievement of basic knowledge and skills is the sole measure of an effective education is a serious threat to the teaching profession. Further, few, if any, measurement experts in the country would argue that we have the techniques at hand to measure student growth and development with sufficient validity and reliability to warrant such a practice, even if one did accept the questionable assumptions upon which such a practice would be based.

As a teacher, you will face the difficult task of resolving the dilemma in using assessment as a tool of good instruction in a context in which results of assessment are used for purposes unrelated to sound instructional decision making. Keeping the welfare of individual students as the primary focus in such a situation will be difficult indeed, and yet this will be your responsibility. Your rewards for deciding in favor of students will be in seeing the development of those students with whom you work. Effective teachers are those who are content with such a reward.

IMPLICATIONS FOR PLANNING

When first planning lessons, identify the objectives and the corresponding assessments (not just tests) used to evaluate student performance on the objectives, and then design activities to accomplish them. Occasionally, you may identify activities first and then develop objectives and assessments. Regardless of the sequence, the objectives, activities, and assessments should all be congruent; that is, the activities should lead to the accomplishment of the objectives and the assessments should evaluate students on the attainment of the objectives.

If you are going to teach and test higher-level understandings, then plan activities that will provide experiences with examples similar but not identical to those to be assessed. For example, if you want students to be able to answer a word problem requiring addition and subtraction at the application level, then introduce examples of word problems requiring addition and subtraction at the application level in the learning activities. You need a sufficient number of examples to ensure that the students learn that kind of application problem. The example used on a test to find out if students could do that task would then need to be an example not previously used during the instruction. Using the same example on the test as during instruction would allow the students to respond simply by having memorized the particular example. You would have no way of knowing if those who answered such an item correctly could apply what they learned to other, similar problems.

When administering tests, plan very carefully the distribution of tests and the directions to be given at the start of tests. When first administering tests, include a list of directions in your plans. You should include not only the directions needed to start the test, but also what students will need to do at the end of the test. If the test is lengthy, then having another activity available for students to work on after they complete their tests is important. You can tell students to bring their test papers to a table in the front of the class and pick up a copy of the activity to be completed at the same table. Provide some incentive for completing the additional activity so that students who finish the test early are not penalized.

When using formal assessment instruments, be sure to study carefully the teacher manuals provided with the instruments. These manuals will provide guidelines for the administration of the instrument and the interpretation of the results. Familiarity with the information in these manuals will help you make better instructional decisions.

When using assessment results to evaluate the effectiveness of activities, use special care. For example, there may be several reasons that children were unsuccessful in learning as a result of a particular activity. Some novice teachers will be quick to assume that the method involved in the activity is at fault, resulting in the incorrect notion that certain methods are inappropriate for children. The fact that children do not learn as a result of an activity is seldom related to the method, unless the method is inconsistent with the children's intellectual development (e.g., using an expository strategy with children who have not had prior experience with the examples being used). More reasonable explanations usually relate to the skill level of the teacher in using a particular method, or the compatibility of the content or skills taught with the ability levels and prerequisite knowledge and skills of the children. Avoid using incomplete assessment information when making instructional decisions. Your best guide in making decisions about instruction is to collect data systematically and then consider the information carefully before acting on it. This requires that you consider all of the possible causes for the assessment results observed before deciding on what you believe to be the actual cause and making an instructional decision.

REFERENCES

Bloom, B. S., ed. 1956. *Taxonomy of educational objectives, handbook I: Cognitive domain.* New York: David McKay.

Blumberg, P., M. D. Alschuler, and V. Rezmovic. 1982. Should taxonomic levels be considered in developing examinations? *Educational and Psychological Measurement, 42:* 1–7.

Chase, C. I. 1968. The impact of some obvious variables on essay test scores. *Journal of Educational Measurement, 5*(4): 315–318.

Diederich, P. B. 1969. Short-cut statistics for teacher-made tests. In *Statistics and measurement in the classroom.* Ed. Hereford, C. F., L. Natalicio, and S. J. McFarland. Dubuque, IA: Kendall/Hunt.

Goodman, Y. M., D. J. Watson, and C. L. Burke. 1987. *Reading miscue inventory.* New York: Richard C. Owen.

Gronlund, N. E. 1977. *Constructing achievement tests* (2d Ed.) Englewood Cliffs, NJ: Prentice-Hall.

Klein, S. P., and F. M. Hart. 1968. Chance and systematic factors affecting essay grades. *Journal of Educational Measurement, 5*(3): 197–206.

Kubiszyn, T., and G. Borich. 1984. *Educational testing and measurement.* Glenview, IL: Scott, Foresman.

Medley, D. M. 1979. The effectiveness of teachers. In *Research on teaching.* Ed. P. L. Peterson and H. J. Walberg. Berkeley, CA: McCutchan.

CHAPTER REVIEW

Assessment: the systematic collection of data useful in making decisions Evaluation: the use of assessment information in making a decision

Types of Evaluation

1. Formative Evaluation
   Of students—decisions that have a direct and immediate effect on the student
   Of curriculum—decisions made during the development of materials
2. Summative Evaluation
   Of students—decisions that do not have immediate effects on student's instruction
   Of curriculum—decisions made about the effectiveness of the curriculum in meeting stated goals

Quality of Tests

1. Efficiency: sampling students' behavior to ensure that no more data than necessary to make a decision is collected
2. Reliability: degree to which a test measures consistently
   a. Tests that are too easy or too difficult tend to have lower reliability.
   b. As the number of items on a test increases, the higher the reliability will tend to be.
3. Validity: degree to which a test measures what it is purported to measure
   a. Concurrent Validity: degree to which the test corresponds to other tests purported to measure the same thing
   b. Construct Validity: degree to which a test conforms to some theoretical model

Types of Tests

1. Informal: tests constructed, administered, and interpreted by the teacher
2. Formal: tests developed by commercial publishers and that have established procedures for administration and interpretation; sometimes referred to as standardized tests
3. Qualitative: designed to provide specific information on the skills and knowledge mastered by the student; also called criterion-referenced tests
4. Quantitative: designed to provide a score for a student that represents a rank or ability level; when used to compare the student with other samples of students, it is called a norm-referenced test.

Types of Scores

1. Raw Score: the number of correct responses
2. Percentile Score: represents the percentage of students from the norming sample that the student taking the test outperformed
3. Normal Curve Equivalent Score (NCEs): similar to percentile scores, but statistically adjusted to minimize the distortions found in percentile scores
4. Grade-Equivalent Score: represents the level at which a student is achieving compared with a sample at the grade level for which the test was designed, but reported as equivalent to the performance at a certain grade level; their use is not recommended

Constructing Informal Cognitive Tests

1. Write items congruent with the instructional objectives.
2. Group like kinds of items together.
3. Decide on the use of a separate answer sheet.
4. Write directions for the test as well as each kind of item.
5. Indicate the value placed on each item of the test.

Cognitive Levels of Questions

1. Knowledge: questions asking the student to remember specific facts, definitions, rules, past trends, sequences, criteria, classifications, generalizations, methodologies, theories, structures, or principles.
2. Comprehension: questions asking the student to translate, interpret, or extrapolate from a message.
3. Application: questions asking the student to
    a. determine which principles are relevant in dealing with a new problem situation
    b. restate a problem so as to determine which principles are necessary for solution
    c. specify the limits within which a particular principle or generalization is true
    d. recognize the exceptions to a particular generalization and be able to identify the reasons for the exceptions

4. Analysis: questions asking the student to examine a novel problem situation from a description provided and break it into component parts, identify the elements, identify the relationships that exist between the parts, and/or recognize organizational principles that might govern the whole.
5. Synthesis: questions asking students to respond to a novel problem, task, or situation and develop a new communication, produce a plan or organization, invent a set of relations, or produce a solution to a problem.
6. Evaluation: questions asking students to make judgments about the relative value or worth of something novel and recognize the evidence and criteria used in those judgments.

Essay Questions

1. Essay questions should
   a. usually require answers of short duration
   b. measure one kind of understanding within one question
   c. include the criteria for scoring
   d. be unambiguous
   e. be scored by scoring one question at a time for all respondents
2. Advantages of Essay Questions
   a. can measure students' organizational skills
   b. can measure all cognitive levels of understanding
   c. take less time to prepare than multiple-choice questions
3. Disadvantages of Essay Questions
   a. scoring can be less reliable than with objective items
   b. difficult to write unambiguous questions
   c. takes more time for students to respond
   d. cumbersome to score

Multiple-Choice Questions

1. Multiple-Choice questions should
   a. be composed of the same number of alternatives
   b. be composed of alternatives of about the same length
   c. list the alternatives in a column
   d. be stated positively
   e. be composed of equally plausible distractors
   f. use reasonable vocabulary
   g. have alternatives logically related to the stem
2. Advantages of Multiple-Choice Questions
   a. little response time is needed for each question
   b. questions can be improved through statistical analysis
   c. can measure a wide variety of cognitive levels
   d. scoring is simple and accurate
3. Disadvantages of Multiple-Choice Questions
   a. time consuming to construct
   b. usually takes training to write items beyond memory/recognition
   c. more paper and typing are required to prepare the test
   d. test-wise students can score higher than others

True-False Questions

1. True-False questions should
    a. not be statements of absolutes
    b. be unambiguous
    c. be evenly distributed between those that are true and those that are false
    d. be stated positively
    e. be relatively short sentences
    f. not be composed of phrases taken directly from the textbook
2. Advantages of True-False Items
    a. short response time
    b. easily scored
3. Disadvantages of True-False Items
    a. writing items that test for significant understanding that are either true or false is difficult
    b. guessing can play a significant role in individual scores

Matching Questions

1. Matching questions should
    a. be composed of numbered items to the left; lettered choices to the right
    b. be composed of stems and choices dealing with similar content
    c. have a larger number of choices than stems
    d. have longer statements composing the stems, and shorter statements composing the choices
    e. have the directions for responding at the beginning of the item
2. Advantages of Matching Questions
    a. response time is short
    b. items are easy and accurate to score
3. Disadvantages of Matching Questions
    a. level of understanding tested is limited to the simple recognition of related items
    b. difficult not to give clues

Completion Questions

1. Completion questions should
    a. have the same length of blank space for each item
    b. not include questions about measured quantities
    c. not have more than one blank per question
    d. not be composed of statements taken directly from the textbook
2. Advantages of Completion Questions
    a. items can be constructed easily
    b. many words for definitions can be tested in a short time
3. Disadvantages of Completion Questions
    a. test only for association of words with phrases
    b. scoring takes longer than for other objective questions
    c. writing unambiguous items is very difficult

Administration of Tests to Whole Classes

1. Copies should be distributed with a minimum of confusion.

2. All students should be silent before they start the examination.

3. Only examination materials should be on the students' desks.

4. Directions should be made clear to students before they begin the examination.

5. Students finishing early should have an assigned task to accomplish.

Characteristics of Effective Tests

1. The test is valid; it measures what it is intended to measure.
2. The test is reliable; it measures consistently.
3. The test is of reasonable difficulty.
   a. Mastery tests should be composed of items that approximately 80 to 100 percent of the students will answer correctly.
   b. Achievement tests should be composed of items that approximately 60 percent of the students will answer correctly.
4. The cognitive levels of the questions vary.
5. The test contains a number of items needed to be reliable, but not excessive.

Other Forms of Assessment

1. Inventories and interviews

2. Observations: anecdotal records, shadowing, and performance sampling

Factors to Consider When Assessing

1. domain being assessed

2. purpose of the assessment

3. economy of time

EXERCISE 28

Evaluating Test Items

This exercise provides you with experience in recognizing deficiencies in test items and correcting those deficiencies.

Directions

1. Read each of the test questions and identify the deficiency exhibited by the item.
2. Rewrite the item to reflect recommended practices.

1. Essay Items
   a. Discuss the different kinds of test question types introduced in this chapter.
   b. List the disadvantages of essay test questions.
2. Multiple-choice Questions
   a. Multiple choice questions should: (a) make frequent use of "all of the above" as a response; (b) have alternative responses of approximately the same length; (c) have some implausible alternatives; (d) never use questions in the stem; (e) all of the above.
   b. An effective multiple-choice question
      (1) is one answered correctly by most students
      (2) can measure students' understanding at a variety of cognitive levels
      (3) these questions should not be used
3. Matching Questions
   A. Longer stems   _____ items in the right column
   B. Shorter stems   _____ homogeneous
   C. Relationship of items _____ items in the left column
   D. Number of items   _____ same in both columns
4. True-False Questions
   a. True-False questions should never use "not," "always," etc.
   b. Negatively worded statements and ambiguity are anathemas.

EXERCISE 29

Validity

This exercise provides you with experience in constructing test items that are congruent with your instructional objectives. For a test to be valid it should measure that which you intended for students to learn.

Directions

1. Choose a topic or sequence of topics that could appropriately be taught in an elementary or middle school classroom in approximately one week. Write four instructional objectives for the topics of poten-

tial lessons that will allow you to write the test items requested below. For example, an objective calling for a response to an essay question would be quite different from an objective calling for a response to a matching question. List and number each instructional objective from 1 to 4.

2. Concurrent with writing the objectives above, also write the corresponding test item(s) that would be used on an achievement test to measure attainment of these objectives.
3. Write one test item of each of the following:
   a. essay question
   b. multiple-choice item
   c. matching question composed of five item stems
   d. true/false item
4. To the left of the number for each test item, in parentheses, indicate the number of the objective being tested by inserting the number corresponding to the objective on your list of objectives.

EXERCISE 30

Test Construction

This exercise provides you with experience in constructing a test using the suggestions provided in this chapter.

Directions

1. Construct a complete test on a topic commonly taught in an elementary or middle school classroom. The test should be neatly printed or typed, and **in a form ready to administer** to a class of students.
2. The test should be composed of the following number and kind of items:
   a. two essay questions (one at a cognitive level above knowledge)
   b. three multiple-choice items (two at cognitive levels above knowledge)
   c. one matching question composed of five item stems
   d. three true/false items
3. Include a separate answer sheet, also correctly formatted, and indicate the answer to each question and any criteria to be used in scoring the essay questions.

EXERCISE 31

A Study of Norm-Referenced Tests

This exercise provides you with some experience in using the teacher's manuals that accompany commercially available norm-referenced tests.

Directions

Read the teacher's manual for a norm-referenced test provided by your instructor. Answer the following questions:

1. What is the test purported to be measuring? What subscales, if any, does the test have?
2. What evidence is provided that the test is valid?
3. What evidence is provided that the test is reliable? What evidence is provided for the reliability of the subscales?
4. What kinds of scores does the test provide?
5. Choose a set of sample scores represented by each of the subscales and the total score. Interpret these scores as you would if using the test to make instructional decisions about the child or informing the parent about the child.

Grading **10**

Teachers observe and judge student performance in order to make a variety of decisions, including that of assigning grades. The context in which elementary and middle school teachers assign grades to their respective students is markedly different in some ways and similar in others.

An elementary teacher is called on to assess students and assign grades in a variety of subject areas, including reading, arithmetic, social studies, language arts, and science. The teacher asks students to perform a variety of tasks to demonstrate proficiency in these areas. In a second grade class, for example, these tasks might include:

- counting the days in a week or month
- counting the months of the year
- counting from 1 to 100
- role-playing the buying and selling of groceries
- measuring distances with a metric ruler
- computing combinations of numbers by using addition and subtraction
- telling stories about out-of-school experiences
- writing simple accounts of out-of-school experiences
- writing reports of some hands-on activity
- reading aloud to a small group of students
- composing simple lyrics
- making a simple musical instrument
- listing the roles of letter carriers, firefighters, police officers, and other similar occupations
- performing in a skit dramatizing the behavior of responsible adults in a family setting
- writing spelling words
- writing sentences applying simple grammar
- reading a calendar
- telling time
- cooking simple food items
- demonstrating setting a table

An elementary teacher may also be concerned with assessing students in order to report their work habits, effort, conduct, citizenship, social adjustment, and other areas that deal with the child's development. A second grade teacher, for example, when assessing development, may observe students to see whether they

- put away materials after using them
- do a task without being distracted
- listen to other students who are talking

- offer suggestions to others, without being domineering, about ways of doing their work
- disrupt other students who are working
- do tasks with efficiency
- take care of personal possessions
- lose or control their tempers
- know how to use the telephone
- observe common sanitation rules
- obey class and school rules
- talk to the teacher and other students with respect
- disagree with others in productive ways
- turn in homework
- talk with other students or stay to themselves
- help others

An elementary teacher observes many things—some formal and some informal—about each child in the course of a day. When grading a child on a task, an elementary teacher is likely to think of the achievement of the child in terms of the web of events surrounding that individual child. For example, the teacher may observe a child do poorly on a reading test. In assessing this performance the teacher will likely remember a chain of events leading up to the test performance. On the day the reading skills were practiced, the child was very distracted because just prior to the lesson she was subjected to ridicule and embarrassment by her peers during recess because she was not dressed properly. The child was not dressed properly because her father was an alcoholic and did not provide adequately for the family. Such knowledge is difficult to ignore when assigning grades. When reporting this child's reading grade, the teacher is likely to grade more leniently or temper any grade with comments in defense of the child. These same observations will also likely be used for decisions not directly related to grades. For example, the teacher, knowing that the child may be subject to ridicule from peers, might manipulate the situation so that the student might be given recognition for some achievement. This might be done as a way to raise the esteem of that child in the eyes of other students. Assessment for grading, then, cannot be separated from the formal and informal assessments constantly going on in an elementary classroom for many other purposes.

The kinds of assessments conducted by a middle school teacher will probably not differ in kind from those of an elementary teacher, but will certainly differ in degree. For example, a middle school teacher will likely teach five different classes for approximately 50 minutes each day. The amount of time each student can be observed will be significantly less than that spent by an elementary teacher. The assigned task of a middle school teacher is to teach one subject field. Occasionally he may also be asked to assess conduct or effort. The number of formal assessment tasks that the teacher will ask students to perform, and the number of informal observations of each student the teacher conducts, will be considerably less than that for an elementary teacher. The grading process for each student is simpler in some ways for the middle school teacher than it is for the elementary school teacher, but the number of students who must be assessed for grading purposes is much larger.

Regardless of the numbers of students to be assessed or the complexity of the assessment, assigning grades or marks is likely one of the most unpleasant, least comfortable, and least understood tasks teachers face. The process is fraught with pitfalls to lead the unwary teacher to unfairness in grading. The mistaken notion that students earn grades is one of the major misconceptions of the grading process because it prevents many teachers from examining the actual process they use in arriving at grades. This chapter examines the processes teachers use to determine grades, identifies some of the mistaken assumptions made in using these processes, and provides alternatives. The grading practices you use should minimize the trauma experienced by students and result in more reliable and fairer estimates of grades.

REASONS FOR USING GRADES

People are concerned about grades. Parents expect their children to receive grades in schools and, thinking they understand what a grade represents, they are comfortable with them. Parents seem to need grades as indicators of their child's achievement and would be uncomfortable without them. Some school systems have successfully replaced grades with alternative systems but only by using a process in which parents were informed and involved. Because you will not likely be working in such a district, alternative systems will not be discussed here.

Students also expect to receive grades and think they understand them. Some have been conditioned into relying on grades for their motivation. Teachers' constant reminders of the importance of grades eventually convince some students that they are important. Some students would feel quite uncomfortable if grades were removed as a source of motivation, and achievement could suffer.

Many businesses, colleges, and universities rely on grades as indicators of a student's potential success. Because grades are moderate predictors of success in institutions of higher education, such use is not without foundation. Although the reliability of predictions based on grades alone is not high, when grades are coupled with standardized test scores and other student data, useful predictions can be made.

Teachers are usually the people most concerned about grades. Imagine what you would face if you taught in a school that did not assign grades to students. What would you do to motivate students who were not interested in what you were trying to teach them? What procedures or instruments would you use to inform parents of students' progress? What would be the nature of the records on each student you would maintain? What mechanisms for quality control would you use? These and many other questions would likely arise in such a circumstance.

Teachers have come to depend on grades. Many teachers have the mistaken notion that grades are an effective form of extrinsic motivation to get students to want to learn. They constantly remind students that they need to learn things in order to "get a good grade." Actually, students who are likely to respond favorably to this form of motivation are already interested in learning. They have probably been achieving success and want to maintain the status quo. They are likely to respond favorably to other forms of motivation. It is unfortunate, but using grades as a form of motivation with these students actually causes them to come to depend on grades for motivation.

The students whom teachers most want to motivate by using low grades as a threat are the very ones least likely to be affected. Uninterested students with histories of failure or low grades know that they will not experience success in most classrooms even if they try. Past failures cause some of them to create situations that will allow them to rationalize their anticipated failure when they enter a new classroom. Such students usually rationalize failure in one of two ways: if they withdraw and don't try, they can always say, "I could have learned it if I tried, but I just couldn't see trying to learn that dumb stuff"; or, if students misbehave and are disruptive, they can say, "She was always picking on me. She gave me a bad grade because she just didn't like me." The threat of a bad grade will not cause these students to want to learn. If anything, such threats make it more likely that they will adopt one of these coping mechanisms.

Some teachers depend on the threat of low grades as a behavioral management tool, indicating that their behavioral management skills are deficient and must be developed. Using threats of poor grades as a way to compensate for inadequate behavioral management does a disservice to children. Grades should be indicators of achievement; when other factors, such as disruptive behavior, are allowed to influence grades, the grades become useless as indicators of achievement. The threat of lower grades seldom motivates students to behave. Students most likely to misbehave—those with histories of little success—are those who are least concerned about grades and least likely to modify their misbehavior as a result of such threats.

In spite of their deficiencies, grades do serve the function of being rough indicators of student achievement on which parents, students, teachers, colleges and universities, and others rely. Beyond this, grades have little to recommend them. However, because they continue to be used and are a necessary obligation of teachers, you must learn to apply the process of assigning grades in ways that will be equitable and will cause the least harm to students.

CHARACTERISTICS OF GRADES

Teachers tend to think of grades as something students earn. They fail to see the role that teacher subjectivity plays in the process of determining grades.

Examine the set of data taken from an actual school situation, shown in figure 10–1, which compares the grade distributions of six different middle school classes in the same subject and in the same school, for each of three teachers. The students in the six classes were randomly assigned, and no reason exists for believing the students in different classes possessed different abilities.

Percentage of Grades

	A	B	C	D	F
Teacher A					
Class 1	8	15	19	31	27
Class 2	8	13	26	33	19
Teacher B					
Class 1	16	25	27	23	9
Class 2	11	27	30	23	8
Teacher C					
Class 1	13	32	37	18	0
Class 2	26	31	32	10	1

Figure 10–1   Grade Distributions

How can the differences among these three teachers be explained? Several explanations are possible. Teacher A may not be as successful as Teachers B and C in getting students to learn (assuming comparable material is being taught, and comparable tests are being administered). If this were the case, should the students in Teacher A's classes be penalized for the teacher's inadequacy?

Another explanation might be that Teacher A has higher expectations for his students than do Teachers B and C. When 58 percent and 52 percent of the students in the two classes receive Ds or Fs, how reasonable are Teacher A's expectations? Any teacher can try to teach material that the majority of students cannot learn or teach the material in such an obscure way that students cannot learn. Is this really setting a higher standard than a teacher who chooses material most students **can** learn or who teaches with clarity so that most students **do** learn?

A third explanation might be that the teachers are teaching the same material and students are achieving equally, but the three teachers have different grading philosophies. Teacher A may feel that giving lower grades will motivate students more. Teacher C may feel that giving higher grades may motivate students. Teacher C may feel that student failure is the result of poor teaching, and that an effective teacher is one who ensures the success of students. Teacher C might be very uncomfortable with large numbers of Ds and Fs; teacher A may be quite comfortable, and even pleased, with such grades. Variation in grading philosophies is the most likely explanation for most of the differences in grade distributions among different teachers (Terwilliger, 1968). Teachers have a preconceived notion about the distribution of grades with which they are comfortable, and they manipulate the system, either consciously or subconsciously, to achieve that distribution. This process is essentially a subjective one, not objective, as many believe.

INDICATORS OF LEARNING

Tests are not the only factors to be considered when arriving at a grade or mark for a grading period. Many kinds of learning that are not easily measured by tests can occur in a classroom. Effective grading practices require that a variety of performances be evaluated for grading purposes. Indicators of learning, other than tests, that can be assessed include homework, written assignments, projects, library research papers, skill performances, oral reports, laboratory reports, term papers, drawings, construction of visual materials, journals, notebooks of classroom notes, anecdotal records of students' ability to respond during drill and practice, and book reports.

To base grades only on test scores is to measure student achievement too narrowly. Other achievement measures, however, introduce even more variability into the process of grading, and so you must take some care to reduce errors as much as possible. For example, when grading written assignments or projects, teachers will have the tendency to give higher grades for the same quality of work to students who are considered disadvantaged, slow, or who have better penmanship, even when penmanship is not one of the stated criteria (Chase, 1968; Klein and Hart, 1968). Knowing these tendencies may help you be more equitable in assigning grades to written work.

Some simple procedures may also help you avoid introducing extraneous criteria into the grading process. First, **establish the criteria to be used in grading the task before the task is assigned**. Define the criteria with enough specificity that the task can be scored objectively. For example, saying that students "will write a paper about their summer vacation" or "make a poster" is too vague. You will need to list all of the factors that will be judged to decide which papers or posters will be given an A, which will be given a B, and so on. Will you be concerned about the length? The format? Application of certain principles or rules? Neatness? Use of colors? Size? You must decide these matters in detail before giving the assignment.

Second, **announce the criteria to the students at the time the task is assigned**. Students must know on what they will be evaluated. This will not only make the evaluation system fairer, but will make the introduction of extraneous variables less likely. If such variables are introduced, students will let you know in a hurry!

Third, **when scoring the task, refer to your criteria**. Score the task for all the students on the first variable, then all students on the second variable, and so on. Extraneous variables will less likely be introduced by this process. Essentially, this is the same process proposed for scoring essay questions on tests.

When measuring student classroom participation for grading purposes, the process should be as systematic as possible. Keeping careful anecdotal records on each student introduces consistency and reduces error. Three-by-five inch cards can be helpful for this purpose. As with all such measures, have specific criteria, and record data related only to those stated criteria. When evaluating participation, try to focus on the quality of thinking involved in students' questions and responses. Because frequency of questions or responses quite often depends on the personality or needs of students, avoid emphasizing frequency. Through the continual use of anecdotal records, you will gain a more accurate perception of the actual participation of students. Without such records, grades on participation would be based on long-term impressions that are usually highly inaccurate.

ASSIGNING GRADES TO TESTS

Teachers, when faced with the task of assigning grades to test scores, will tend to use one of two options: based on some percentage of correct responses, or on a "curve" so that some percentage of students receives each grade.

Some teachers score the test and then assign grades on the basis of predetermined percentages of correct responses based on two common distributions of percentages.

90–100	A		90–100	A
80– 89	B		80– 89	B
70– 79	C	or	70– 79	C
60– 69	D		0– 69	F
0– 59	F			

(Ds may be assigned to students with scores below 69 if the pupils tried "their best.")

At first this seems to be an objective method for determining grades; students receive whatever grade they "earn." However, such thinking is fallacious. When teachers write an examination, they choose the content to test and then put the content to be tested into questions. Will they try to anticipate the difficulty level of questions? Will they choose levels of difficulty for questions that will likely result in a distribution of scores with which they are comfortable? The answer is usually yes to both questions. If on the preceding examination students had particularly high scores, the teacher will be likely to increase the difficulty level of the questions on the next test so that the scores (and, hence, the grades) average out to a distribution with which he is more comfortable. On the other hand, if the scores on the preceding examination were very low, the same teacher would be more likely to choose easier questions for the next test, or spend more time teaching the content in order to try to attain a more acceptable distribution of scores. If this seems like a subjective process to you, your perception is correct. Teachers will consciously or subconsciously manipulate the system to achieve an approximate grade distribution with which they are comfortable.

Relying on set percentage distributions to determine grades on tests also involves the questionable assumptions that the instruction provided is always of equal effectiveness and that the level of difficulty for different examinations does not vary. To assume otherwise is to grade students not only on their achievement, but also on the teacher's teaching effectiveness and the variation in difficulty of tests. Both practices would be unfair. Unfortunately, teaching effectiveness is seldom without variation, and tests rarely have the same level of difficulty. Although the practice of using a set distribution of scores to determine grades seems objective and fair, it turns out to be neither.

A second popular method of assigning grades to a set of test scores is to "curve" the scores so that a preset percentage of students receives each grade. A common example of curving is based on the normal curve.

Top 10%   A
Next 20%   B
Next 40%   C
Next 20%   D
Next 10%   F

This method avoids some of the problems inherent in using fixed scores to determine grades. The assumptions of equal levels of difficulty for tests and unvarying effectiveness of instruction are unnecessary. However, curving grades is not without problems. The choice of percentages of students to receive each grade is subjective. The ability levels of the students in a class are assumed to be normally distributed, which seldom occurs in small groups. When using this system, no matter how hard students try to succeed, some will always fail. Because the distribution of scores on most tests will correlate highly with the ability levels of the students, usually the same ones will fail. These students will quickly realize the trap they are in and will either withdraw from the competition or become disruptive. The process of ensuring the failure of some students is inherently destructive.

Any system you adopt for assigning grades to test scores will be subjective. If your test is reliable (not always a safe assumption), students will earn a rank in a group of students by the score they receive on a test. The assignment of a grade to that ranking is going to be subjective and fraught with difficulty. Recognizing this, you may want to consider the following procedure when assigning grades to test scores:

1. Make out a key for a test before administering the examination. Then examine each item on the test and decide which items are measuring basic understandings. Estimate the number of questions measuring basic understandings you feel a student with a "passing" knowledge should be able to answer. (Note: realize that any student will miss approximately 10 percent of the items on an achievement test by misreading them, misplacing their intended answer, or in some way accidentally missing the items.) Now determine the minimum score you feel a student should make to pass, as well as the maximum score likely to be attained. Then arrange, at approximately equal intervals, the cutoff scores (those scores that indicate the breaking point between grades) for other grades between these two scores. With this process you are using your professional judgment to establish some standard with which to compare scores.

2. After the test is administered and scored, arrange the test papers from the highest score to the lowest. Calculate the average or mean for the test. (Note: at this point assume that from test to test, unless there is strong reason to believe that some outside event significantly affected the students' performance, students as a group will exert about the same amount of effort to learn and to succeed on tests.) If the mean

varies greatly from the one you anticipated, either the test varied in difficulty or the instruction varied in effectiveness. Because neither factor should influence the grades, adjust your cutoff scores to reflect these variations.

3.   Again examine the passing cutoff score. If the number of students failing to achieve this score is greater than that with which you are comfortable, then you may wish to adjust the cutoff score downward. If some of the students attempted to complete **all** of the learning activities provided and were still not able to score well on the examination, then the learning activities provided were probably ineffective or the test was too difficult. You may wish to adjust the cutoff scores downward to include these students.

4.   In situations requiring percentage scores to coincide with certain grades, translate the grades assigned into the required standard scores. Record these adjusted scores along with the assigned grade rather than the raw scores and assigned grades.

When deciding on cutoff scores for grades, recognize that the cutoff score should allow for errors in measurement. For example, if 70 percent is chosen as a passing score, recognize that a student with a score of 69 may know just as much or more than the student who received a 70 or 71 or even higher. Unreliability in testing could be a significant factor in determining differences between students. Allowing for this error when deciding on grades to be assigned to scores is recommended (Drayer, 1979).

Some experts feel that grades should not be assigned to individual test scores but should be assigned only at the end of a grading period (Terwilliger, 1971). This practice may have the advantage of reducing the emphasis on grades, but you will still need to inform students about their performance on individual tests, as well as some indication of the score's ultimate effect on their grades. Failure to inform students of their performance on tests could create anxiety and uncertainty that would be counterproductive.

DETERMINING GRADES FOR A GRADING PERIOD

Some experts like to refer to the symbols used to indicate achievement on individual tasks as "grades," and the symbols used to indicate achievement for a grading period as "marks" (Kubiszyn and Borich, 1987). Such a distinction is not made here.

Arriving at a grade for the grading period involves comparing a student's performance to some criteria. The following comparisons are possible:

□ student's achievement compared to the student's ability

□ student's achievement compared to the student's effort

□ student's achievement compared to that of other students

□ student's achievement compared with some standard

□ the change in the student's achievement (improvement) compared to the student's effort or ability, other students', or some standard.

Considering final grades

Achievement vs. Ability

Grades based on ability are assigned depending on how well a student achieved compared to how well she could be expected to achieve. A student with average potential who achieves at an above-average level would be given a high grade; a student with low ability who achieved at an average level also would be given a high grade. On the surface this appears to be a reasonable system; however, some problems do arise. If a student with high ability achieves at an average level, she should be given a low grade because she is not achieving to potential. Let's say that this student is therefore given a grade of D. Suppose another student with low ability also has an achievement equivalent to that of the high-ability student. Such an achievement might be well beyond that which would be expected for that student. This student would then be given a grade of A. What do these two grades represent? Clearly, the two students have nearly the same level of achievement in absolute terms, yet their grades do not reflect this similarity. How are others to know how to interpret grades from such a system? Also, what measures will be used to determine ability? What system of calculations would be used to ensure objectivity? What weight should reading ability play in judging achievement in mathematics, music, and so on? Will all students need to be given ability or aptitude measures in all areas each year? Would comparing a student's achievement to her ability be fair if such measures were not used? Such a system is not without severe difficulties and is not recommended.

Achievement vs. Effort

Grades based on effort require a teacher to adjust the achievement of each student by some factor dependent on the amount of effort each student exerted. A low-ability student who exerted a great deal of effort and achieved at the expected low level would be given a high grade, possibly an A. A high-ability student who achieved at the expected high level with average effort would be given a grade of C. Even though the low-ability student learned far less than the high-ability student, the grade assigned gives a quite different impression. The teacher who uses such a system has the intention of rewarding students for effort exerted. This is a noble goal; however, it creates serious problems. As in the case of comparing ability with achievement, what does a grade mean in such a system? If a teacher wishes to evaluate effort, then establishing a system (common in elementary schools) calling for separate achievement and effort grades would better serve the purpose. Such a system has many advantages and should be given serious consideration.

If such a separate effort grade is to be assigned, then do not attempt to grade effort strictly on incidental things students say to you. Because some students are more willing than others to mention the effort they put into school work, to depend solely on incidental student comments as indicators of effort is to ensure that some students' efforts are overlooked. If you intend to estimate a grade based on effort, then keep systematic anecdotal records on each student, using predetermined and announced criteria. This means you will record similar data on each and every student so that you can make valid comparisons.

Achievement vs. Other Students

Assigning a grade based on the relationship of the achievement of a student to other students in the class is commonly referred to as grading on a curve. As already mentioned, this system is based on some assumptions that may inherently be unfair, that in every class some students will get high grades and some will get low grades or will not pass. When two classes have quite dissimilar populations, the students in a high-ability class who achieve at an average level when compared to students in a low-ability class who achieve at an average level, may have very different absolute achievements but receive the same grades. This system suffers from an inherent unfairness, unless classes are all equivalent and similar distributions of grades are adopted. Such a system will also assure the failure of a certain segment of the student population. No matter how much a teacher is willing to work with these low-ability students, and no matter how much they achieve, if they are still at the bottom of their class in absolute achievement, they will fail. This would be demoralizing to both teacher and student. Students suffering under such a system will quickly lose their self-esteem, become alienated from the school, and will either become disruptive or will withdraw.

Improvement vs. Other

Teachers sometimes determine grades by attempting to measure the change in achievement from the beginning of the grading period to the end of the period. This measurement is then compared to a measure of the student's ability or effort, to the improvement of other students, or to some predetermined standard. This system has little to recommend it. Pretests and posttests used to measure achievement will both measure with error. To use the difference between the scores merely magnifies the error. In addition, those who score high on the pretest have fewer items on which to demonstrate improvement. Those who score low on the pretest can increase their posttests scores more easily because many more items are available for them to answer correctly on the posttest. The phenomenon called **regression toward the mean** operates in such a situation. Those who scored high on the pretest in part scored high because they were on the positive side of the random errors being made. Those who scored low were on the negative side of random errors. On subsequent tests, those who scored high on the pretest will, by chance, score lower on the posttest; those who scored lower on the pretest will score higher on the posttest—scores for both groups will move toward the mean. This phenomenon makes demonstrating improvement for those who initially scored high very difficult. Accounting for regression toward the mean is difficult at best. Due to these and other factors, avoid the use of improvement as a basis for assigning grades.

Achievement vs. A Standard

The teacher who measures a student's achievement against a standard establishes criteria for each grade. Students meeting the criteria for a certain grade are assigned that grade. In theory, no preconceived distribution of grades is used. All students who meet the criteria for a grade of A would be given an A, all who meet the criteria for a B would be assigned a B, and so on. No inherent reasons exist for limiting the number of As or any other grades students in a class are assigned. This system has many advantages to recommend it, and is recommended over other systems.

Rarely do elementary and middle school teachers want to know only that a student has attained a certain standard for the purpose of a grade. Teachers usually want to know by how much a student has exceeded or fallen short of a predetermined level of performance. This allows teachers to adjust the curriculum in response to the performance of individual students. Because teachers are already diagnosing student learning compared to certain performance standards, using the same observation for grading purposes usually follows.

Using teacher-determined standards and comparing student performance to these standards for grading purposes is not without difficulties, however. Teachers have a preconceived notion about the distribution of grades with which they are comfortable and will modify the criteria used as a standard so that, with time, the distribution of grades for their classes will be that with which they are comfortable. Establishing a standard, then, is anything but an objective process. A teacher can make the standards anything he wishes them to be. Achievement that would be considered an A for one teacher may well be a B for another teacher. And how long do you think an administrator would allow you, as a teacher, to assign all As or some other "distorted" (in his mind) distribution of grades? In spite of these pitfalls, if grades are to be assigned, using carefully developed and reasonable standards as the basis for grades has the best chance of being fair and flexible.

A RECOMMENDED PHILOSOPHY OF GRADING

Working effectively with students requires that each student be provided an opportunity to succeed. One way to provide that opportunity is to structure grading so that it does not ensure failure. If tests are the only measure of achievement used for grading purposes, then some students may be doomed to failure.

A question often raised is, "But, how do I ensure against failure for students and still assign grades in some legitimate fashion acceptable to parents and the school administration?" The answer is not easy for many teachers to accept because it involves a rather significant change in both basic philosophy and practice.

Confidence comes from success.

Basis Assumptions

Two basic assumptions must be made about students and teaching in order to put this grading philosophy into proper perspective.

1. Students are capable of learning if they are provided with learning experiences that use effective methodology of adequate duration and if they are presented with content within their ability levels.

2. Students are capable of demonstrating this learning if assessed with appropriate measures.

Too often, when a student's score falls below the chosen cutoff score, the student is assumed to be at fault. The student, not the instruction or the test, is called into question. In reality, if a student has made an honest attempt to complete **all** classroom activities and homework assignments and does not demonstrate "passing" achievement, then the teacher can safely assume that:

1. the methodology was ineffective

2. the instruction was of too short a duration

3. the student lacked the prerequisite knowledge, skills, or intellectual development to learn the content being taught

4. the test was too difficult or did not measure that which was taught

Should a student be failed through no fault of her own? Such a practice is intuitively and actually unfair. When faced with that situation, you should examine the four possible causes of failure listed **before** you decide something is wrong with the student. The factors causing the student's lack of success should be changed. Any student who conscientiously does **all** you ask should be able to demonstrate acceptable learning. If she cannot, and none of the four factors listed are the cause, then she may be inappropriately placed at that grade level or in that course.

If you cannot accept the fact that all students are capable of learning when appropriate learning experiences are provided, then you will be unable to accept this philosophy of grading and the practices it implies. To accept the grading philosophy being proposed requires that you have confidence in the quality of the learning experiences you provide. You must believe that those who complete all of the activities provided in your classroom have learned the minimum expected of all students. Teachers with this kind of confidence will have little difficulty in accepting this grading philosophy. They also will have little difficulty in being able to justify their grading practices to parents and school administrators.

Recommended Procedures

In using this philosophy of grading, there are several recommended procedures. All students must have the assurance of at least a grade of C, or satisfactory, **if and only if they make an honest attempt to complete all of the activities,** including tests, that are expected of all students. These suggestions also assume that the students have been placed at a grade level consistent with their abilities. If these criteria are met, then students must have an absolute assurance that they cannot fail, and if their test grades warrant, they are eligible to receive higher grades. Students must recognize that they are not being "given" anything: they must do the activities to receive any credit and they must attend class if they are going to do the activities. Students should never be given anything they have not earned. Neither should they be denied credit they earn simply to satisfy someone's arbitrarily imposed grading standards.

Choosing to do or not to do things is in reality **the student's** option. All you as a teacher can do is assure them that if they attend class and make an honest effort to do the activities, credit will not be denied. If they fail to do the activities reasonably, then they will not earn credit for those activities. To earn credit, they must demonstrate acceptable knowledge of the subject through test scores, assignment, projects, and other evaluated activities.

Some will say that this will result in grade inflation. It will not. Grade inflation results when teachers raise the average grades of students while achievement is not raised. In this case we are allowing students to achieve at higher levels and recognizing that achievement in our grade structure.

To accept this grading scheme, and to make it work successfully, you must have confidence that if you provide learning experiences appropriate for all students, they will learn. You must also have the ability to provide learning experiences that ensure that students who make an honest effort to learn will learn the minimum required of all students for passing.

GUIDELINES FOR GRADING

Grades are single symbols conveying the teacher's evaluation of a student's performance. As single symbols, they have serious limitations in communicating the various factors that go into determining the grade. A teacher cannot compress all of the necessary judgments into one letter grade and expect it to represent a student's progress and development. In essence, very little is communicated other than a simple categorization of a student's achievement. Grades, when used improperly, can be dehumanizing and destructive. The grading process is neither pleasant nor easy. Trying to build in as much accuracy and humaneness into the process as possible is something on which teachers should place high priority. To accomplish this goal, the following guidelines are suggested:

1. Establish standards consistent with the prerequisite knowledge and skills students bring to your classroom. Base your grades on these standards and avoid trying to compare achievement of a student with others, or with the student's effort or ability.

2. Choose content consistent with the intellectual development of students. If you choose to teach abstract content beyond the intellectual development of students,

then you ensure their failure (Deutsch, 1979; Lawson and Renner, 1978; Sayre and Ball, 1978).

3.   Explain your grading policies early in the year and remind students of those policies periodically (Drayer, 1979).

4.   Inform students of the criteria to be used in an evaluation prior to each task to be evaluated.

5.   Base grades for a grading period on a variety of objective evidence systematically obtained on each student. To use incidentally obtained subjective evidence does a disservice to many students due to the unfairness of such a practice.

6.   Tie grades to important objectives, not merely to trivial memorization of facts. Also, avoid assigning high grades only to those who conform to your views in situations where other views could be reasonably held (Bostrum, Vlandis, and Rosenbaum, 1961). Remember, students will tend to try to accept and/or learn those things on which they are graded.

7.   Provide credit and/or recognition for students for those parts of work successfully completed. Students will be encouraged to sustain effort as a result.

8.   Remember that all measurement involves error. Try to allow for this error when making distinctions between the grades assigned different students.

9.   Grades assigned for achievement should be indicators of achievement only. If other factors such as effort or behavior are to be evaluated, then use separate grades for these factors. Do not allow extraneous factors to influence grades meant to communicate achievement.

IMPLICATIONS FOR PLANNING

The assessment of students requires careful planning. When identifying goals and objectives for units or lessons, be sure to identify the tasks to be assessed. Because some assessments such as effort or work habits require anecdotal records, you must develop the instruments on which these will be recorded beforehand. Each day you should observe a selected sample of students, but you must plan this carefully if you are to observe students equally on each criterion.

Schedule tests and major assignments so that outside events will not significantly affect students' performance. Also, consider the prompt return of tests when scheduling tests. For example, you would not want to schedule a test the day before a Christmas or spring holiday.

REFERENCES

Bostrum , R. N., J. W. Vlandis, and M. E. Rosenbaum. 1961. Grades as reinforcing contingencies and attitude change. *Journal of Educational Psychology, 52:* 112–115.

Chase, C. I. 1968. The impact of some obvious variables on essay test scores. *Journal of Educational Measurement, 5*(4): 315–318.

Deutsch, M. 1979. Education and distribution justice: Some reflections on grading systems. *American Psychologist, 39:* 391–401.

Drayer, A. M. 1979. *Problems in middle and high school teaching: A handbook for student teachers and beginning teachers.* Boston: Allyn & Bacon.

Klein, S. P., and F. M. Hart. 1968. Chance and systematic factors affecting essay grades. *Journal of Educational Measurement, 5*(3): 197–206.

Kubiszyn, T., and G. Borich. 1987. *Educational testing and measurement: Classroom application and practice* (2d Ed.). Glenview, IL: Scott, Foresman.

Lawson, A. E., and J. W. Renner. 1975. Relationships of science subject matter and developmental levels of learners. *Journal of Research in Science Teaching, 12*(4): 347–358.

Sayre, S., and D. W. Ball. 1975. Piagetian cognitive development and achievement in science. *Journal of Research in Science Teaching, 12*(2): 165–174.

Terwilliger, J. S. 1968. Individual differences in the marking practices of secondary teachers. *Journal of Educational Measurement, 5*(1): 9–15.

Terwilliger, J. S. 1971. *Assigning grades to students.* Glenview, IL: Scott, Foresman.

CHAPTER REVIEW

Functions of Grades

1. They communicate students' academic achievement to parents, institutions of higher education, businesses, and others.
2. They serve as crude predictors of future academic success.

Characteristics of Grades

1. Grades are based on a teacher's subjective process.
2. Grades are not directly earned by students, but are assigned by teachers.
3. As single symbols, grades have serious limitations in communicating the factors determining the grade.

Assigning Grades to Tasks

1. Establish the criteria to be used for grading before the task is assigned.
2. Announce the criteria to the students at the time the task is assigned.
3. When scoring the task, score all students for the first criterion before going on to the next.

Assigning Grades to Achievement Tests

1. Make a key to be used in scoring the test prior to the administration of the test.
2. Determine a passing cutoff score based on an analysis of the number of questions measuring basic understanding.
3. Determine other cutoff scores.
4. After the test is administered, adjust cutoff scores based on the distribution of scores.

Determining Grades for a Grading Period

1. Evaluate a variety of performances, not just tests.
2. Collect objective data on all measures systematically so that the same kinds of data are collected for each student.
3. Determine the relative weightings to be given to each measure and ensure the final grade reflects these weightings.
4. The basic criteria chosen for passing should provide all students with the opportunity for success if they complete all assigned tasks.
5. Avoid comparing the achievement of a student with others or with the student's effort or ability.
6. Tie grades to important objectives, not merely trivial memorization of facts and performance of basic skills.
7. Provide credit and/or recognition to students for those parts of work successfully completed.
8. Remember that all measurement involves error. Try to allow for this error when making distinctions between the grades assigned different students.
9. Grades assigned students for achievement should be indicators of achievement only. If other factors such as effort or behavior are to be evaluated, then use separate grades for these factors.

EXERCISE 32

Assigning Grades to Test Scores

One of the tasks you will face as a teacher is assigning grades to test scores. In this exercise you will be given descriptions of students taking a test and their test scores. You will then assign grades to each student for this test.

Directions.   Record the results of the following tasks on the answer sheets provided.

1. Using any criteria, process, and/or procedures you wish, assign a grade, using A, B, C, D, and F, to each of the scores recorded for each student on the test.
2. Count how many As you assigned, how many Bs, and so on.
3. After you have completed giving each student a grade, and you have arrived at a distribution of grades, answer the following questions in the spaces provided on the answer sheet.
   a. What are the cutoff scores between the grades A and B, and also between D and F? Give one reason used in arriving at each of the cutoff scores listed.
   b. Did you make any exceptions for individual students to the cutoff scores chosen between any of the grades? If so, list the name of the student for each exception and give the reason for each exception.
4. During the next class period your instructor will have you discuss the following questions.
   a. What set of decisions were used in arriving at the cutoff scores?
   b. How did your assigned grades for selected students differ? What were some of the reasons for these differences? Were all of the reasons equally valid?
   c. How did your grade distributions vary? What were some of the reasons for the differences? Were all of the reasons equally valid?

Pupil Description.   You may use these descriptions for both exercise 32 and 33 if you choose

1. Aleck, Smart. Has an easy time in school. IQ about 140. Comes from a broken Anglo family. Doesn't seem to work hard at school, but turns everything in.

2. Black, Bart. Constantly disrupts class, and puts little effort into his work. IQ about 130. Upper-middle-class Anglo family, and wears the latest designer fashions.

3. Bell, Dumb. Has consistently been assigned to "slow" groups. IQ about 85. Comes from a broken Anglo home, and lives with a grandmother. Makes an attempt to do all activities, but says she is not able to do homework because her grandmother makes her work.

4. Guy, Nice. A fairly friendly Black boy. IQ about 90. Lives with his widowed mother. Says he tries hard, and really wants to do well.

5. Glass, Looking. Consistently good student in all of her classes. IQ about 120. Both parents are professional people. Looking is a very popular Black girl, and seems to enjoy school.

6. Heavy, Very. A well-behaved girl who is not popular with her peers. A good student who tries hard. IQ about 110. Comes from a middle-class Anglo family.

7. Jones, Davey. A typical "goof-off." Makes little attempt to do assignments. IQ about 100. Comes from a middle-class Anglo family. Likes cars and doing mechanical things.

8. Juice, Orange. Says she really tries hard, but has trouble learning. IQ about 90. Lives with her divorced mother. She is Hispanic and has some problems with English.

9. Makeit, Willie. Has consistently been assigned to "slow" groups. IQ about 90. Comes from a middle-class Anglo family. Turns in all homework and says he tries his best on everything.

10. Nutt, Ima. Very friendly and well-behaved Black girl. IQ about 110. Lives with her divorced mother. Seems well-intentioned, and is always willing to answer questions.

11. Ray, Violet. Average Anglo student. IQ about 110. Very quiet, and seldom talks in class. Lives with her divorced father.

12. Seedy, Pretty. Just doesn't seem able to grasp the subject. IQ about 95. Comes from a poor Anglo family. Has given up trying to do class assignments.

13. Sharp, Kinda. Seems to do well in most classes. IQ about 120. Comes from a middle-class Hispanic family. Says her cheer leading keeps her from spending needed time on her homework.

14. Sore, Cold. A dirty, smelly little girl. IQ about 95. From a poor Anglo family. Very quiet and shy. Seldom says anything in class.

15. Vendor, Street. An average student. IQ about 100. Lower-middle-class Anglo family. Occasionally misbehaves, but tries to do most classroom activities.

16. Welk, Larry. An Anglo who talks with an accent. IQ about 140. Likes to get up in front of the class and show off. Tends toward the artistic.

17. Won't, Betty. Rarely comes to class. IQ about 120. Lower-middle-class Hispanic family. Seems more interested in things other than school.

Test Scores

Name _____

Maximum score possible is 50.

Pupil	Score	Grade
Aleck, Smart	50	
Black, Bart	45	
Bell, Dumb	29	
Glass, Looking	44	
Guy, Nice	39	
Heavy, Very	41	
Jones, Davey	25	
Juice, Orange	38	
Makeit, Willie	39	
Nutt, Ima	44	
Ray, Violet	40	
Seedy, Pretty	27	
Sharp, Kinda	42	
Sore, Cold	34	
Vendor, Street	36	
Welk, Larry	42	
Won't, Betty	29	

Grade Distribution

Grade	Number
A	
B	
C	
D	
F	

Answer the following questions:

1. What are the cutoff scores between the grades A and B and between D and F? Give one reason used in arriving at each of the cutoff scores listed.

2. Did you make any exceptions to the cutoff scores chosen between any of the grades? If so, list the name of each exception and give the reason for each.

3. Examine the test scores and grades for each student. Were any students given different grades for the same score? If so, for what reason?

EXERCISE 33

Gradebook Assignment

Maintaining a gradebook is a task all teachers face. You will use the information recorded in your gradebook to arrive at grades for a grading period. This exercise will allow you to use information found in a gradebook to determine a set of grades. An examination of the decisions you make in this process, along with the reasons used in arriving at those decisions, can be of value to you. This examination will help you recognize any faulty or unfair logic you used in arriving at your grades.

Directions

1. Examine the data recorded in the gradebook provided in this exercise. Assume this data relates to some academic area such as social studies, mathematics, or science. Also examine the data on each student given in exercise 32. Use any procedures you wish to arrive at a grade for each student. Record a grade in the gradebook for each student.
2. Count the number of As, Bs, etc., given and record the distribution of grades for the class you graded in the spaces provided.
3. After you have completed giving each student a grade and arriving at a distribution of grades, answer the following questions.
   a. What are the cutoff scores between grades A and B and between D and F? Give one reason used in arriving at each of the cutoff scores listed.
   b. Did you make any exceptions to the cutoff scores chosen between any of the grades? If so, list the name of each student who was an exception and give the reason for each.
4. During the next class period your instructor may have you discuss the following questions either as a small group or as a whole class.
   a. What set of decisions were used in arriving at the cutoff scores? Were different decisions made by different members in your class or group?
   b. How did your assigned grades for selected students differ among members in your class or group? What were some of the reasons for these differences? Were all of the reasons equally valid?
   c. How did your grade distributions vary among members in your group? What were some of the reasons for the differences? Were all of the reasons equally valid?
   d. What weights were assigned the different tasks? What were some reasons for assigning different weights?

Your Gradebook

Name _____

Student	I	II	III	IV	V	VI	VII	VIII	IX	X	Grade
Possible points	50	75	100								
Aleck, Smart	50	69	75	B+	+	+	*	+	70		
Black, Bart	45	71	87	B	+	+	+	+	65		
Bell, Dumb	29	68	63	C−	0	0	0	0	82		
Glass, Looking	44	74	93	A−	+	*	+	+	95		
Guy, Nice	39	55	72	B	-	-	-	*	86		
Heavy, Very	41	65	77	A+	-	-	*	*	92		
Jones, Davey	25	52	66	D	0	0	0	0	45		
Juice, Orange	38	49	71	C	*	*	-	*	64		
Makeit, Willie	39	38	65	D+	-	-	-	-	93		
Nutt, Ima	44	67	82	B	*	*	*	*	91		
Ray, Violet	40	57	74	B−	*	-	*	+	72		
Seedy, Pretty	27	39	59	F	0	0	0	0	63		
Sharp, Kinda	42	59	83	A	-	-	-	0	86		
Sore, Cold	34	52	69	C−	-	*	-	*	66		
Vendor, Street	36	56	72	B−	*	*	*	*	74		
Welk, Larry	42	72	99	A+	+	*	+	+	97		
Won't, Betty	29	53	58	D−	0	0	0	0	55		

Explanation:

		Homework:	
I	Weekly Test	+	Excellent
II	Weekly Test	*	Acceptable
III	Major Test	-	Unacceptable
IV	Written Project	0	Not turned in
V-VIII	Homework		
IX	Participation		
X	Final ranking		

Grade Distribution

Grade	Number
A	_____
B	_____
C	_____
D	_____
F	_____

Answer the following questions:

1. What are the cutoff scores between grades A and B and between D and F? Give one reason used in arriving at each of the cutoff scores listed.

2. Did you make any exceptions to the cutoff scores chosen between any of the grades for individual students? If so, list the name of each exception and give the reason for each.

3. In what way was the homework assessment used to determine grades? What were the reasons?

4. Would the tasks assessed allow each student to pass if they completed all of the activities in class as well as homework? In what ways would you recommend the tasks that were assessed be changed?

OBSERVATION EXERCISE 34

Analyzing a Report Card

This exercise provides you with an opportunity to think about the kinds of assessments that might be used in arriving at grades for report cards. You will also begin to develop a rationale for the choices in assessments to be used.

Directions. Obtain a blank report card from the teacher with whom you are working in the school. Make a photocopy of the report card to attach to this exercise. Complete the following tasks:

    1.   Choose one of the academic areas on the report card and list the kinds of assessments you would use to arrive at a grade in that academic area for one grading period. Describe each of the assessments and give one reason for including each.

    2.   Each kind of assessment used in arriving at a grade may be weighted differently; that is, each may have different effects on the final grade. For each assessment used in the preceding item, indicate the relative effect it will have on the final grade for a grading period. Give one reason to support the weighting given each assessment.

    3.   Repeat the above two tasks, but choose a nonacademic area such as citizenship, conduct, effort, etc.

PART SIX

PRACTICUM TEACHING OR OBSERVATION EXERCISES

This part of the textbook provides some practical experience with the skills of teaching. The exercises are designed to be used in one of three possible ways: teaching students in the classroom; teaching peers; or observing model teaching lessons. In addition to the practice or observation of skills, you will learn some of the skills in observing and analyzing teaching behavior, which will help you learn how to make needed changes in behavior to improve teaching effectiveness.

Learning to teach is a lifelong process. The information and practice provided in this book are merely the beginning of that process. Developing the skills of observing and analyzing teaching behavior will help you become more self-reliant in solving your problems. Such self-reliance will allow you to continue to grow as a teacher without total dependence on others.

PRACTICUM TEACHING OR OBSERVATION EXERCISES

Because not all of you are in situations that will allow you to use these exercises as practices in teaching, some of you will use them for observations and analysis purposes only. If you are going to be using these exercises in a teaching situation with students or peers, skip ahead to the section Practicum Teaching Exercises. If you are going to be restricted to observing classrooms, continue reading the next section, Observing Classrooms.

OBSERVING CLASSROOMS

These exercises have been designed so that in the absence of actual teaching practice you can still learn some of the skills involved in observing teaching and then analyzing that teaching for strengths and weaknesses. Your instructor will provide the teaching to be observed in one of three ways: by playing a videotape of a teaching situation, teaching a model lesson, or having one or more of you demonstrate the lesson. Your instructor will assign some or all of you to observe certain skills being demonstrated in the lesson. Following the observations, you will complete part or all of the Observation Guide and Observer-Analysis for that lesson.

The sections Preparation for Observations, Preparing Observer Analysis and Observation Guide, and Observing Teaching Behaviors found in this introduction provide information necessary for you to do the exercises. When preparing for observing particular lessons, you will need to study the section Observing the Lesson provided in each exercise. You will also follow any directions given to the observer within each exercise. You will make the same observations as the observer and complete the Observation Guide and Observer Analysis, unless your instructor divides the tasks among the class members. Your analyses will be discussed in your class after your observations.

PRACTICUM TEACHING EXERCISES

The practicum teaching exercises provide practice with some of the skills introduced in this textbook in situations that allow you to concentrate on skills emphasized in each exercise. The complexity of the teaching situation is minimized by reducing the number of tasks required and/or the number of students to be taught. These exercises, when used as teaching exercises, are rarely complete in the way that teaching lessons would be conducted in the actual classroom. Students used for these exercises may be either your peers or actual elementary or middle school students. Since actual classrooms for practice with children are not always available to beginning education students, the exercises have been written so that they can be used while teaching your peers. For those of you in situations that do not allow actual practice of the skills, the exercises have been designed to allow you to observe and analyze the teaching behaviors of teachers in classrooms. These observations will help you develop the skills of observing teaching and then analyzing observations to recognize strengths and weaknesses. These observation and analysis skills will be useful later when you begin to practice teaching in the classroom.

Teaching these lessons will differ in some respects from being the teacher responsible for a classroom of students. You will not need to worry about disruptive behavior, because either you will be teaching your peers, or, if in a classroom, the teacher will deal with all disruptive behavior. This should make these exercises less intimidating. Even then, teaching in these exercises may seem threatening, but those feelings will pass. If teaching your peers, the choice of content and the nature of your interactions will be different from those found in the classroom. Then, too, the eagerness and willingness of your peers to learn will also not be representative of most classrooms. In spite of these differences and the artificiality they introduce, the advantages outweigh the disadvantages in this approach to learning basic skills.

If you are fortunate enough to be able to work with small groups of elementary or middle school students, the situation will not be as artificial as that of working with your peers. Although the teacher will assume responsibility for behavioral management, the content and interactions that occur will be the same as in an actual classroom.

These practicum exercises limit the complexity of the tasks you will be asked to use in your teaching, thus allowing you to practice a limited number of skills without being concerned with all of the complexities of the teaching process. Learning to teach is somewhat similar to learning how to write a novel. One doesn't learn how to write a novel in one lesson; rather, one learns the simple and complex skills involved in writing a novel in situations of reduced complexity. For example, one must first learn the meaning of words and how to spell them, and then proceed from there. Expecting students during the early stages of learning to produce a novel would be out of the question. Practicum teaching exercises will limit the number of skills in much the same way. You will not be asked to teach the master lesson. Instead, you will practice limited sets of skills until they become familiar. Later, in student teaching, you will continue practicing these skills until you become competent.

Avoid practicing skills during these exercises unthinkingly. What distinguishes effective from ineffective teachers is not simply whether or not they use certain skills. The effective teacher is an effective decision maker and knows when and how to use certain skills. Not all skills and strategies can be used in all settings with all students. Therefore, you must not only be able to use the skills you are learning, but, just as important, you must think about and learn when and when not to use them.

Learning complex and higher-order skills like those being introduced in the practicum exercises involves trial and error. You cannot learn enough through merely reading and talking to eliminate all errors. Just as you cannot learn to type or play golf without actually practicing, making errors, and correcting them, you cannot learn how to teach without making errors. Do not feel threatened when you make errors; expect them. Identifying these errors yourself, or with the help of others, is an integral part of the practicum exercises. **This focus on errors is not personal criticism.** Although we will want to reinforce those things you are doing well, we will not want to let errors go uncorrected just for the sake of making you feel good. Accepting constructive criticism is part of becoming a professional. Remembering this during your feedback sessions after the completion of these exercises may help you to be more open to accepting suggestions and less likely to be defensive. Welcome the constructive criticisms that result from your errors: they are opportunities for learning. Correcting errors now will ensure later success in the classroom.

PLANNING TIPS

Planning lessons for these exercises is similar to planning for classroom instruction, but with obvious differences. At first, planning a 15-to-20 minute lesson is going to seem strange. You are accustomed to the 50-to-60 minute university class periods, and planning for shorter periods will seem different. In middle school when planning for 45-to-60 minute periods, you must think of that period in terms of short 10-to-15 minute segments. Middle school teachers commonly provide two or three different activities each class period in order to maintain the students' attention. Elementary teachers at the primary levels also plan relatively short activities lasting 15 to 30 minutes. At the upper elementary grades, 30-to-45 minute periods devoted to a subject are usually broken down into shorter activities. Therefore, when planning, think of these lessons as being composed of short activities. This is excellent practice for later classroom planning.

Normally, when planning for instruction, a teacher identifies the instructional objectives and then chooses appropriate learning activities. This is the desired sequence and one that you will want to practice as a teacher. However, in order for you to practice certain teaching skills in these exercises, this sequence will need to be reversed. Not all content and instructional strategies will be equally effective in allowing you to practice certain teaching skills in an assigned lesson. **Be sure to analyze the nature of the skills involved in each lesson before choosing the content or skills to be**

taught. Try to choose content or skills that fit the particular set of skills being practiced. If you have difficulty doing this, seek help from your instructor well in advance of teaching your lesson. Your instructor can help you modify existing plans in advance, and she can more likely ensure a satisfying experience for you.

Many of you may have difficulty choosing an appropriate amount of material to be taught in the time available. **Teachers have a tendency to attempt to teach far too much material in the time available.** You will tend to underestimate the time needed for students to learn what you are teaching with understanding. Merely memorizing nonsense symbols or some simple skill may take little time, but coming to a reasonable understanding of ideas or being able actually to know when and how to use a certain skill takes considerable time. In planning lessons, try to limit the amount of material to be taught.

When planning these exercises, some of you will tend to develop sequential lessons as a teacher in the normal classroom would do. Planning sequential lessons in actual teaching situations is very desirable, but planning sequential lessons for practicum exercises can be a distinct disadvantage. Therefore, do not be concerned with teaching a logical sequence of content or skills from one lesson to the next, but **approach each lesson as an independent lesson designed to allow you to practice those skills assigned.**

Because these practicum exercises may be your first attempt at teaching, judging the amount and detail of planning necessary to teach successful lessons may be difficult. You may underestimate the amount of time needed to plan a lesson adequately. Expect to spend **at least** 3 to 4 hours planning each lesson. Some individuals will need to spend significantly more time than others, so defining a maximum time is not possible.

Each of the practicum exercises will have distinct objectives identified in the Observation Guide for each lesson. When planning your lesson, attempt to achieve the assigned objectives.

Trying to improve on or practice all of the possible skills involved in the teaching process would be overwhelming and would defeat the purpose of these exercises. Focusing only on those tasks assigned for a given lesson will help to ensure that you are able to gain practice on them.

A suggested list of tasks to be included in your lesson plans will be included in the description of each practicum exercise. Including each of these items in your plans will help you to demonstrate all parts of each lesson.

MODEL TEACHING

During a class period preceding your practicum lesson, your instructor may ask you to demonstrate the upcoming lesson by teaching it to the entire class of your peers. The purposes of these model teaching lessons are to provide an opportunity to teach the whole class and to allow the class to see someone actually attempt to teach the lesson.

Students teaching model lessons will likely make errors similar to those made by most students. By seeing a fellow student teach the lesson and analyzing what he did, the class can benefit from the mistakes identified. If you are called on to do a model teaching lesson, you will not be graded on your demonstration lesson. You will have the benefit of having practiced the practicum lesson before doing it in the classroom with elementary or middle school students or your peers. This practice should help your ultimate performance. Finally, this situation provides your instructor an opportunity to teach you some of the skills of observing teaching behavior, analyzing observations, and learning to plan for change.

If you volunteer to do a model teaching lesson, plan the lesson to last approximately the same time as the practicum lesson. Do not try for perfection, but plan the lesson just as you would any other lesson. Expect to make mistakes and don't worry about them; if you do not make any mistakes, the model lesson will not be useful in the ways intended.

Your instructor may also demonstrate some model teaching if she feels you have had limited experiences observing the skills being practiced in the lesson. Your instructor will also make some mistakes. Teaching is a lifelong learning process, and you should not expect yourself or anyone else to be perfect.

CONDUCTING PRACTICUM TEACHING EXERCISES

There are a few simple suggestions you should follow when conducting practicum lessons. First, do not play the role of teacher, but teach and interact with the students as naturally as possible. Be yourself!

When planning your lessons, try to incorporate the skills to be practiced as listed in the descriptions of the practicum lessons as well as those listed in the Observation Guide found with each practicum exercise.

For each lesson, some or all of you will be expected to turn in a copy of your lesson plan. Follow the format suggested for that lesson. Your instructor will tell you if the lesson plan is to be turned in prior to or following the lesson.

Following the lesson, and before the next class period, listen to a tape of your lesson or view a videotape of your lesson and complete an Observation Guide and Self-Analysis. You may be asked to turn them in at the next class meeting. This process of analyzing your teaching behavior is meant to help you identify those skills that you do well and those that need to be improved. A second and possibly more important purpose is to help you develop the skills needed to study your teaching behavior for self-improvement. These self-improvement skills will be invaluable to you during student teaching and later as a classroom teacher.

Before completing the Observation Guide and Self-Analysis, record the requested observations. When checking your behaviors on the Observation Guide, try to reflect your performance accurately. You will likely do some tasks better than you do others. The position of your check mark on the scale should reflect these differences. When answering the questions about your performance and possible changes in your behavior on subsequent lessons, try to be as specific as possible. Avoid vague words or phrases such as **more, less, improve, increase participation, do better,** or **try harder.** Also avoid the use of evaluative words such as **better, poor, good,** or **lousy.** With practice you will be able to describe those things you said and did and arrive at specific changes likely to be more effective in the classroom.

During each subsequent practicum teaching exercise, you will be expected to incorporate the skills introduced in earlier lessons. Continued practice of these skills is the only mechanism available for self-improvement.

Teaching Peers

It is hoped that you will be practicing these exercises in school classrooms. Some of you, however, may need to do these exercises using peers as students. When you are teaching peers, the members of each group will be as heterogeneous as your instructor can make them to give you the opportunity of teaching a group of individuals not majoring or deeply interested in your field. The peers with whom you are working will not be inherently interested in learning the content being taught. This should provide you many opportunities to select content or skills appropriate for the general population and to practice motivational techniques to interest students in the content or skills.

When choosing content or skills for lessons taught to your peers, you will be restricted to choosing content or skills commonly taught in the schools that could appropriately be taught to a general population of adults. **You are restricted to teaching topics normally taught in the school. Do not teach topics dealing with teaching.** Your instructor will allow you some time to discuss the appropriateness of your choices of content with your peer group prior to early lessons.

Because members of your peer group are not likely to be majors in your field, they will likely have little or no interest in its technical aspects. On the surface, teaching such a group may seem like a difficult task and unlike what you will need to do as a classroom teacher, but, in fact, it is identical. If you are fortunate enough to be teaching students in the classroom, you will not sense this artificiality. Few students in the elementary or middle school grades will later major in your field and will have little or no interest in its technical aspects. Too many classroom teachers fail to recognize this fact and force students to learn a great deal of meaningless content. You will learn early the importance of making appropriate choices of content. Choosing appropriate content for elementary or middle school students, just as with your peers, will not be an easy task. You have had little opportunity to practice the kind of thinking necessary in choosing content or skills appropriate for the general population. Much of the university coursework in content areas is designed to meet the needs of researchers or scholars in the field. This makes the process of choosing content or skills for elementary or middle school students very difficult. The difficulty of selecting appropriate content will diminish but will not disappear with experience.

Avoid referring to peers as you would young people. When you are the student, act as any normal adult. Do not play the role of an imaginary student. If you feel bored, act bored. If you are interested, act interested. The only restriction on your behavior is that **you will not ask questions during the lessons** unless you need to have the teacher clarify something. Each "teacher" has a limited amount of time, and if you interject too many questions, the "teacher" may not have time to finish the planned lesson.

Plan a lesson for each of the exercises except the lesson for which you are assigned to be an observer. A description of your responsibilities as an observer is in the section of this chapter called The Observer.

Your class will be split into small groups for the lessons. Usually each group will go to a separate area or room to conduct the teaching lessons. Once your group has arrived in the teaching area, be sure to check that all needed equipment is present and in working order. If any piece of equipment is missing or not functioning, notify your instructor at once. Decide on the order in which your lessons will be taught. When preparations are complete, divide the remaining time equally among those teaching lessons that day. Each of you should restrict the length of your lesson to the time available. The observer has been directed to stop you when you reach the maximum time allowed. Allowing those teaching early to use the time of those students teaching later would be unfair; therefore, **you will be stopped at the end of your allotted time whether finished or not.** During the teaching lesson, the observer will be busy with other tasks, so he will not be one of the students. Before starting your lesson, give a copy of the Observation Guide for the lesson to the observer.

If Teaching Students

In cooperation with the teacher and your instructor, choose objectives and activities that fit the practicum lessons as well as the needs of the students in the classroom. Recognize that the teacher has the final word on what will be done in his classroom. Your teacher will need to approve your lesson plan before you can teach the practicum lesson.

Two of you will be conducting each exercise in the same classroom. While one is teaching the lesson, the other will be the observer. You may do your lessons on the same day or on different days, depending on your particular situation. A description of your responsibilities as an observer is in the section of this chapter called The Observer. Before starting your lesson, give a copy of the Observation Guide for the lesson to the observer.

The practicum exercises will usually be scheduled after you have completed certain parts of the textbook. The sequence should be:

1. Unstructured Microteaching—to be done before any organized instruction occurs in the course
2. Teaching for Instructional Objectives—to be done following instruction on the first two chapters
3. Presenting I—to be done following instruction on Chapter 3, Some Basic Teaching Tasks

4. Presenting II—to be done following instruction on Chapter 3, Some Basic Teaching Tasks, and after feedback on practicum exercise Presenting I

5. Discussion I—to be done following instruction on Chapter 4, Questioning

6. Discussion II—to be done following instruction on Chapter 4, Questioning, and following feedback on practicum exercise Discussion I

7. Inductive Strategy I—to be done following instruction on Chapter 6, Teaching Concepts and Generalizations

8. Inductive Strategy II—to be done following instruction on Chapter 6, Teaching Concepts and Generalizations, and feedback on practicum exercise Inductive Strategy I

THE OBSERVER

Because your instructor cannot observe each of you during each lesson, you will be assigned the task of observing your peers during their lessons. This ensures that each of you will receive some suggestions for improvement for each lesson. Carefully directed peer feedback, as used in this approach, provides valid suggestions for improving the skills being practiced. Carefully observing teachers and then analyzing these observations can also help you learn how to analyze your own teaching. This should enable you to make more rapid improvement on later teaching lessons.

Responsibilities of the Observer

1. If teaching peers, you will be assigned one group to observe during the semester. If teaching in the classroom, you will observe another of your peers during his lessons. Usually, your instructor will assign observers so that you will not observe anyone who has also observed you. You will collect observations and complete an Observation Guide for each person observed.

2. You will audiotape each lesson and collect data during the lesson and from the audiotape that will allow you to complete an Observation Guide and Observer Analysis for each individual. Each item on the Observation Guide should describe the behavior of the teacher on that item. Comparing the performance of individuals is unnecessary and undesirable. **Do not rate an individual the same in all categories.** Let the person know which skills met the criteria and which skills may still need to be improved.

3. You will share your observations the next day during a feedback session with the individual or individuals you have observed. You will offer **at least** one specific suggestion for improvement directly related to one or more of the items on the Observation Guide to each individual.

4. Following the feedback session, you will turn in to the instructor a copy of each completed Observation Guide with the suggestion for improvement made to

each individual at the bottom of the form. You are also responsible for turning in an audiotape of all the teaching lessons you observed. **Ensuring that there is a clear recording of each person teaching is your responsibility**.

5. As observer, you will be graded primarily on the quality of your observations and suggestions.

Procedures for the Observer

Tape Recorders

1. Obtain two tape recorders sometime before you are to make your observations. Your instructor will indicate where these recorders can be obtained. If a videotape recorder is to be used, check out only one audiotape recorder and a videotape recorder.

2. Place a tape in each of the two recorders and be sure that both are working properly before the observation is to begin. Replace faulty recorders.

3. Do not place recorder microphones on or near an overhead projector if the overhead projector is to be used during the teaching lesson.

4. Place the microphone of the tape recorder near the person doing the teaching so that his voice is recorded clearly.

5. Place your tape in one recorder and your peer's audio- or videotape in the other recorder before beginning the teaching lesson.

6. If you think that you will not be able to remember the names of your peers when observing them, have the person doing the teaching say his name before beginning the lesson.

7. Give the instructor a clearly audible tape of each teaching lesson during the next class period.

Timing

1. If observing a group of peers, once all preparations for teaching the exercise are completed, determine how much time is left in the period assigned for the exercise. Divide the remaining time by the number of persons doing a lesson on that day. That time is the **maximum time** allowed each individual. **No one may be allowed to continue beyond this length of time**. Ensuring that no one exceeds his allotted time is your responsibility.

2. If observing in a classroom, merely work out a set of signals with the person teaching the lesson. Try to let the person know the amount of time remaining at least 5 minutes before the alloted time expires.

Preparation for Observations

1. Study your text, class notes, and the forms to be used for the practicum exercises. You must know more about what is expected of individuals teaching the lesson than they do.

2. Decide what you need to observe during the actual lesson and what you can observe later by listening to the tape.

3. Decide how and when all data will be collected. Studying Observing the Lesson, found in each Practicum Teaching Exercise, will help you with this task.

4. Prepare an observation instrument that will enable you to record the necessary observations.

Preparing Observer Analysis and Observation Guide

1. Review your observations and then place a check mark on the scale for each task on the Observation Guide consistent with your observations.

2. Answer each of the questions on the Observer Analysis. Use words that describe teaching behaviors specific to the tasks being practiced. These descriptions should meet the following criteria:

   a. Avoid words and phrases that are open to many different interpretations such as "enthusiasm," "participation," "involvement," "more," "less," "adequate," "not enough," "too much," "fast-paced," "many," "most," and "effective."

   b. Evaluative words such as "great," "dull," "interesting," "enjoyable," "excellent," "good," "poor," and "slow" should not be part of these statements.

   c. The behaviors described should deal directly with the tasks found on the Observation Guide. All other teaching behaviors are to be ignored.

Feedback to Your Peers

1. During the next class period, you will again meet with the individual or individuals you observed during the practicum lesson. Be prepared to share your observations and suggestions with them during this feedback session.

2. The feedback session will be sequenced as follows:

   a. The person who did the teaching lesson will briefly describe those things he thinks he did well and those things he thinks could be improved. He may also indicate areas on which he would like some feedback.

   b. If a group of peers observed the lesson, those in the group may now offer their observations and suggestions to the teacher. Be advised to avoid evaluative phrases such as "good" and "not very good." Some discussion of the appropriateness and amount of material included in the lesson should take place. If the observer is giving feedback to one person, the observer will then share observations with the teacher. Avoid evaluative phrases such as "very good" and "poor." The teacher is given a copy of the Observation Guide as well as the observational data completed by the observer to examine before it is turned into the instructor.

3. Avoid criticizing individuals. Identify helpful suggestions that will enable the individual to improve his teaching.

4. During the feedback discussion, focus only on those tasks found on the Observation Guide. The individual receiving feedback cannot assimilate suggestions about every aspect of his teaching; therefore, do not discuss extraneous observations and recommendations. To do so would defeat the purpose of limiting practicum teaching to a few skills to be practiced.

5. Give the instructor copies of your Observation Guide, your observational data, and your tape recording of the lesson following this feedback session. Your instructor

may need to analyze further the teaching of individuals who seem to be demonstrating particular problems or who feel a need for additional assistance. Your data and tapes can be valuable to the instructor for this purpose.

OBSERVING TEACHING BEHAVIORS

Every practicum exercise will require you to collect data on your teaching behaviors in order to complete the Observation Guide and Self-Analysis or, as an observer, to complete the Observation Guide and Observer Analysis. Research has shown that individuals can profit from a study of their teaching behavior if the information is specific to certain tasks and is studied in a nonthreatening environment (Tuckman, McCall, and Hyman, 1966; Tuckman and Oliver, 1968). Learning the process of analyzing teaching behavior is valuable for these exercises and for later classroom use. One reason for providing this experience in analysis is to teach you the kind of thinking involved in productive self-analysis.

Observations should be restricted to the tasks being practiced on that particular lesson. Since the tasks assigned individual lessons are extensive enough to challenge the best students, adding feedback on additional tasks would do nothing but overwhelm those receiving the feedback.

Observations for Practicum Exercises

Each practicum exercise will introduce you to some methods for observing specific skills. Review the methods for observing skills found in descriptions for each practicum teaching exercise, titled Observing the Lesson, before making observations on a lesson. If you need additional information on how to observe for a specific behavior, check with your instructor.

REFERENCES

Tuckman, B. W., K. M. McCall, and R. T. Hyman. 1966. The modification of teacher behavior: Effects of dissonance and coded feedback. *American Educational Research Journal, 6:* 607–620.

Tuckman, B. W., and W. F. Oliver. 1968. Effectiveness of feedback to teachers as a function of source. *Journal of Educational Psychology, 59:* 297–301.

PRACTICUM TEACHING EXERCISE 1

Unstructured Lesson

Until this course, most of you have been students sitting passively at your desks waiting to be taught. Now you must move to the other side of the desk so that you can begin thinking about the teaching process. This is the purpose of this first teaching exercise.

During the next class period, you will teach a short lesson to a small group of your peers.

Description of the Lesson
Choose and prepare to teach a topic you think would be relevant and interesting to a small group of your peers. Your lesson should last no longer than 10 minutes. You will not be observed or evaluated on this teaching lesson.

These are all the directions that will be provided. Your instructor will not help you decide on a topic or any further planning or provide any additional information about the nature of the task. You are on your own.

Observing the Lesson
Observations on this teaching lesson will not be made. Your instructor may ask you to audio- or videotape this lesson and save it for later analysis. Comparing your behavior on this lesson with your behavior on the last teaching lesson will help you recognize your growth through this course.

PRACTICUM TEACHING EXERCISE 2

Teaching for Instructional Objectives

In this teaching exercise you will conduct a lesson in which the students will achieve your instructional objective. Look over the criteria listed in the Observation Guide. These define your objectives for this practicum exercise. In your planning, try to address each of these criteria. Complete the following tasks:

1. Write one instructional objective that could be reasonably achieved in a 10-15 minute lesson.
2. Design a lesson not to exceed 15 minutes that will accomplish this objective. Take special care to ensure that the learning activity is congruent with your objective.
3. When planning and teaching the lesson, consider the following:
    a. At some point in the lesson, your instructional objective should become clear to the observer and the students.
    b. Teach the lesson using an instructional mode and instructional materials congruent with the objective.
    c. At the end of the lesson, but within the 15-minute time frame, ask the class questions that will let you know whether you have accomplished your instructional objective. Plan these questions carefully so that they will be congruent with your instructional objective. Keep in mind that in a regular

teaching situation you would also use some written or performance assessment instrument in addition to the brief informal assessment at the end of a lesson.

4. Write a lesson plan using the following format:
   a. State your instructional objective(s) at the beginning of the lesson plan.
   b. Describe your learning activity in enough detail so the instructor can judge the congruence between your objective and the learning activity provided.
   c. List the questions you will ask to assess the attainment of the objective at the end of the lesson.

Observing the Lesson

The three tasks to observe in this lesson are listed on the Observation Guide. You will be asked to record additional data on the Self-Analysis.

Recording data on the amount of teacher-talk versus the amount of student-talk will also be a part of the observations for this exercise. To accomplish this task set up a small table as follows:

Teacher-Talk

Student-Talk

Silence or Confusion

As you listen to an audiotape of the lesson, place a check mark on the table approximately every 2 seconds (the exact time is unimportant, but try to keep a regular interval) that represents who was talking during that period. If no one was talking, or if many people were talking simultaneously, place a check in the Silence or Confusion category. When you have finished listening to the lesson, count the number of checks in the categories of teacher- and student-talk combined. Use the following formula to determine the percent of teacher-talk:

$$\frac{\text{Checks under teacher-talk}}{\substack{\text{Total number of checks} \\ \text{teacher-} + \text{student-talk}}} \times 100 = \% \text{ of Teacher-Talk}$$

When recording observations of your verbal mannerisms for the Self-Analysis, recording verbatim each time you use a mannerism such as "you know," "all right," or "OK" is recommended. You will thus become sensitive to their use and more able to eliminate them. Developing this sensitivity is the first step if you are to break any undesirable verbal habits. Count the number of times you use these filler words and/or phrases from the list you record.

If you are the observer, you will be asked to make a judgment about the clarity with which the teacher communicated the objective. A simple method for making this judgment is to record the objective at the completion of the lesson without having been told what the objective is. After the lesson, ask the teacher to give you a written statement of his objective. Comparing the two will enable you to better judge the clarity of the objective.

A verbatim recording of the questions asked at the end of the lesson can be compared with the teacher's objective. This comparison will enable you to make a judgment about the adequacy of the questions in assessing the attainment of the objective. A brief anecdotal description of the nature of the lesson and the ways it contributed to the objective should be sufficient to make the other judgments requested.

If you need additional guidance in how to observe this lesson for purposes of the Self-Analysis, Observer Analysis, or Observation Guide, check with your instructor.

TEACHING FOR INSTRUCTIONAL OBJECTIVES

Observation Guide

The items in this Observation Guide are designed to help you systematically describe the behavior of the teacher on the tasks of this lesson. Place a check mark on the line above the listed behaviors to indicate the bahavior exhibited on each of the following tasks:

1. The teacher either stated the objectives of the lesson or in some other manner made the objectives clear by the end of the lesson.

The objective was clear to all students	The objective was clear to some students	The objective was not clear to any students

2. The lesson focused directly on the achievement of the objectives.

All discussion was directed at the objectives	There were a few digressions from the objectives	There was little related to the objectives

3. The teacher asked questions at the end of the lesson to assess the degree to which the students achieved the intended objective.

The teacher asked questions that clearly demonstrated that most students achieved the objective of the lesson		The teacher asked no questions to assess students' achievement of the objective

TEACHING FOR INSTRUCTIONAL OBJECTIVES

Self-Analysis

The items in the Observation Guide and this Self-Analysis are designed to help you identify the tasks of this lesson that you are doing well and those that you need to improve. Listen to an audiotape of your lesson and record the data that will allow you to complete this Self-Analysis and an Observation Guide. **Attach the observational raw data to your report.** From your observations, answer the following questions on a separate sheet of paper, using the number corresponding to the item to identify it on your paper.

1. How many times did the lesson digress from accomplishing the objective?
2. How many questions did you ask at the end of the lesson to assess the extent to which the students learned what you intended in your objectives?
3. How many students did you call on to respond to the questions assessing student learning?
4. State your objective and then list your reasons for choosing this particular objective to teach to this group of students. Do these reasons still seem valid to you? If not, why not?
5. Were students able to demonstrate that they learned what you intended them to learn? If so, what evidence leads you to this conclusion?
6. What specific changes will you make in your behavior during the next teaching lesson as a result of your analysis?

Additional Considerations

The items here are not directly related to the tasks assigned in this exercise but are included to help you identify any general behaviors that might be interfering with your effectiveness. Listen to an audiotape of your lesson and tally the following, and then record the frequencies or answer the item on a separate sheet of paper. Use the number corresponding to the item to identify it on your paper.

1. How many filler words or sounds did you use ("OK," "you know," or "uh")?
2. How many times did you address students by name? (You should have used each student's name several times.)
3. How many times did you pause for students to think about what you said? (Pauses are important for learning.)
4. What percentage of time did you talk? (Some student-talk is desirable.)
5. What will you do before and during the next teaching lesson to help yourself modify any of these behaviors that need to be improved?

TEACHING FOR INSTRUCTIONAL OBJECTIVES

Observer Analysis

Using the observations of this lesson you have already made, complete an Observation Guide and the Observer Analysis. Attach your observations to this analysis. Ignore any behaviors not listed on the Observation Guide.

1. List the objective of the lesson as best you can determine it **without** asking the teacher or looking at his lesson plan.
2. Offer at least one suggestion for improving the statement of this objective.
3. Offer at least one suggestion of something the teacher could have done during the lesson to improve the effectiveness of the lesson. Do not be concerned with all aspects of the teaching process but merely the teacher's attempt to accomplish the tasks of the lesson. Consider only those tasks listed on the Observation Guide.

PRACTICUM TEACHING EXERCISE 3

Presenting I

In this exercise you will teach a lesson using the presentation method. Incorporate what you learned in Practicum Teaching Exercise 2 on instructional objectives; continue to teach for the achievement of a clearly defined instructional objective. Study the Observation Guide for this lesson, and attempt to practice the skills listed. Before teaching the lesson, complete the following tasks:

1. Plan a lesson that requires you to present information.
2. Incorporate a set induction strategy at the start of the lesson.
3. Ask some brief questions at the beginning to preassess students' knowledge of the material to be presented if you are not confident about what they currently know.
4. Ask some questions during the presentation to check the students' understanding of something you have said. **Do not ask questions with the intent of starting a discussion.**
5. Close the presentation by asking questions that assess students' accomplishment of your instructional objective. Do not ask, "Do you understand?" for this purpose.
6. Allow yourself approximately 15 minutes for your lesson.
7. The lesson plan to be presented to your instructor should
   a. list your instructional objectives
   b. list the preassessment questions you will ask
   c. describe the set induction you will use
   d. include an outline of the content you will be presenting
   e. list the questions you will ask during the lesson to check immediate understanding
   f. list points you will include during your closing comments
   g. list questions you will ask at the end of the lesson to assess the attainment of the objective(s)

Observing the Lesson

Much of the data needed to assess this lesson will be written descriptions of what the teacher sequentially said and did. If you are an observer, you may also need to make an outline of the lesson from an audiotape to enable you to identify specific aspects of the presentation that seemed out of place or were unclear. The same can be said of the set induction, unless it was strictly verbal. In the latter case a verbatim transcript of the set induction could be useful in offering suggestions for change. Use the same procedure as that in lesson 2 to determine the clarity of the objective.

The additional tasks on the Observer Analysis, Self-Analysis, and Observation Guide can be done by listening to an audiotape and tallying the occurrences of the behaviors being analyzed. If you have additional questions, check with your instructor before proceeding with the analysis.

PRESENTING I

Observation Guide

The items in this Observation Guide are designed to help you systematically describe the behavior of the teacher on the tasks of this lesson. Place a check mark on the line above the listed behaviors to indicate the behavior exhibited on each of the following tasks:

Skills/tasks specific to this exercise

1. The set induction of the lesson created an interest in the lesson.

Attention of the students was effectively gained	Some attempt was made to get the students' attention	There was little or no attempt made to get students' attention

2. The set induction of the lesson gave direction to the rest of the lesson by indicating the ultimate goal and the importance of that goal to the students.

Overall direction or purpose of the lesson was clear	Overall direction or purpose of the lesson was somewhat clear	Direction or purpose of the lesson was unclear

3. The presentation was clear and well organized.

Information being presented was understandable to the students at all times	Information being presented was somewhat unclear at times	Information being presented was seldom clear to the students

4. The lesson focused directly on the achievement of the objectives.

All discussion was directed at the objectives	There were a few digressions from the objectives	There was little related to the objectives

5. The teacher closed the lesson in a way that reinforced, reviewed, and clarified the objectives and the importance or usefulness of the learning outcomes of the lesson.

Objectives were reinforced and the importance of the lesson to the students was made clear	Some attempt to review the lesson and its relevance to the students was made	Little or no attempt was made to review the lesson

6. The content was appropriate in both amount and relevancy

| Content was appropriate in both amount and relevancy | Content was appropriate in one but not the other | Content was excessive and irrelevant |

Skills/tasks applied from previous exercises

7. The teacher either stated the objectives of the lesson or in some other manner made the objectives clear by the end of the lesson.

| The objective was clear to all students | The objective was clear to some students | The objective was not clear to any students |

PRESENTING I

Self-Analysis

The items in the Observation Guide and this Self-Analysis are designed to help you identify the tasks of this lesson that you are doing well and those that you need to improve. Listen to an audiotape of your lesson and record the data that will allow you to complete the Observation Guide and this Self-Analysis. **Attach the observational raw data to your report.** If you decide to try to change some teaching behaviors as a result of this analysis, do not attempt to change more than two or three behaviors simultaneously. Answer the following on a separate sheet of paper, using the number corresponding to the item to identify it on your paper.

1. Describe any distracting verbal mannerisms.
2. How many times did I use distracting verbal mannerisms?
3. How many times did I pause noticeably in order to think about what I was going to say next (usually undesirable)?
4. How many questions did I ask to check student understanding of what was being said during the presentation?
5. How many questions did I ask during the close of the lesson to assess student learning of the objectives of the lesson?
6. What particular behavior related to the tasks of this lesson did you exhibit that seemed particularly effective? In what way did the response of students cause you to think it was effective?
7. What specifically did you do or fail to do related to the tasks of this lesson that caused your lesson to be less effective than it could have been?
8. What will you do or not do differently (behaviorally) in your next practicum teaching lesson?
9. What specific changes will you make in your **lesson plan** to help yourself accomplish these changes?

PRESENTING I

Observer Analysis

Prepare your observation instrument before the day of the lesson. Either record data during the teaching lesson or record data from a videotape following the lesson. Then complete an Observation Guide and the Observer Analysis. **Attach your observational data to this report.** Ignore any teaching behaviors not listed on the Observation Guide.

Complete the following items:

1. Describe one particular behavior related to the tasks under Skills/Tasks Specific to this Exercise that you thought was particularly effective and that you feel the teacher would be advised to continue.

2. Describe one particular behavior related to the tasks under Skills/Tasks Applied from Previous Exercises that you thought was particularly effective and that you feel the teacher would be advised to continue.

3. Offer at least one specific suggestion about what the teacher could have done differently related to the tasks under Skills/Tasks Specific to this Exercise to improve the lesson.

4. Offer at least one specific suggestion about what the teacher could have done differently related to the tasks under Skills/Tasks Applied from Previous Exercises to improve the lesson.

PRACTICUM TEACHING EXERCISE 4

Presenting II

This lesson will provide another opportunity to practice the strategy of presenting, along with some emphasis on refocusing skills. The only difference between Presenting I and Presenting II is the addition of refocusing skills to be practiced in Presenting II.

The Teaching Task

1. You will have approximately 15 minutes available for your lesson.
2. Include a set induction in the lesson.
3. A major part of the presentation will be teacher-talk. Feel free to ask some questions during this lesson, but confine them to simple questions to check students' comprehension of something you just said. Do not become involved in a discussion.
4. Attempt to incorporate what you learned in the preceding teaching exercises.
5. Throughout this lesson, try to incorporate refocusing skills. Be conscious of the reactions of students, and try to provide the appropriate refocusing skill at the appropriate time. Use as many different refocusing tactics as the situation will allow.
6. Ask questions to assess the students' attainment of your objective(s) just before your closing statements. Bring the lesson to a close by summarizing important parts that relate directly to your instructional objective(s). Also refer to your set induction and emphasize the relevance of those things taught.
7. The lesson plan to be presented to your instructor should
   a. list your instructional objectives
   b. list the preassessment questions to be asked
   c. describe the set induction to be used
   d. include an outline of the content to be presented
   e. list the questions to be asked during the lesson to check immediate understanding at the point in the lesson they will be asked
   f. list points to be included during your closing comments
   g. list questions you will ask at the end of the lesson to assess the attainment of the objective(s)
   h. list notes to yourself to include refocusing skills at appropriate points throughout the lesson plan

Observing the Lesson

The data for this lesson is similar to that if the preceding lesson but with some additional observations necessary. Review the explanations for making observations included in the prior lessons before you develop your observation instrument for this lesson.

You will be recording the gestures used during the lesson. As the observer, you will need to record them during the lesson at the time they occur, or have access to a videotape recording of the lesson. As the teacher, you will need to rely on the use of a videotape recording for this purpose. Making a distinction between purposeful and distracting gestures would be helpful. Use some kind of shorthand symbols such as:

Purposeful pointing   —   PP

Purposeful movement of hands   —   PH

Random, distracting gestures   —   DG

You may also add a description of each kind of distracting gesture by creating symbols for each kind and recording the modified symbol rather than this general symbol. Then record each gesture as it occurs. Occasionally noting the time to the left of the column of symbols for gestures will help you recognize the frequency of the gestures. If too frequent use of gestures is made, you may merely need to record the frequency of each use by tallying them in a table similar to the one following. Prepare such a table beforehand.

Puposeful Gestures

Distracting Gestures

When recording the use of the different senses that students are being asked to use, keep a record of the time in a column on the left and the sensory channels being used by the students in a corresponding column to the right.

Time	Senses Used
0–2 minutes	Hearing or Listening
2–6 minutes	Hearing and Speaking
6–8 minutes	Hearing and Seeing
8–9 minutes	Hearing
9–10 minutes	Hearing and Speaking

PRESENTING II

Observation Guide

The items in this Observation Guide are designed to help you systematically describe the behavior of the teacher on the tasks of this lesson. Place a check mark on the line above the listed behaviors to indicate the behavior exhibited on each of the following tasks:

Skills/tasks specific to this exercise

1. The expression of the teacher's voice was effectively modified during the lesson.

The teacher varied his or her voice to focus and/or maintain attention	The teacher varied his or her voice only occasionally	The teacher rarely varied his or her voice during the lesson

2. Gestures were used to emphasize major points or to focus the students' attention to some location.

Gestures were effective in focusing students' attention at a variety of times during the lesson	Gestures were occasionally used to focus attention	Gestures were not used or were not effective in focusing students' attention

3. Students were required to use several sensory channels during the lesson.

The lesson required students to use at least two different senses, each for about equal times	The lesson required students to use at least two senses, but one predominated	Students were required to use only one sensory channel

4. The set induction of the lesson created an interest in the lesson.

Attention of the students was effectively gained	Some attempt was made to get the students' attention	There was little or no attempt made to get students' attention

5. The set induction of the lesson gave direction to the rest of the lesson by indicating the ultimate goal and the importance of that goal to the students.

Overall direction or purpose of the lesson was clear	Overall direction or purpose of the lesson was somewhat clear	Direction or purpose of the lesson was unclear

6. The lesson focused directly on the achievement of the objectives.

All discussion was directed at the objectives	There were a few digressions from the objectives	There was little related to the objectives

7. The presentation was clear and well organized.

Information being presented was understandable to the students at all times	Information being presented was some-what unclear at times	Information being presented was seldom clear to the students

8. The teacher closed the lesson in a way that reinforced, reviewed, and clarified the objectives and the importance or usefulness of the learning outcomes of the lesson.

Objectives were reinforced and the importance of the lesson to the students was made clear	Some attempt to review the lesson and its relevance to the students was made	Little or no attempt was made to review the lesson

9. The teacher either stated the objectives of the lesson or in some other manner made the objectives clear by the end of the lesson.

The objective was clear to all students	The objective was clear to some students	The objective was not clear to any students

10. The content was appropriate in both amount and relevancy.

Content was appropriate in both amount and relevancy	Content was appropriate in one but not the other	Content was excessive and irrelevant

PRESENTING II

Self-Analysis

The items in the Observation Guide and this Self-Analysis are designed to help you identify the tasks of this lesson that you are doing well and those that you need to improve. Observe a videotape of your lesson for purposes of this self-analysis. Record data that will enable you to describe the behaviors requested. **Attach your raw observational data to your Self-Analysis report**. From your observations, record the frequencies of the following behaviors and answer the questions on a separate sheet of paper. Use the number corresponding to the item to identify it on your paper.

1. How many times did I pause to allow students time to think about what I said?
2. How many times did I change the volume of my voice noticeably to emphasize an expression?
3. How many filler words or sounds such as "OK," "you know," or "uh" did I use?
4. What were the gestures I used repetitiously, if any, that could be considered distracting?
5. List the senses students were called on to use (list all in sequence as they occurred and the duration of each).
6. What specific changes will you make in your behavior during the next teaching lesson as a result of this analysis?
7. What specific changes in your written lesson plans will you make to help yourself accomplish these changes during your next lesson?

PRESENTING II

Observer Analysis

Prepare your observation instrument before the day of the lesson. Either record data during the teaching lesson or record data from a videotape following the lesson. Then complete an Observation Guide and the Observer Analysis. **Attach your observational data to this report.** Ignore any teaching behaviors not listed on the Observation Guide.

Complete the following items:

1. Describe one particular behavior related to the tasks under Skills/Tasks Specific to this Exercise that you thought was particularly effective and that you feel the teacher would be advised to continue.
2. Describe one particular behavior related to the tasks under Skills/Tasks Applied from Previous Exercises that you thought was particularly effective and that you feel the teacher would be advised to continue.

3. Offer at least one specific suggestion about what the teacher could have done differently related to the tasks under Skills/Tasks Specific to this Exercise to improve the lesson.

4. Offer at least one specific suggestion about what the teacher could have done differently related to the tasks under Skills/Tasks Applied from Previous Exercises to improve the lesson.

PRACTICUM TEACHING EXERCISE 5

Discussion I

In this exercise you will practice the skills of using open and divergent questions, probing, silence, and reinforcement. Read chapter 4, "Questioning," before planning this lesson. The basic purpose of this lesson, to encourage student talking and thinking rather than your own, takes time and should not be rushed. Restrict the complexity of the discussion by limiting the content of the lesson. Trying to discuss too much in a short time invites superficial examination of a topic.

Questions are used in many situations in addition to discussions. You are being asked to use them in a discussion because they allow you to practice most, if not all, of the skills involved in using questions effectively. You will use discussions in the actual classroom only occasionally, but the skills you will be practicing in this exercise are those you will use whenever you use questions in the classroom.

The Teaching Task

1. During this lesson, you should encourage equal participation of all students.
2. Reduce the amount of time you talk and increase the amount of time the students talk. Ensure that the time the students are discussing the questions of the lesson exceeds the time you are talking during the lesson.
3. Use each kind of probe approximately equally. Although this introduces some artificiality, with practice you will find more than enough opportunities to use probing, and this attempt at equality can be dropped. Ideally, you should use probing whenever a child says something that is incomplete, ambiguous, or seems to lack justification.
4. Use an eliciting pattern of asking the question and then calling on a student by name to respond. Do not accept responses from students who have not been called on to respond.
5. Use approximately 3 to 4 seconds of silence following each student's response when the response is unclear, incomplete, or an unsubstantiated assertion. Recognize that the actual amount of silence will likely be much less than 3 to 4 seconds if students are eager to respond.
6. Refer to something students contributed earlier, using their names, and then incorporate the students' earlier ideas into your lesson. Sometimes this can most easily be done during the process of drawing generalizations from the discussion or in coming to a summary of the discussion. You will need to plan for this and include some reminders in your lesson plan if you expect to be able to incorporate this skill into your lesson.
7. During this lesson, have some objective in mind, but **do not let this be your primary focus**. The primary focus of this lesson should be increased student-talk and reduced teacher-talk.
8. Review the Observation Guide and attempt to incorporate all of the skills and tasks included on that form.

9. Lesson sequence:
   a. Begin the lesson with a set induction that includes at least one open or divergent question to start the discussion. Call on several students using the same question. Probe these students as needed.
   b. Follow this lead question with divergent questions to cause the students to consider alternatives before you narrow the discussion down to convergent and closed questions.
   c. Bring closure to the interaction through the use of convergent or closed questions and through a summary of important ideas identified during the interaction.
10. The lesson plan to be turned in to your instructor should include the following:
    a. a statement of your instructional objective
    b. a description of the set induction you will use, including your initial question to start the discussion
    c. in order of their use, all of the questions other than probes you intend to ask; to the left of each question classify it as open, divergent, convergent, or closed
    d. summarizing statements you intend to make at the end of the discussion
    e. the convergent or closed questions you will ask at the end of the lesson to assess the attainment of the objective; to the left of each question classify the cognitive level of the question
    f. notes to yourself throughout the lesson plan to help you incorporate the assigned tasks in your lesson

Observing the Lesson

Review Observing the Lesson for all previous lessons before planning your observations for this lesson. In determining whether questions are open or divergent versus convergent or closed, listen to a tape recording and write a verbatim transcript of the actual questions asked. This list will allow you not only to make a judgment about the openness but will also allow you to study the questions for possible ambiguity. This process will also make needed changes to questions more apparent.

Tallying the number of times each probe is used is not particularly helpful. A verbatim transcript of each probe asked will allow an analysis of the kind of probe and the sequence and clarity of the probes. Students' verbatim responses to questions will help identify when the teacher used ambiguous language in his questions or when student responses needing to be probed were left unprobed. Record only those responses that would illustrate some needed change.

At least three possible patterns of eliciting student responses are possible.

1. The teacher asks a question and students respond without being called.

2. The teacher calls on a student by name and then asks the question.

3. The teacher asks a question and then calls the student by name to respond.

These three patterns can be symbolized for recording purposes as

Q—R

N—Q—R

Q—N—R

When recording eliciting patterns used by the teacher, record each pattern in the order that it occurs. Rather than using the symbol "N" for the name of the student, substitute the actual name of the student. Merely recording the frequency of each pattern used hides some very useful information. For example, consider the following two observations:

Observation #1	Observation #2
Q—R	Q—Mary—R
Q—R	Q—Bob—R
Q—R	Q—Mary—R
Bob—Q—R	Q—Bob—R
Mary—Q—R	Q—Bob—R
Q—R	Q—R
Q—R	Q—Al—R
Alice—Q—R	Q—Bob—R

This first sequence demonstrates a teacher's tendency to revert to the N—Q—R pattern when students start calling out answers without permission. This pattern would not be apparent from a mere tally of frequencies. The second sequence shows the frequency with which patterns are used, which students were called on, and in what sequence. The second observation also shows that a few students dominated the discussion. This information, when transferred to a seating chart, can also help a teacher recognize when he is concentrating on only certain parts of the room, a common tendency for beginning teachers.

Because not all of the behaviors to be observed for this lesson can be observed simultaneously by one person, a tape recording is absolutely necessary for later analysis. Plan your observations and observation instrument carefully so you are clear about those things that need to be observed live and those things that can later be retrieved from a tape.

DISCUSSION I

Observation Guide

The items in this Observation Guide are designed to help you systematically describe the behavior of the teacher on the tasks of this lesson. Place a check mark on the line above the listed behaviors to indicate the behavior exhibited on each of the following tasks:

Skills/tasks specific to this exercise

1. The teacher asked open or divergent questions during the early part of the lesson.

Teacher asked only open questions during the first half of the lesson	Teacher asked few open questions during the first half of the lesson	Teacher asked no open questions during the first half of the lesson

2. The teacher used each open or divergent question to increase student participation.

Teacher elicited responses from more than one student on each of the open questions asked	Teacher elicited responses from more than one student for at least two open questions asked	Teacher elicited responses from only one student for each open question asked

3. The teacher used an appropriate eliciting pattern.

Almost all were Q-N-R patterns	About an equal mix of Q-R, N-Q-R, and Q-N-R	Almost all were Q-R and N-Q-R

4. The phrasing of the teacher's questions reflected the intent of the question clearly and unambiguously.

All questions were clear and unambiguous	About one-half of the questions were clear and unambiguous	Few questions were clear and unambiguous

5. The teacher made use of extending, clarifying, and justifying probes when students' responses were unclear, incomplete, or unsubstantiated assertions.

Teacher made use of all three kinds of probes when needed	Teacher used probes about half the time when needed	Teacher used few if any probes

6. The teacher made use of silence following students' responses to encourage additional thinking.

Three to five seconds on the average	One to two seconds on the average	Less than one second on the average

7. The teacher made proper use of verbal and nonverbal reinforcement.

Teacher frequently used labeled praise or used student ideas as forms of reinforcement	Teacher used some verbal and nonverbal reinforcement, but it was somewhat repetitious	Teacher rarely used verbal or nonverbal reinforcement

Skills/tasks applied from previous exercises

8. The set induction of the lesson created an interest in the lesson.

Attention of the students was effectively gained	Some attempt was made to get the students' attention	There was little or no attempt made to get students' attention

9. The set induction of the lesson gave direction to the rest of the lesson by indicating the ultimate goal and the importance of that goal to the students.

Overall direction or purpose of the lesson was clear	Overall direction or purpose of the lesson was somewhat clear	Direction or purpose of the lesson was unclear

10. The teacher closed the lesson in a way that reinforced, reviewed, and clarified the objectives and the importance or usefulness of the learning outcomes of the lesson.

Objectives were reinforced and the importance of the lesson to the students was made clear	Some attempt made to review the lesson and its relevance to the students	Little or no attempt was made to review the lesson

11. The teacher either stated the objectives of the lesson or in some other manner made the objectives clear by the end of the lesson.

The objective was clear to all students	The objective was clear to some students	The objective was not clear to any students

12. The content was appropriate in both amount and relevancy.

Content was appropriate in both amount and relevancy	Content was appropriate in one but not the other	Content was excessive and irrelevant

DISCUSSION I

Self-Analysis

The items in the Observation Guide and this Self-Analysis are designed to help you identify the tasks of this lesson that you are doing well and those that you need to try to improve. Observe a videotape of your lesson for purposes of this self-analysis and record the observations requested. Read Observing the Lesson for the exercises Teaching for Instructional Objectives, Presenting I, and Presenting II for ways of observing some of the behaviors you are being asked to observe. **Attach your raw observational data to your Self-Analysis report.**

From your observations, record the frequencies requested for the following behaviors and answer the questions on a separate sheet of paper. Number your responses to correspond to the number for each of the items.

1. How many open or divergent questions did I ask during the first half of the lesson?
2. How many times did I use each of the following eliciting patterns:
   a. Question—Name—Response
   b. Name—Question—Response
   c. Question—Response
3. How many times did I use each of the following probes:
   a. Extending
   b. Clarifying
   c. Justifying
4. How many times did I merely repeat a student's response?
5. What was the percentage of teacher-talk and student-talk?
6. Record each of your eliciting questions verbatim. Do not include probing questions.
   a. If any questions are ambiguous or in any other way inadequate, indicate the nature of the inadequacy beneath each question.
   b. Rephrase all inadequate questions to remove the inadequacy.
   c. Format your analysis for each question as follows:
      (1) eliciting question written verbatim
      (2) identification of the inadequacy (or write "No inadequacy")
      (3) rephrased question (or write "No modifications necessary")
7. What specific skills practiced during this lesson would you like to improve in your next lesson? Be specific about the skill to be changed and the extent to which you will change your behavior.

DISCUSSION I

Observer Analysis

Prepare your observation instrument before the day of the lesson. Either record data during the teaching lesson or record data from a videotape following the lesson. Then complete an Observation Guide and the Observer Analysis. **Attach your observational data to this report.** Ignore any teaching behaviors not listed on the Observation Guide.

Complete the following items:

1. Describe one particular behavior related to the tasks under Skills /Tasks Specific to this Exercise that you thought was particularly effective and that you feel the teacher would be advised to continue.

2. Describe one particular behavior related to the tasks under Skills/Tasks Applied from Previous Exercises that you thought was particularly effective and hat you feel the teacher would be advised to continue.

3. Offer at least one specific suggestion about what the teacher could have done differently related to the tasks under Skills/Tasks Specific to this Exercise to improve the lesson.

4. Offer at least one specific suggestion about what the teacher could have done differently related to the tasks under Skills/Tasks Applied from Previous Exercises to improve he lesson.

PRACTICUM TEACHING EXERCISE 6

Discussion II

In the last lesson, you have the opportunity to practice the skills involved in a discussion situation: open, divergent, convergent, and closed questions; set induction; eliciting; probing; silence; closure; and reinforcement. In this lesson you will have the opportunity to continue practicing these skills in a discussion to be controlled by you, the teacher, in an effort to achieve a specific instructional objective. This is commonly called a teacher-directed discussion. The major difference between this lesson and the Discussion I lesson is the attempt to accomplish a particular objective.

This lesson is a complex series of tasks that will require careful preparation if you are to be effective. Give each question careful consideration, plan on when and how to probe, build reminders in your plans to do certain things at certain times, and study your plans and mentally rehearse what you intend to do until you are familiar with all aspects of what you want to do. If the discussion is to proceed smoothly, however, do not be overly dependent on your plans. To ensure effectiveness, a few practice runs with friends may be helpful.

The Teaching Task

1. Incorporate an effective set induction strategy into the lesson to start the discussion.
2. Use an appropriate pattern (Q—N—R 100%) in eliciting responses from students.
3. Start the discussion with open or divergent questions and call on more than one student to respond to each question.
4. Talk less than half of the time during the first half of the discussion.
5. Use all forms of probing approximately equally or when student responses are unclear, incomplete, or unsubstantiated assertions.
6. Use a variety of cognitive questions that will help you accomplish your objective.
7. Formulate well-phrased questions that are unambiguous and directed toward the topic. Students should have no need to ask questions for clarification, and you should have no need to rephrase questions that students do not understand.
8. Use silence **after** student responses when the responses are unclear, incomplete, or unsubstantiated assertions.
9. Use student ideas expressed in the first half of the discussion to arrive at conclusions during the last half of the discussion. Refer to the student by name when using that student's idea. (Try to do this at least twice.)
10. Use closed questions as part of your summary to assess attainment of objectives. Try to have an objective and a closed question that involves a cognitive level beyond the knowledge level.
11. Because this lesson is an attempt to achieve a particular objective through a discussion method, the objective should become clear to all of the students.
12. The discussion should stay centered on the topic at hand, and, should it stray from the topic, you will respond in ways that will return discussion to the topic without delay. (Note: If a peer is teaching and you are the student, **do not ask questions or interject comments** about the lesson **unless** some question asked by the teacher is unclear. Then feel free to ask him questions to clarify his question.)
13. Follow the same sequence as in the last lesson. Start with open or divergent questions and then, after exploring the topic, begin to use the convergent questions in order to focus in on your objective. The close of the lesson may include a brief presentation in order to summarize the discussion. This summary is then followed by closed or convergent question to check for the attainment of the objective.
14. The lesson plan to be turned in to your instructor should include the following:
    a. a statement of your instructional objective
    b. a description of the set induction you will use, including your initial question
    c. in order of their use, all of the question other than probes you intend to ask; to the left of each question classify the question as open, divergent, convergent, or closed
    d. any summarizing statements you intend to make at the close of the discussion
    e. the closed or convergent questions you will ask at the end of the lesson to assess the attainment of the objective; to the left of each question classify the cognitive level of the question
    f. notes to yourself throughout the lesson plan that will help you incorporate the assigned tasks in your lesson

Observing the Lesson

Two additional observations will be made for the Self-Analysis in this lesson in addition to those for Practicum Teaching Exercise 5. First, make a verbatim recording when students' ideas were used. Second, make a verbatim list of the questions asked (other than probes) and categorize each question by cognitive level.

If you are the observer you will need to review all Observing the Lesson sections found in preceding exercises, including how to calculate the percent of teacher-talk found in Practicum Teaching Exercise 2.

DISCUSSION II

Observation Guide

The items in this Observation Guide are designed to help you systematically describe the behavior of the teacher on the tasks of this lesson. Place a check mark on the line above the listed behaviors to indicate the behavior exhibited on each of the following tasks:

Skills/tasks specific to this exercise

1. The teacher's eliciting questions during the first half of the lesson were open or divergent.

Teacher asked open or divergent questions	Teacher asked some open or divergent questions	Teacher asked few open or divergent questions

2. The phrasing of the teacher's questions reflected the intent of the question clearly and unambiguously.

All questions were clear and unambiguous	About one-half of the questions were clear and unambiguous	Few questions were clear and unambiguous

3. The teacher asked a variety of cognitive questions.

Teacher used five categories of questions	Teacher used three categories of questions	Teacher used knowledge questions only

4. The teacher used an appropriate eliciting pattern.

Almost all were Q-N-R patterns	About an equal mix of Q-R, N-Q-R, and Q-N-R	Almost all were Q-R and N-Q-R

5. The teacher made use of silence following students' responses to encourage additional thinking.

Three to five seconds on the average	One to two seconds on the average	Less than one second on the average

6. The teacher made use of extending, clarifying, and justifying probes when students' responses were unclear, incomplete, or unsubstantiated assertions.

Teacher made use of all three kinds of probes when needed	Teacher used probes about half the time when needed	Teacher used few if any probes

323

7. The teacher made use of student ideas as a form of reinforcement by mentioning students by name when identifying and using their contributions.

Four or more times	Two times	Not at all

8. The lesson focused directly on the achievement of the objectives.

All discussion was directed at the objectives	There were a few digressions from the objectives	There was little related to the objectives

9. The teacher used closed or convergent questions as part of the summary of the lesson to assess the objectives of the lesson.

Teacher asked a sufficient number of questions to assess the objectives	Teacher assessed some of the objectives	Teacher asked no closed questions to assess the objectives

10. The teacher made the objective of the lesson clear.

The objective of the lesson was clear	The objective of the lesson was somewhat clear	The objective of the lesson was unknown

Skills/tasks applied from previous exercises

11. The set induction of the lesson created an interest in the lesson.

Attention of the students was effectively gained	Some attempt was made to get the students' attention	There was little or no attempt made to get students' attention

12. The set induction of the lesson gave direction to the rest of the lesson by indicating the ultimate goal and the importance of that goal to the students.

Overall direction or purpose of the lesson was clear	Overall direction or purpose of the lesson was somewhat clear	Direction or purpose of the lesson was unclear

13. The content was appropriate in both amount and relevancy.

Content was appropriate in both amount and relevancy	Content was appropriate in one but not the other	Content was excessive and irrelevant

DISCUSSION II

Self-Analysis

The items in the Observation Guide and this Self-Analysis are designed to help you identify the tasks of this lesson that you are doing well and those that you need to try to improve. Observe a videotape of your lesson for purposes of this self-analysis. Record data that will enable you to describe the behaviors requested. **Attach your raw observational data to your Self-Analysis report**.

Complete the following tasks on separate sheets of paper:

1. Record verbatim all questions on the probes you asked, and list them in the sequence they were asked. Record everything from the time you first started to formulate the question to the time you actively elicited a response from a student, including all attempts to rephrase a question until it was in a form that was understandable.
2. Record verbatim the probes that you used with each question immediately following the question. Indent the probes so that they will not be confused with the question.
3. Record, in sequence after each eliciting question, the pattern for each elicit you made. The three patterns are:
   a. teacher question—spontaneous student response
      Symbol: Q—R or Q—MR (for multiple responses)
   b. teacher question—name of student—student response
      Symbol: Q—(Name)—R (Use the actual name.)
   c. student name—question—student response
      Symbol: (Name)—Q—R (Use the actual name.)
4. To the right of each question, indicate by the word "cutoff" the times you cut off a student's response by immediately beginning to talk. Combine the data from the four tasks to look something like this:

   Question: What are some foods you dislike?   Q—(Barb)—R Cutoff
      Probe: What do you think might be some of the causes for your dislike of spinach?
      Probe: Bob, what are some reasons other than those Barb has suggested for disliking foods? Cutoff

5. What specific improvements on the above tasks will you make in your next microteaching lesson?

DISCUSSION II

Observer Analysis

Prepare your observation instrument before the day of the lesson. Either record data during the teaching lesson or record data from a videotape following the lesson. Then complete an Observation Guide and the Observer Analysis. **Attach your observational data to this report**. *Ignore any teaching behaviors not listed on the Observation Guide.*

Complete the following tasks on separate sheets of paper:

1. Percentage of time the teacher was talking during the first 10 minutes of the lesson.

2. Describe one particular behavior related to the tasks under Skills/Tasks Specific to this Exercise that you thought was particularly effective and that you feel the teacher would be advised to continue.

3. Describe one particular behavior related to the tasks under Skills/Tasks Applied from Previous Exercises that you thought was particularly effective and that you feel the teacher would be advised to continue.

4. Offer at least one specific suggestion about what the teacher could have done differently related to the tasks under Skills/Tasks Specific to this Exercise to improve the lesson.

5. Offer at least one specific suggestion about what the teacher could have done differently related to the tasks under Skills/Tasks Applied from Previous Exercises to improve the lesson.

PRACTICUM TEACHING EXERCISE 7

Teaching a Complex Skill

In previous lessons you practiced some basic skills in the context of presentations and discussions. This lesson will provide additional practice with these skills in the context of the strategy of teaching complex skills.

The practice of some of the steps used in teaching complex skills will of necessity be incomplete. The first step of reviewing prerequisite skills will be omitted in this exercise. If working with children in the classroom, you will need to be sure that this task is accomplished by either you or the teacher before you practice this exercise. If teaching peers, assume that they have the needed prerequisites.

The last steps of teaching complex skills, including independent practice, review, and reteaching, will also not be part of this exercise. If you are working in the classroom, you will want to be sure that either you or the teacher follow up on these two steps. To teach a complex skill to students without incorporating these last two steps into the lesson would be inappropriate.

This exercise will consist of the following steps used when teaching complex skills:

1. do a set induction including a statement of the objective(s) and its (their) importance

2. present instructions for performing the skill

3. model the skill following the steps of your instructions

4. guide the students through an initial practice

5. provide a brief review of the steps of the complex skill

6. assess the attainment of your objective(s), either orally or in writing, and close the lesson

The Teaching Task

1. Design a lesson that will allow you to teach a complex skill using the steps outlined.
2. Continue to use and practice the appropriate teaching skills from earlier lessons, particularly those found on the Observation Guide.
3. Use closed or convergent questions as part of the conclusion to assess the attainment of your objective.
4. The lesson plan to be turned in to your instructor should
   a. state your instructional objectives at the beginning of the plan
   b. briefly describe your set induction, including a verbatim script of anything you are going to say
   c. name the complex skill and list the sequence of the steps needed to perform it
   d. briefly describe the practice you will provide
   e. list the examples you will use for practice
   f. list the closed or convergent questions you will use at the conclusion of the lesson to assess attainment of the objectives. These may be used orally or in writing.

Observing the Lesson

For the Self-Analysis, a sequential description of the instructions given on the steps to follow when performing the skill would be helpful. This allows you to analyze the clarity with which the steps were introduced. As the observer, you will need to record this same sequence of instructions. Some of the instructions given by the teacher may need to be recorded verbatim in order to describe some particular problems with clarity.

Record the steps followed when modeling the complex skill for the students. Compare these with the steps introduced in the initial description of the skill. Record any discrepancies.

Both the observer and the teacher will need to record the directions given that describe the task students are to perform when practicing the skill. This data may be useful if students experience difficulty in following the directions.

The rest of the observations will be the same as in earlier lessons, so read sections of Observing the Lesson from earlier practicum teaching lessons. Examine particularly those observations described in the two preceding exercises on discussions.

TEACHING A COMPLEX SKILL

Observation Guide

The items in this Observation Guide are designed to help you systematically describe the behavior of the teacher on the tasks of this lesson. Place a check mark on the line above the listed behaviors to indicate the behavior exhibited on each of the following tasks:

Skills/tasks specific to this exercise

1. The instructions provided were adequate for illustrating the essential steps of the complex skill taught in this lesson.

Instructions included all of the steps	Instructions included some of the steps	Instructions included few of the steps

2. Model of the steps of the skill was consistent with the steps included in the instructions.

Model included all of the steps	Model included some of the steps	Model included none of the steps

3. The practice provided the pupils was adequate for initial learning of the skill.

Practice was sufficient	Practice was sufficient in part	Practice was insufficient

4. Review of the steps was consistent with the steps included in the initial instruction and practice.

Review included all of the steps	Review included some of the steps	Review included none of the steps

Skills/tasks applied from previous exercises

5. The set induction of the lesson created an interest in the lesson.

Attention of the students was effectively gained	Some attempt was made to get the students' attention	There was little or no attempt made to get students' attention

6. The set induction of the lesson gave direction to the rest of the lesson by indicating the ultimate goal and the importance of that goal to the students.

Overall direction or purpose of the lesson was clear	Overall direction or purpose of the lesson was somewhat clear	Direction or purpose of the lesson was unclear

7. The phrasing of the teacher's questions reflected the intent of the question clearly and un-ambiguously.

All questions were clear and unambigu-ous	About one-half of the questions were clear and unambiguous	Few questions were clear and unambiguous

8. The teacher used an appropriate eliciting pattern.

Almost all were Q-N-R patterns	About an equal mix of Q-R, N-Q-R, and Q-N-R	Almost all were Q-R and N-Q-R

9. The teacher made use of silence following students' responses to encourage additional thinking.

Three to five seconds on the average	One to two seconds on the average	Less than one second on the average

10. The teacher made use of student ideas as a form of reinforcement by mentioning students by name when identifying and using their contributions.

Four or more times	Two times	Not at all

11. The teacher made use of extending, clarifying, and justifying probes when students' responses were unclear, incomplete, or unsubstantiated assertions.

Teacher made use of all three kinds of probes when needed	Teacher used probes about half the time when needed	Teacher used few if any probes

12. The teacher used closed or convergent questions as part of the summary of the lesson to assess the objectives of the lesson.

Teacher asked a sufficient number of questions to assess the objectives	Teacher assessed some of the objectives	Teacher asked no closed questions to assess the objectives

TEACHING A COMPLEX SKILL
Self-Analysis

The items in the Observation Guide and this Self-Analysis are designed to help you identify the tasks of this exercise that you are doing well and those that you need to improve. Observe a videotape of your lesson for purposes of this self-analysis. Record data that will enable you to describe the behaviors requested. **Attach your raw observational data to your Self-Analysis report.**

Complete the following items:

1. Of the four tasks listed under Skills/Tasks Specific to This Exercise, which one do you think you did the best? What observations support your opinion?
2. Which one of these four tasks do you think you were least effective in accomplishing? What observations support this opinion?
3. In what ways would you change what you did in performing the four tasks specific to this exercise if you were to teach this same lesson again?
4. In what ways would you change what you did in performing the eight tasks under Skills/Tasks Applied From Previous Exercises if you were to teach this same lesson again?

TEACHING A COMPLEX SKILL
Observer Analysis

Prepare your observation instrument before the day of the lesson. Either record data during the teaching lesson or record data from a videotape following the lesson. Then complete an Observation Guide and the Observer Analysis. **Attach your observational data to this report.** *Ignore any teaching behaviors not listed on the Observation Guide.*

Complete the following items:

1. Describe one particular behavior related to the tasks under Skills/Tasks Specific to This Exercise that you thought was particularly effective and that you feel the teacher would be advised to continue.
2. Describe one particular behavior related to the tasks under Skills/Tasks Applied from Previous Exercises that you thought was particularly effective and that you feel the teacher would be advised to continue.
3. Offer at least one specific suggestion about what the teacher could have done differently related to the tasks under Skills/Tasks Specific to this Exercise to improve the lesson.
4. Offer at least one specific suggestion about what the teacher could have done differently related to the tasks under Skills/Tasks Applied from Previous Exercises to improve the lesson.

PRACTICUM TEACHING EXERCISE 8

Teaching a Higher Order Skill in a Process Curriculum Area

In the previous lesson you practiced teaching a complex skill. In this lesson you will practice some of the steps used in teaching higher-order skills in a process curriculum area using direct teaching. Direct teaching of a higher-order skill from one of these areas will follow the same steps as those used in teaching complex skills. As with the exercise in teaching complex skills, this practice will of necessity be incomplete. The first step of reviewing prerequisite skills will be omitted. If working with children in the classroom, be sure that this task is accomplished by either you or the teacher before you practice this exercise. If teaching peers, assume that they have the needed prerequisites.

The last steps of teaching complex skills, including independent practice, review and re-teaching, will also not be part of this exercise. If you are working in the classroom, be sure that either you or the teacher follow up on these two steps. To teach a complex skill to students without incorporating these last two steps into the lesson would be inappropriate.

This exercise in direct teaching higher-order skills will consist of the following steps:

1. do a set induction including a statement of the objective(s) and its (their) importance
2. present instructions for performing the skill
3. model the skill following the steps of your instructions
4. guide the students through an initial practice
5. provide a brief review of the steps of the complex skill
6. assess the attainment of your objective(s), either orally or in writing, and close the lesson

The Teaching Task

1. Design a lesson that will allow you to teach a higher-order skill using the steps outlined.
2. Continue to use and practice the appropriate teaching skills from earlier lessons, particularly those found on the Observation Guide.
3. Use closed or convergent questions as part of the conclusion to assess the attainment of your objective.
4. The lesson plan to be turned in to your instructor should
   a. state your instructional objectives at the beginning of the plan.
   b. briefly describe your set induction, including a verbatim script of anything you are going to say.
   c. list the higher-order skill and the steps of the skill to be taught
   d. briefly describe the practice you will provide
   e. list the examples you will use for practice f. list the closed or convergent questions you will use at the conclusion of the lesson to assess attainment of the objectives. These may be used orally or in writing.

Observing the Lesson

For the Self-Analysis, a sequential description of the instructions given on the steps to follow when performing the skill would be helpful. This allows you to analyze the clarity with which the steps were introduced. As the observer, you will need to record this same sequence of instructions. Some of the instructions given by the teacher may need to be recorded verbatim in order to describe some particular problems with clarity.

Record the steps followed when modeling the higher-order skill for the students. Compare these steps with the steps introduced in the initial description of the skill. Record any discrepancies.

Both the observer and the teacher will need to record the directions given that describe the task students are to perform when practicing the skill. This data may be useful if students experience difficulty in following the directions.

The rest of the observations will be the same as in earlier lessons, so read sections of Observing the Lesson from earlier practicum teaching lessons. Examine particularly those observations described in the three preceding exercises on discussions.

TEACHING A HIGHER ORDER SKILL IN A PROCESS CURRICULUM AREA

Observation Guide

The items in this Observation Guide are designed to help you systematically describe the behavior of the teacher on the tasks of this lesson. Place a check mark on the line above the listed behaviors to indicate the behavior exhibited on each of the following tasks:

Skills/tasks specific to this exercise

1. The instructions provided were adequate for illustrating the essential steps of the higher order skill taught in this lesson.

Instructions included all of the steps	Instructions included some of the steps	Instructions included few of the steps

2. Model of the steps of the skill was consistent with the steps included in the instructions.

Model included all of the steps	Model included some of the steps	Model included none of the steps

3. The practice provided the pupils was adequate for initial learning of the skill.

Practice was sufficient	Practice was sufficient in part	Practice was insufficient

4. Review of the steps was consistent with the steps included in the initial instruction and practice.

Review included all of the steps	Review included some of the steps	Review included none of the steps

Skills/tasks applied from previous exercises

5. The set induction of the lesson created an interest in the lesson.

Attention of the students was effectively gained	Some attempt was made to get the students' attention	There was little or no attempt made to get students' attention

6. The set induction of the lesson gave direction to the rest of the lesson by indicating the ultimate goal and the importance of that goal to the students.

Overall direction or purpose of the lesson was clear	Overall direction or purpose of the lesson was somewhat clear	Direction or purpose of the lesson was unclear

7. The phrasing of the teacher's questions reflected the intent of the question clearly and unambiguously.

All questions were clear and unambiguous	About one-half of the questions were clear and unambiguous	Few questions were clear and unambiguous

8. The teacher used an appropriate eliciting pattern.

Almost all were Q-N-R patterns	About an equal mix of Q-R, N-Q-R, and Q-N-R	Almost all were Q-R and N-Q-R

9. The teacher made use of silence following students' responses to encourage additional thinking.

Three to five seconds on the average	One to two seconds on the average	Less than one second on the average

10. The teacher made use of student ideas as a form of reinforcement by mentioning students by name when identifying and using their contributions.

Four or more times	Two times	Not at all

11. The teacher made use of extending, clarifying, and justifying probes when students' responses were unclear, incomplete, or unsubstantiated assertions.

Teacher made use of all three kinds of probes when needed	Teacher used probes about half the time when needed	Teacher used few if any probes

12. The teacher used closed or convergent questions as part of the summary of the lesson to assess the objectives of the lesson.

Teacher asked a sufficient number of questions to assess the objectives	Teacher assessed some of the objectives	Teacher asked no closed questions to assess the objectives

TEACHING A HIGHER-ORDER SKILL

Self-Analysis

The items in the Observation Guide and this Self-Analysis are designed to help you identify the tasks of this exercise that you are doing well and those that you need to improve. Observe a videotape of your lesson for purposes of this self-analysis. Record data that will enable you to describe the behaviors requested. **Attach your raw observational data to your Self-Analysis report**.

Complete the following items:

1. Of the four tasks listed under Skills/Tasks Specific to This Exercise, which one do you think you did the best? What observations support your opinion?

2. Which one of these four tasks do you think you were least effective in accomplishing? What observations support this opinion?

3. In what ways would you change what you did in performing the four tasks specific to this exercise if you were to teach this same lesson again?

4. In what ways would you change what you did in performing the eight tasks under Skills/ Tasks Applied From Previous Exercises if you were to teach this same lesson again?

TEACHING A HIGHER-ORDER SKILL

Observer Analysis

Prepare your observation instrument before the day of the lesson. Either record data during the teaching lesson or record data from a videotape following the lesson. Then complete an Observation Guide and the Observer Analysis. **Attach your observational data to this report**. Ignore any teaching behaviors not listed on the Observation Guide.

Complete the following items:

1. Describe one particular behavior related to the tasks under Skills/Tasks Specific to this Exercise that you thought was particularly effective and that you feel the teacher would be advised to continue.

2. Describe one particular behavior related to the tasks under Skills/Tasks Applied from Previous Exercises that you thought was particularly effective and that you feel the teacher would be advised to continue.

3. Offer at least one specific suggestion about what the teacher could have done differently related to the tasks under Skills/Tasks Specific to this Exercise to improve the lesson.

4. Offer at least one specific suggestion about what the teacher could have done differently related to the tasks under Skills/Tasks Applied from Previous Exercises to improve the lesson.

PRACTICUM TEACHING EXERCISE 9

Inductive Strategy I

In previous lessons you used questions in the context of presentations and discussions. This lesson will acquaint you with an inductive strategy in which questions play a critical role.

In this lesson you are going to provide some experience for the students and, through questioning about that experience, lead them to some understanding of a **concept.** You will encourage students, through the use of questions, to discuss, examine, and analyze the experience. The use of questions is critical to the success of an inductive strategy.

Questions will not necessarily follow any particular pattern as they did in a directed discussion; however, you will need to use a sequence of questions that will allow you to lead the students from the experience you provided to the point where **you will present the definition and name of the concept** being taught. The questions may be observational in character; you may have the students describe what they see, feel, smell, hear, or taste. Some questions may ask them to identify similarities and differences or draw conclusions from evidence. Most questions will require thought and understanding of the experience beyond mere recall. For guidance in planning, review the kinds of cognitive questions and use those needed to achieve your plans.

Some information-giving (presentation or lecture) will be needed at the end of the questioning to define and name the concept. In rare instances, students will be able to do this without being told, but expecting students to discover the definition and name of the concept strictly on their own is usually not reasonable.

The Teaching Task

1. Design a lesson that will allow you to teach a concept using an inductive strategy.
2. Use a combination of cognitive questions to arrive at a point where you can present the definition of a concept.
3. Continue to use and practice the appropriate skills from earlier lessons. Do not feel that you need to conduct a directed discussion, but do practice effective eliciting patterns and the use of silence, probing, and student ideas.
4. Use closed or convergent questions as part of the conclusion to assess the attainment of your objective.
5. The lesson plan to be turned in to your instructor should
   a. state your instructional objectives at the beginning of the plan
   b. briefly describe your set induction, including a verbatim script of anything you are going to say
   c. define the concept you will teach, including all necessary critical and variable attributes
   d. describe how the direct experience will be used, including:
      (1) list of materials
      (2) directions (verbatim) to be given
      (3) teaching procedures
   e. list in proper sequence the questions you will ask during and following the direct experience
   f. list the closed or convergent questions you will ask at the conclusion of the lesson to assess attainment of the objectives
   g. integrate items (a) through (f) into a useful and coherent lesson plan

Observing the Lesson

For the Self-Analysis, a verbatim transcript of the questions (other than probes) in order of sequence will be helpful. This sequence can be used to analyze the clarity of the questions, cognitive level of the questions, and the logic of the sequence. As the observer, you will need to record an anecdotal description of the direct experience so that deficiencies in the experiences can be identified. You will also need to record data that allows you to calculate the percentage of teacher-talk found in Practicum Teaching Exercise 2. The rest of the observations will be the same as in earlier lessons, so read sections of Observing the Lesson from earlier practicum teaching lessons.

INDUCTIVE STRATEGY I

Observation Guide

The items in this Observation Guide are designed to help you systematically describe the behavior of the teacher on the tasks of this lesson. Place a check mark on the line above the listed behaviors to indicate the behavior exhibited on each of the following tasks:

Skills/tasks specific to this exercise

1. The direct experience provided was adequate for illustrating the essential characteristics of the concept taught in this lesson.

Direct experience was adequate	Direct experience was adequate in part	Direct experience was inadequate

2. An understanding of the concept was derived from the direct experience before the definition and name were introduced.

Teacher clearly waited until understanding was assured to introduce symbols	Teacher mixed the sequence of observations and introduction of symbols	Teacher introduced symbols before understanding occurred

3. The questions leading to the development of the concept were logically sequenced.

Questions led directly to the idea	There was some confusion in the sequence of questions	There was little or no logic in sequence of questions

Skills/tasks applied from previous exercises

4. The set induction of the lesson created an interest in the lesson.

Attention of the students was effectively gained	Some attempt was made to get the students' attention	There was little or no attempt made to get students' attention

5. The set induction of the lesson gave direction to the rest of the lesson by indicating the ultimate goal and the importance of that goal to the students.

Overall direction or purpose of the lesson was clear	Overall direction or purpose of the lesson was somewhat clear	Direction or purpose of the lesson was unclear

6. The phrasing of the teacher's questions reflected the intent of the question clearly and unambiguously.

All questions were clear and unambiguous	About one-half of the questions were clear and unambiguous	Few questions were clear and unambiguous

7. The teacher asked a variety of cognitive questions.

Teacher used five categories of questions	Teacher used three categories of questions	Teacher used knowledge questions only

8. The teacher used an appropriate eliciting pattern.

Almost all were Q-N-R patterns	About an equal mix of Q-R, N-Q-R, and Q-N-R	Almost all were Q-R and N-Q-R

9. The teacher made use of silence following students' responses to encourage additional thinking.

Three to five seconds on the average	One to two seconds on the average	Less than one second on the average

10. The teacher made use of student ideas as a form of reinforcement by mentioning students by name when identifying and using their contributions.

Four or more times	Two times	Not at all

11. The teacher made use of extending, clarifying, and justifying probes when students' responses were unclear, incomplete, or unsubstantiated assertions.

Teacher made use of all three kinds of probes when needed	Teacher used probes about half the time when needed	Teacher used few if any probes

12. The expression of the teacher's voice was effectively modified during the lesson.

The teacher varied his or her voice to focus and/or maintain attention	The teacher varied his or her voice only occasionally	The teacher rarely varied his or her voice during the lesson

13. The teacher used closed or convergent questions as part of the summary of the lesson to assess the objectives of the lesson.

Teacher asked a sufficient number of questions to assess the objectives	Teacher assessed some of the objectives	Teacher asked no closed questions to assess the objectives

14. The teacher made the objective of the lesson clear.

The objective of the lesson was clear	The objective of the lesson was somewhat un-clear	The objective of the lesson was unknown

15. The content was appropriate in both amount and relevancy.

Content was appropriate in both amount and relevancy	Content was appropriate in one but not the other	Content was excessive and irrelevant

INDUCTIVE STRATEGY I

Self-Analysis

The items in the Observation Guide and this Self-Analysis are designed to help you identify the tasks of this lesson that you are doing well and those that you need to improve. Observe a videotape of your lesson for purposes of this self-analysis. Record data that will enable you to describe the behaviors requested. **Attach your raw observational data to your Self-Analysis report**.

Complete the following items on separate sheets of paper:

1. Listen to an audiotape or watch a videotape of this teaching lesson. Record verbatim each question you asked in the sequence they were asked. Record everything from the time you first started to formulate the question to the time you actively elicited a response from a student. Include all attempts at rephrasing a question until it was understandable.

2. Record verbatim each probe that you used immediately following the question with which it was used. Indent the probe so that it will not be confused with the eliciting question.

3. Study the questions and probes you used. Could the wording of questions be changed to help make the intent of the questions clearer? If so, rewrite the particular questions or indicate the change in phrasing you would make to improve the questions.

4. What specific changes will you make for your Inductive Strategy II Practicum Teaching Exercise? What specifically will you do prior to the lesson, as well as during the lesson, to ensure that you will be successful in making these changes? For example, when you have analyzed your probing, your reply might look similar to this:

> Changes in the number and kinds of probes:
> > From 2 clarifying to 4 clarifying
> > From 0 extending to 2 extending
> > From 0 justifying to 4 justifying
> > From 1 redirecting to 3 redirecting
>
> To accomplish this change, I will write the name of the probe or probes that I intend to use with that question in my lesson plans. I will also record the student replies from this tape, and then identify those that could have been probed and were not. This process will help me to become more sensitive to using probes when I hear students use ambiguous words or phrases (which they need to clarify), make conclusion-type statements (which they need to justify), or offer seemingly incomplete answers (which they need to extend).

Do not restrict your reply to the example given. Include in your reply all those behaviors that you feel need to be changed.

INDUCTIVE STRATEGY I

Observer Analysis

Prepare your observation instrument before the day of the lesson. Either record data during the teaching lesson or record data from a videotape following the lesson. Then complete an Observation Guide and the Observer Analysis. **Attach your observational data to this report.** Ignore any teaching behaviors not listed on the Observation Guide.

Complete the following items:

1. Percentage of time the teacher was talking   _____
2. Describe one particular behavior related to the tasks under Skills/Tasks Specific to this Exercise that you thought was particularly effective and that you feel the teacher would be advised to continue.
3. Describe one particular behavior related to the tasks under Skills/Tasks Applied from Previous Exercises that you thought was particularly effective and that you feel the teacher would be advised to continue.
4. Offer at least one specific suggestion about what the teacher could have done differently related to the tasks under Skills/Tasks Specific to this Exercise to improve the lesson.
5. Offer at least one specific suggestion about what the teacher could have done differently related to the tasks under Skills/Tasks Applied from Previous Exercises to improve the lesson.

PRACTICUM TEACHING LESSON 10

Inductive Strategy II

This teaching lesson will provide further practice in the use of an inductive teaching strategy. An inductive strategy is a valuable tool in helping students learn with comprehension. More students enjoy learning in this fashion than with expository or didactic methods. Examining your own and other students' reactions to the inductive strategy used in these exercises should verify this assertion.

The Teaching Task

1. Design a lesson that will allow you to teach a concept using an inductive strategy.
2. Use a combination of cognitive questions to arrive at a point where you can define the concept.
3. Continue to use and practice the appropriate skills used from prior lessons. Do not feel that you need to conduct a directed discussion, but do use effective eliciting patterns, silence, probing, and student ideas.
4. Use closed or convergent questions as part of the conclusion to assess the attainment of your objective.
5. The lesson plan to be turned in to your instructor should
   a. state your instructional objectives at the beginning of the plan.
   b. briefly describe your set induction, including a verbatim script of anything you are going to say.

    c. describe how you will use the direct experience, including:
       (1) list of materials
       (2) directions (verbatim) to be given
       (3) teaching procedures
    d. list in proper sequence the questions you will ask during and following the direct experience.
    e. write out the critical and variable attributes defining the concept you are teaching.
    f. list the closed or convergent questions you will ask at the conclusion of the lesson to assess attainment of the objectives.
    g. integrate items (a) through (f) above into a useful and coherent lesson plan.

Observing the Lesson

For the Self-Analysis, a verbatim transcript of the questions (other than probes) in order of sequence will be helpful. This sequence can be used to analyze the clarity of the questions, cognitive level of the questions, and the logic of the sequence.

As the observer you will need to record an anecdotal description of the direct experience so that deficiencies in the experiences can be identified. You will also need to record data that allows you to calculate the percentage of teacher-talk found in Practicum Teaching Exercise 2. The rest of the observations will be the same as in earlier exercises, so read sections of Observing the Lesson from earlier exercises.

INDUCTIVE STRATEGY II

Observation Guide

The items in this Observation Guide are designed to help you systematically describe the behavior of the teacher on the tasks of this lesson. Place a check mark on the line above the listed behaviors to indicate the behavior exhibited on each of the following tasks:

Skills/tasks specific to this exercise

1. The direct experience provided was adequate for illustrating the essential characteristics of the concept taught in this lesson.

Direct experience was adequate	Direct experience was adequate in part	Direct experience was inadequate

2. An understanding of the concept was derived from the direct experience before the definition and name were introduced.

Teacher clearly waited until understanding was assured to introduce symbols	Teacher mixed the sequence of observations and introduction of symbols	Teacher introduced symbols before understanding occurred

3. The questions leading to the development of the concept were logically sequenced.

Questions led directly to the idea	There was some confusion in the sequence of questions	There was little or no logic in sequence of questions

Skills/tasks applied from previous exercises

4. The set induction of the lesson created an interest in the lesson.

Attention of the students was effectively gained	Some attempt was made to get the students' attention	There was little or no attempt made to get students' attention

5. The set induction of the lesson gave direction to the rest of the lesson by indicating the ultimate goal and the importance of that goal to the students.

Overall direction or purpose of the lesson was clear	Overall direction or purpose of the lesson was somewhat clear	Direction or purpose of the lesson was unclear

6. The phrasing of the teacher's questions reflected the intent of the question clearly and un-ambiguously.

All questions were clear and unambigu-ous	About one-half of the questions were clear and unambiguous	Few questions were clear and unambiguous

7. The teacher asked a variety of cognitive questions.

Teacher used five categories of questions	Teacher used three categories of questions	Teacher used knowledge questions only

8. The teacher used an appropriate eliciting pattern.

Almost all were Q-N-R patterns	About an equal mix of Q-R, N-Q-R, and Q-N-R	Almost all were Q-R and N-Q-R

9. The teacher made use of silence following students' responses to encourage additional thinking.

Three to five seconds on the average	One to two seconds on the average	Less than one second on the average

10. The teacher made use of student ideas as a form of reinforcement by mentioning students by name when identifying and using their contributions.

Four or more times	Two times	Not at all

11. The teacher made use of extending, clarifying, and justifying probes when students' responses were unclear, incomplete, or unsubstantiated assertions.

Teacher made use of all three kinds of probes when needed	Teacher used probes about half the time when needed	Teacher used few if any probes

12. The expression of the teacher's voice was effectively modified during the lesson.

The teacher varied his or her voice to focus and/or maintain attention	The teacher varied his or her voice only occasionally	The teacher rarely varied his or her voice during the lesson

13. The teacher used closed or convergent questions as part of the summary of the lesson to assess the objectives of the lesson.

Teacher asked a sufficient number of questions to assess the objectives	Teacher assessed some of the objectives	Teacher asked no closed questions to assess the objectives

14. The teacher made the objective of the lesson clear.

The objective of the lesson was clear	The objective of the lesson was somewhat un-clear	The objective of the lesson was unknown

15. The content was appropriate in both amount and relevancy.

Content was appropriate in both amount and relevancy	Content was appropriate in one but not the other	Content was excessive and irrelevant

INDUCTIVE STRATEGY II

Self-Analysis

The items in the Observation Guide and this Self-Analysis are designed to help you identify the tasks of this lesson that you are doing well and those that you need to improve. Observe a videotape of your lesson for purposes of this self-analysis. Record data that will enable you to describe the behaviors requested. **Attach your raw observational data to your Self-Analysis report**.

Complete the following items on separate sheets of paper:

1. Listen to an audiotape or watch a videotape of this teaching lesson. Record verbatim all eliciting questions in the sequence in which you ask them. Record everything from the time you first started to formulate the question to the time you actively elicited a response from a student. Include all attempts at rephrasing a question until it was understandable.

2. Record verbatim each probe that you used immediately following the question. Indent the probe so that it will not be confused with the eliciting question.

3. Could the phrasing of some questions or probes be improved to make their intent clearer? If so, rewrite the particular questions or probes to improve the phrasing.

INDUCTIVE STRATEGY II

Observer Analysis

Prepare your observation instrument before the day of the lesson. Either record data during the teaching lesson or record data from a videotape following the lesson. Then complete an Observation Guide and the Observer Analysis. **Attach your observational data to this report**. Ignore any teaching behaviors not listed on the Observation Guide.

Complete the following items:

1. Percentage of time the teacher was talking ;oblr;cb

2. Describe one particular behavior related to the tasks under Skills/Tasks Specific to this Exercise that you thought was particularly effective and that you feel the teacher would be advised to continue.

3. Describe one particular behavior related to the tasks under Skills/Tasks Applied from Previous Exercises that you thought was particularly effective and that you feel the teacher would be advised to continue.

4. Offer at least one specific suggestion about what the teacher could have done differently related to the tasks under Skills/Tasks Specific to this Exercise to improve the lesson.

5. Offer at least one specific suggestion about what the teacher could have done differently related to the tasks under Skills/Tasks Applied from Previous Exercises to improve the lesson.

EXERCISE 35

Final Appraisal

ALthough you have learned many skills during the Practicum Teaching Exercises, you have much more to learn. Taking the time to identify those skills you have learned, as well as those yet to be learned, can be productive. In this exercise, you will examine both these aspects in detail.

Directions

On a separate sheet of paper, titled "Final Appraisal," do a self-appraisal on the teaching tasks listed here. **Use complete sentences only, and use behavioral language**.

Avoid the use of vague expressions such as, "I am doing well in this area"; "I need to improve on phrasing questions"; or "I'm satisfied (or dissatisfied) with." In your appraisal of each task include:

1. a specific assessment of your competence in doing the task, titled Competence
2. specific improvements you feel you still need to make, titled Needed Improvements

Teaching Tasks

1. teaching for an instructional objective with clarity
2. asking closed questions at the end of lessons to assess attainment of objectives
3. creating a set induction that creates interest, gives direction to a lesson, and relates the current lesson to past knowledge and experiences
4. organizing the content of presentations in logical sequence
5. choosing a reasonable amount of content to include in lessons
6. choosing content relevant to the students being taught
7. maintaining an adequate volume in my voice
8. interjecting changes of expression in my voice
9. using gestures and other refocusing tactics to maintain student interest
10. closing lessons in ways likely to reinforce and clarify the lesson
11. asking interesting and effective open or divergent questions at the start of discussions
12. utilizing probes when students respond to questions incompletely, unclearly, or with unsubstantiated assertions
13. asking clear and unambiguous questions
14. using silence following student responses
15. using student ideas by mentioning the student's name and the idea and then incorporating the idea into the lesson
16. using labeled praise effectively
17. using only the eliciting pattern of asking the question and then calling on a student by name to respond

18. incorporating a variety of cognitive levels of questions into lessons
19. providing direct experiences that are sufficient to allow the development of concepts when using an inductive strategy
20. ordering questions in a sequence that will allow the development of concepts when using an inductive strategy

Index

WE VALUE YOUR OPINION—PLEASE SHARE IT WITH US

Merrill Publishing and our authors are most interested in your reactions to this textbook. Did it serve you well in the course? If it did, what aspects of the text were most helpful? If not, what didn't you like about it? Your comments will help us to write and develop better textbooks. We value your opinions and thank you for your help.

Text Title _____ Edition _____

Author(s) _____

Your Name (optional) _____

Address _____

City _____ State _____ Zip _____

School _____

Course Title _____

Instructor's Name _____

Your Major _____

Your Class Rank _____ Freshman _____ Sophomore _____ Junior _____ Senior

_____ Graduate Student

Were you required to take this course? _____ Required _____ Elective

Length of Course? _____ Quarter _____ Semester

1. Overall, how does this text compare to other texts you've used?

_____ Superior _____ Better Than Most _____ Average _____ Poor

2. Please rate the text in the following areas:

	Superior	Better Than Most	Average	Poor
Author's Writing Style	_____	_____	_____	_____
Readability	_____	_____	_____	_____
Organization	_____	_____	_____	_____
Accuracy	_____	_____	_____	_____
Layout and Design	_____	_____	_____	_____
Illustrations/Photos/Tables	_____	_____	_____	_____
Examples	_____	_____	_____	_____
Problems/Exercises	_____	_____	_____	_____
Topic Selection	_____	_____	_____	_____
Currentness of Coverage	_____	_____	_____	_____
Explanation of Difficult Concepts	_____	_____	_____	_____
Match-up with Course Coverage	_____	_____	_____	_____
Applications to Real Life	_____	_____	_____	_____

3. Circle those chapters you especially liked:
   1   2   3   4   5   6   7   8   9   10   11   12   13   14   15   16   17   18   19   20
   What was your favorite chapter? _____
   Comments:

4. Circle those chapters you liked least:
   1   2   3   4   5   6   7   8   9   10   11   12   13   14   15   16   17   18   19   20
   What was your least favorite chapter? _____
   Comments:

5. List any chapters your instructor did not assign. _____

6. What topics did your instructor discuss that were not covered in the text?_____

   _____

7. Were you required to buy this book? _____ Yes   _____ No

   Did you buy this book new or used? _____ New   _____ Used

   If used, how much did you pay? _____

   Do you plan to keep or sell this book? _____ Keep   _____ Sell

   If you plan to sell the book, how much do you expect to receive? _____

   Should the instructor continue to assign this book? _____ Yes   _____ No

8. Please list any other learning materials you purchased to help you in this course (e.g., study guide, lab manual).

   _____

9. What did you like most about this text? _____

   _____

10. What did you like least about this text? _____

    _____

11. General comments:

    May we quote you in our advertising? _____ Yes   _____ No

    Please mail to: Boyd Lane
                      College Division, Research Department
                      Box 508
                      1300 Alum Creek Drive
                      Columbus, Ohio 43216

    Thank you!